MW00999377

The Magnificent Ambersons

A RECONSTRUCTION

HOLLYWOOD'S MOST AMAZING
CITIZEN NOW BRINGS YOU HIS
SUCCESSOR TO "CITIZEN KANE"

THE STORY OF A WOMAN IN
LOVE—FROM THE FAMOUS
PULITZER PRIZE NOVEL BY
BOOTH TARKINGTON

RKO Radio Pictures Present

ORSON WELLES'

Mercury Production

The Magnificent
Ambersons

With JOSEPH COTTEN · DOLORES COSTELLO · ANNE BAXTER · TIM HOLT
AGNES MOOREHEAD · RAY COLLINS · ERSKINE SANFORD · And RICHARD BENNETT
Screen Play, Production and Direction by Orson Welles

The Magnificent Ambersons

A RECONSTRUCTION

Robert L. Carringer

UNIVERSITY OF CALIFORNIA PRESS
Berkeley   Los Angeles   Oxford

The publisher gratefully acknowledges the contribution provided by the General Endowment Fund of the Associates of the University of California Press.

University of California Press
Berkeley and Los Angeles, California

University of California Press
Oxford, England

Copyright © 1993 by The Regents of the University of California

Library of Congress Cataloging-in-Publication Data

Carringer, Robert L.
    The Magnificent Ambersons: a reconstruction / Robert L. Carringer
        p.   cm.
    Includes bibliographical references.
    ISBN 0-520-07857-8 (cloth : alk. paper)
    1. Magnificent Ambersons (Motion picture) I. Title.
PN1997.M25433C37   1993
791.43'72—dc20   92-4410
                                                       CIP

Printed in the United States of America

1 2 3 4 5 6 7 8 9

The paper used in this publication meets the minimum requirements of American National Standard for Information Sciences—Permanence of Paper for Printed Library Materials, ANSI Z39.48-1984 ∞

for Sonia

CONTENTS

ACKNOWLEDGMENTS

In a series of interviews in 1979, Orson Welles related to me his version of the events surrounding the fate of *The Magnificent Ambersons*. Two of his closest associates in the golden years of the Mercury Theatre, William Alland and the late Richard Wilson, freely shared their recollections with me. Robert Wise extended the courtesy of several interviews to me and never failed to respond to additional inquiries. Other former RKO employees associated with *The Magnificent Ambersons* provided valuable first-hand information: Amalia Kent, John Mansbridge, James G. Stewart, Linwood Dunn, the late Howard Schwartz, and the late Maurice Seiderman.

Vernon Harbin, Archivist Emeritus of RKO, instructed me in innumerable ways, especially on legal issues and on matters of studio history and politics. John Hall, RKO West Coast Manager, was a tireless champion of the book, especially where it mattered most, with the New York corporate hierarchy. These two steadfast custodians of the studio's legacy have both since passed away, and I feel their loss deeply.

It is always a pleasure to express appreciation to dedicated professionals such as the following: Saundra Taylor and Rebecca Campbell Cape, Lilly Library, Bloomington, Indiana; Lois Bader-Stein, Kenosha Historical Society; Brigitte Kueppers, Theater Arts Library, UCLA; Ned Comstock, Archives of Performing Arts, University of Southern Calfornia; and Emmet Chisum, Western Heritage Center, Laramie, Wyoming.

I owe a special debt to: Bette LeVine, former business manager of RKO Pictures, for the original approval of this project; the Booth Tarkington Literary Properties, for clearance on the underlying story rights; Alan Rose, who spent countless hours attempting to instruct a novice like me in the mechanics of book production and the vagaries of the world of book publishing; Bill Simon, who presented me with the opportunity to read an early draft of the "Oedipus in Indianapolis" essay at the International Orson Welles Conference at New York University in May, 1988; and the Graduate Research Board, University of Illinois at Urbana-Champaign, for supplementary financial assistance.

Chick Callenbach, my editor at the University of California Press, treated my less inspiring ideas with gentle forbearance and always tried to help me find a better way. James Naremore and Al LaValley, specialist readers for the Press, wrote conscientious, immaculately reasoned, and eminently fair reports; they will discover that I did not take their counsel lightly.

Michelle Nordon was an exemplary production editor.

Sharon Decker heroically typed the manuscript.

I am also grateful to my research assistants, Kim Worthy, George Scheetz, and Mark Cummings, to fellow Welleseans Richard France and Charles Higham, and to Ruth Warrick, Christopher Husted, Kathryn Kalinak, and Grace Blum.

This project was underwritten by a grant from the Research Programs Division of the National Endowment for the Humanities.

INTRODUCTION

THE FATE of *The Magnificent Ambersons* is one of film history's great tragedies. From the studio's standpoint, it was a risky proposition from the beginning—a downbeat regional period drama, expensive to produce, and with no star attraction. Indeed, it had been necessary for Welles to grant additional dispensations on his obligations to the studio to get RKO President George Schaefer's permission to proceed in the first place. Shooting on the film began on October 28, 1941, at the RKO-Pathé studios in Culver City, RKO's second lot across town from its main operation on Gower Street in Hollywood. Exactly one month later, Welles arranged a special screening for Schaefer of the work in progress. Three especially powerful sequences had been completed by this time—the Ambersons ball, the dinner for Eugene Morgan, and George and Aunt Fanny on the stairs afterwards. The preview left Schaefer considerably relieved. Although the film continued to represent what in the trade is called a "hard sell," with careful handling it might show a respectable return. Schaefer, a veteran distributor, took charge of the marketing strategy himself. To maximize box-office potential, *The Magnificent Ambersons* would have a major opening at RKO's flagship theater, Radio City Music Hall, during Easter week (one of the best times of the year for the picture business) followed by a quick saturation playoff in RKO theaters around the country. Shooting was completed on *The Magnificent Ambersons* on January 22, 1942, in sufficient time to make possible the implementation of Schaefer's plan. Almost immediately after, Welles departed for South America (at the urging of the State Department and with Schaefer's blessing) to make a film on local customs and themes, leaving postproduction on *The Magnificent Ambersons* in the hands of the film's editor, Robert Wise.

A completed version of the film, edited according to Welles's precise instructions, was put into preview at Pomona, a small town on the edge of the desert forty-five minutes east of Hollywood, on March 17, 1942. Schaefer attended, expecting to see the promise of October fulfilled. To the contrary, the Pomona preview was an unmitigated disaster. Schaefer wrote to Welles in South America that it was the most painful experience in his twenty-eight years in the industry. "I have never been present in a theater where the audience acted in such a manner. They laughed at the wrong places, talked at the picture, kidded it, and did everything that you can possibly imagine."

A second preview at Pasadena on March 19 went better (a less rowdy audience, and only about a fourth of the preview cards negative vs. three-fourths at Pomona), but this was small comfort to Schaefer. Pasadena, with its rarefied, upscale audience, was the exception. If the picture would not play in Pomona, it could not even come near to recouping its extravagant $1,000,000 cost. Reluctantly, Schaefer ordered the studio, independently of Welles, to take whatever action was necessary to make the film more palatable to a mass audience. (The additional time entailed now made an Easter release out of the question.) The task was entrusted to Wise, who removed almost fifty minutes of Welles's footage and arranged for several scenes to be rewritten and reshot. Wise's original cut had run 131 minutes, 45 seconds. The recut version ran 88 minutes, 10 seconds. In the meantime, Schaefer was deposed as head of the studio in favor of a new regime that was openly hostile to Welles. The short version received a perfunctory release, and the picture was retired to the vaults showing a loss of $625,000 (roughly 75% of the total *cost* of *Citizen Kane*).

As a protection against possible legal complications, the negative trims and outtakes were held for a time in the vaults, but were eventually burned because of a shortage of storage space. (The leftover material from Hitchcock's *Suspicion* was destroyed at the same time, making it unlikely that this was a selective act of vindictiveness toward Welles.) The duplicate print sent to Welles in South America was deemed useless and was also destroyed. As a consequence, not even a frame of the extracted footage is known to survive. The only complete record of the 131-minute version of the film which does survive is a cutting continuity (a script transcribed from what appears on the screen) of March 12, 1942. The cutting continuity is the basis for the reconstruction undertaken in this volume. It is supplemented with various materials pertaining to the missing footage, including storyboards (cartoon-like drawings which are preliminary visualizations of a shot), detailed sketches, blueprints of the sets, still photographs representing the film's action, the script supervisor's editing notes made during the shooting, cues for the musical score, information in studio documents, and recollections of several of the original participants in the shooting. A graphic and annotational network correlates the shots and scenes which are lost to the portion of the film which survives.

A cutting continuity is a technical document containing shot and footage counts, dialogue, and extremely scant descriptions of the action. The first necessity in preparing the reconstruction was to convert a purely functional document of this sort into a readerly one. This involved such matters as rearranging the format, correcting errors, making the text internally consistent, and rewriting for clarity and, sometimes, for accuracy. This process has been carried out in accord with, I would hope, editorially responsible principles. These are explained in "A Note on Textual Practice."

The survival of crucial records related to the production has made possible a lengthy addendum, "Editing *Ambersons:* A Documentary History." There are also a chronology of the story events, an extensive cast list (including players in deleted scenes), and a critical introduction, "Oedipus in Indianapolis."

The critical introduction is likely to be controversial. *The Magnificent Ambersons* has traditionally been considered a prime instance of the Hollywood system's total disdain for mature artistry and its unrelenting commitment to its destruction. To the contrary, I argue that Welles himself must bear the ultimate responsibility for the film's undoing. While it is undeniable that Schaefer's decision to recut *The Magnificent Ambersons* was primarily a business judgment, I believe it was a string of questionable judgments and rash actions on Welles's part that predisposed this outcome.

If events had turned out differently, it might well be that *The Magnificent Ambersons,* rather than *Citizen Kane,* would be regarded as "the greatest film of all time." Even in the film's truncated form, it is clear that one of Welles's primary motives was to outdo the achievement of his first film. This book has two goals: to account for the failure of the film's execution, and to bring the reader into as close touch as possible, from such materials as survive, with a masterwork that might have been.

1

OEDIPUS IN INDIANAPOLIS

After a thunderous beginning like *Citizen Kane*, Welles's choice of a serene and elegiac story like *The Magnificent Ambersons* for his second film may appear something of a puzzle. In fact, *The Magnificent Ambersons* came about almost as an afterthought. Welles had originally intended to follow up *Citizen Kane* with *The Way to Santiago*, an espionage thriller set in Mexico which would co-star his current inamorata, Dolores Del Rio. The script was almost completed and production plans were well under way when the Mexican government announced its objection to the project. With most foreign markets already shut off because of the war, RKO was unwilling to risk jeopardizing any of the few territories remaining and withheld its assent. Once again, Welles was in the same situation he had been faced with at the inception of *Citizen Kane*—several months of preproduction activity without even a story idea in hand. To help things along, RKO studio President George Schaefer ordered a search of the files for available properties that might be suitable for Welles, and this produced a list of more than three dozen items ranging from Hemingway's *To Have and Have Not* to a life of Beethoven. Welles dutifully reviewed each item with an RKO story editor but could find nothing that ignited a spark. When the situation was at its bleakest, Welles suddenly hit on the idea for the Tarkington novel, which the Mercury Theatre had done as a radio show. From Welles's point of view, it seemed an eminently sensible choice. Virtually forgotten in the postwar era, Tarkington once had a wider following than probably any other writer in American history and could provide the commercial drawing power the studio was demanding from Welles. The radio production was considered one of the Mercury's best, and the experience gained from it would help to speed the progress of the film and make up for lost time. There were also deeper currents of attraction: although Welles probably did not fully sense it at this early stage, one of the central preoccupations of the Ambersons story is the same as that in *Citizen Kane*. *The Magnificent Ambersons*, however, is not the kind of property one associates with RKO. Recognizing that he faced a difficult selling job, Welles took a phonograph and a re-

The gestation of a legend: a 1925 precocious schoolboy item from a local paper, reprinted in the 1940 *Saturday Evening Post* "How to Raise a Child" series.

Cartoonist, Actor, Poet, and only 10

Orson G. Welles
—Photo by De Longe

A POET, artist, cartoonist, and actor at 10 years old.

Orson G. Welles, a pupil in the fourth grade at the Washington school, is already attracting the attention of some of the greatest literary men and artists in the country.

Orson has a background and

cording of the radio broadcast and went alone to see Schaefer. In later years, Welles took a certain mischievous glee in relating that during his presentation, one of the finest performances of his career, he quipped, Schaefer fell asleep. In any case, he came away with the necessary permission to proceed.

1

It was André Bazin who first put the matter in clear perspective. *Citizen Kane* and *The Magnificent Ambersons* are so profoundly interrelated as to constitute a distinct phase in Welles's film output. Indeed, Bazin suggests, it may justifiably be considered the major phase. The two films are centrally related by such general traits as the long take, deep focus style, and a somewhat Balzacian view of American life, but there is a more elemental link. In Kane's attachment to Rosebud and in George Minafer's extreme solicitousness toward his mother, we see manifestations of the same "egotistic fixation"—"the obsession with, or, if one prefers, nostalgia for childhood." The impetus, Bazin felt, was Welles's own childhood. Not, however, because it was troubled—quite the opposite, "it was a happy childhood *par excellence*"—but because it was too brief. "Too many good fairies hovered over his cradle, not leaving the child time enough to live his childhood."[1]

"A happy childhood *par excellence*"—that is exactly the conclusion Welles would have expected Bazin to draw. Matters had been carefully contrived so that he would. Welles had been feeding glorified accounts of his childhood to the press for so long that they had come to be accepted as fact. It was a conspicuous feature of what critic Kenneth Tynan called his "lifelong task . . . of inventing himself."[2] It involved embellishment, outright fabrication, and selective concealment. It may be seen at its most characteristic in the portrait of the boy genius astonishing and confounding the adult world that is presented in the *Saturday Evening Post* feature series, "How to Raise a Child" (1940),[3] which was to be a fountainhead of Welles biography for decades. Attempts to get behind the mask were invariably brushed aside, though with the insouciance and utterly disarming politeness of which Welles was master. To Tynan, who had remarked on the anomaly that Welles heroes usually have no fathers:

> I had a father whom I remember as enormously likable and attractive. He was a gambler, and a playboy who may have been getting a bit old for it when I knew him, but he was a marvelous fellow, and it was a great sorrow to me when he died. No, a story interests me on its own merits, not because it's autobiographical.[4]

To British reviewer Dilys Powell:

> Is *Citizen Kane* autobiographical? Not for a minute. I can't think why that legend persists. Kane was born poor. I was born rich and became poor about the time in life Mr. Kane came into a fortune. His childhood was lonely and starved for love. Mine was the opposite. I had no "Rosebuds."[5]

---

1 André Bazin, *Orson Welles*, translated by Jonathan Rosenbaum (New York: Harper and Row, 1978), pp. 65–66.

2 Kenneth Tynan, "Portrait: Orson Welles," in *Show* (November 1961), p. 60. Reprinted in *Profiles* (New York: Harper Perennial, 1990), p. 158.

3 Alva Johnston and Fred Smith, "How to Raise a Child," in *The Saturday Evening Post*, January 20, 27, and February 3, 1940.

4 Kenneth Tynan, "Playboy Interview: Orson Welles," in *Playboy*, March 1967, p. 56.

5 Dilys Powell, "The Life and Opinions of Orson Welles," in the London *Sunday Times*, February 3, 1963, p. 21.

On the contrary, Welles's childhood had overflowed with family emotional traumas.[6] His parents were flagrantly mismatched and quarreled constantly and bitterly. When Welles was a baby, a second male adult entered the family circle. Welles's mother encouraged the outsider's attentions and before long he had effectively supplanted Welles's real father as head of the household. His father went into a professional and personal decline that was undoubtedly precipitated by the presence of the male rival, and he never recovered. When Welles was six, his parents separated and thereafter he was shuttled back and forth between them. When with his father, he had ample opportunity to observe firsthand the elder Welles's boozing and philandering. He was living with his mother when she contracted a debilitating illness and she died in agony when he was nine. When he was thirteen, his father had his older brother committed to a mental institution. When he was fifteen, his father died of alcoholism.

As a young man, Richard Head Welles (1872–1930) was a small-town entrepreneur with spectacular promise. He liked to tinker with mechanical things and apparently had genuine talent. One of his early inventions, a solar bicycle headlamp that generated its own gas, earned him a modest fortune. He married Beatrice Ives (1882–1924), an exquisite beauty from a once-prosperous Springfield, Illinois, mercantile family that had fallen on hard times. She had well-developed artistic tastes, some musical talent, and a mind of her own. Dr. Maurice Bernstein, a Kenosha physician of some repute, came into their lives when he was summoned to care for Beatrice Welles's mother, who was dying of cancer. On his visits to the house, he began to take special notice of the baby, Orson, whom he recognized as a prodigy. Bernstein was well connected in Chicago's cultural community and represented an opportunity for Beatrice Welles to further her musical ambitions. In 1919, Richard Welles, then in his forties, disposed of his business interests and spent the rest of his life indulging his weaknesses. Around the same time, Beatrice Welles arranged for the family to relocate to Chicago, where she was soon presiding over a salon that catered to the musically and otherwise artistically gifted. Inevitably, permanent separation came. If Kenneth Tynan's characterization of the relationship was tasteless, it was nonetheless correct: "where mother had her *salon*, father favored the saloon."[7] The family spent the summers at the resort town of Grand Detour, an hour's drive west of Chicago, but Beatrice lived in a rented house while Richard stayed at the town's famous old hotel.

On May 10, 1924, at forty-two, Beatrice Welles died of hepatitis, for which there was then no effective cure. According to her wishes, Welles was placed under the joint guardianship of his father and Bernstein, but it was the latter who assumed chief responsibility, and with whom he lived, because of Richard Welles's instability. After Beatrice's death, Richard Welles moved to Grand Detour and bought its famous hotel, which he managed and ran for a time until it was burned to the ground through an employee's carelessness. His drinking grew worse, and Bernstein enjoined his young charge, now away at boarding school, from associating with his father in this condition. Richard Welles died alone of acute alcoholism in a Chicago hotel room on December

---

[6] The following account of Welles's parentage and childhood is taken principally from Barbara Leaming, *Orson Welles: A Biography* (New York: Viking, 1985); Charles Higham, *Orson Welles: The Rise and Fall of an American Genius* (New York: St. Martin's Press, 1985); conversations with Lois Bader-Stein, archivist of the Kenosha Historical Society, and documents compiled by her; unpublished letters of Todd School headmaster Roger Hill; and original materials in the Charles Higham Welles Research Collection, Archives of Performing Arts, University of Southern California (hereafter *HRC*). *HRC* is of special interest for its public and legal documents pertaining to the Welles family, clippings from Kenosha, Milwaukee, and Chicago newpapers, and a family scrapbook kept by Welles's governess Sigrid Jacobsen.

[7] Tynan, *Show*, October 1961, p. 68. Reprinted in *Profiles*, p. 155.

27, 1930. As Welles remarked in reaction to Rita Hayworth's characterization of her life with him, "If this was happiness, I wonder what the rest of [it] had been."[8]

It is understandable why anyone might want to keep family skeletons of this sort securely locked in the closet. Nor would there be anything out of the ordinary in altering an occasional fact to protect the concealment. What makes Welles's case unusual is the matter of degree. He went to extraordinary lengths to control the story of his childhood. This trait persisted to the end of his life.

Joseph Cotten, his friend of fifty years, identified, probably unwittingly, one of his principal strategies. "I know little about Orson's childhood," Cotten wrote in his autobiography, "and seriously doubt that he was ever a child."[9] If it had been left up to Welles himself, he never would have been. His accounts of childhood events almost never involve peers and usually present him in the company of adults who accept him as one of their own. In a familiar variant, he proves himself their superior. The "How to Raise a Child" series, subtitled "The Education of Orson Welles, Who Didn't Need It," is a compendium of such anecdotes repeated without any discernible trace of skepticism: Welles escaped kindergarten by feigning appendicitis; resisted being sent to ordinary school because it would interfere with his works in progress, a universal history of the drama and a critical analysis of *Thus Spake Zarathustra;* was singled out as a special subject of study by an eminent psychologist but faked his answers because of his disdain for what he regarded as a pseudoscience; and, at twelve, wrote a series of papers refuting the work of one of the world's leading Egyptologists. "His main ambition was to escape from childhood," the authors editorialized. "From the first, Orson was a full-fledged member of [his mother's] circle . . . of artists and intellectuals."

One such anecdote is especially enlightening. The *Post* authors report that when Dr. Bernstein first encountered Welles on a professional call to the family home, the "infant Confucius" was "uttering wisdom in polished sentences."[10] Bernstein himself gave a very different account: "Orson at that time didn't talk, as since reported, like a college professor. He talked like a 2 year old, somewhat precocious."[11] Welles preferred the more flattering story and constantly repeated it. Late in his life, he would even recount it in precise detail: One day, at eighteen months, he was alone in his nursery when Bernstein happened to look in on him. From his crib, he addressed an observation to the startled doctor: "The desire to take medicine is one of the greatest features which distinguishes men from animals." Bernstein rushed to announce the news to the family.[12] While it may seem a typical Welles whopper, its symbolic implications are profound. It is a fable of personal origin, an account of the birth of the version of Welles he wished himself to be. Its psychological dynamic is that the prelapsarian child is enabled to advance directly to adulthood, bypassing the painful developmental phases in between. In this respect, it is significant that only the baby and his "Dadda" (Welles's childhood name for Bernstein), and none of the disruptive forces from Welles's real childhood, are present in the fable.

---

[8] Barbara Leaming, *If This Was Happiness: A Biography of Rita Hayworth* (New York: Viking, 1989), prefatory inscription.

[9] Joseph Cotten, *Vanity Will Get You Somewhere* (San Francisco: Mercury House, 1987), p. 30.

[10] All the preceding examples are from the first installment of *The Saturday Evening Post* series, January 20, 1940.

[11] Kirk Bates, "When Welles Loses Sleep He Makes It Up, and How!" Milwaukee *Journal*, February 7, 1940, p. 1. Bernstein was interviewed for the second in a series of three articles in the Milwaukee *Journal* (February 6, 7, and 8) intended as a corrective to the *Post* series. Roger Hill was interviewed for the first article, "Hollywood Jeers While Watching Orson Welles on Slippery Limb." In the third, "Kenosha Is Indignant Over Some Orson Welles Stories," Welles's former townspeople called into question much of what he had said in the *Post* series about his early years.

[12] Reported by Leaming, *Orson Welles*, p. 8.

A 1922 photograph signifies the Welles family situation at the time. Dr. Bernstein stands in the far right foreground, next to Beatrice Welles, clutching the seven-year-old boy in front of him. (The older brother, Richard, is inexplicably absent.) In the center are an elderly neighbor couple, smiling. Next, to the left, is Sigrid, the boy's governess, turned sideways to cast a solicitous glance at her charge. At the far left, behind and apart from the others, is Richard Welles, 50, taut and unsmiling.

One such force would be Beatrice Welles. In her artistic cultivation, singlemindedness, and disdain for conventional values, she was so positive a model for her son that one might expect he would have reveled in being so fortunate.[13] Yet he remained impassively silent in regard to her for much of his life. Actor William Alland, production assistant, chief aide, and personal fixer for Welles from his early days in theater through *Citizen Kane* and, some say, closest of all to him in these years, told me that in all that time he cannot recall a single instance when Welles even mentioned his mother.[14] The occasional obligatory commentary to the press had all the feeling of an encyclopedia entry: "My mother was a famous beauty, active in politics, a champion rifle shot and a gifted concert pianist."[15] Not until late in life did he begin speaking more freely. À propos his own status in her Chicago salon, he told an interviewer, "children could be treated as adults as long as they were amusing. The moment you became boring, it was off to the nursery."[16] In 1982 he published the first (and only) installment of his memoirs. It was in two parts, one devoted to Richard Welles ("My Father Wore Black Spats") and one to Beatrice ("A Brief Career as a Musical Prodigy"). The latter is without question the most moving piece he ever wrote. On his ninth birthday, he was called to his mother's deathbed. The room was dark except for the faint glow from the tiny candles on the cake which flickered in her strong green eyes. She fixed him in a piercing look ("these could be quite terrible—I'd seen my father wither under them into a crisp, brown, winter's leaf"), addressed him as "Georgie-Porgie"—the dread nickname his playmates taunted him with, and recited lines from *A Midsummer Night's Dream,* the primer she had used to teach him to read. Then she turned to the purpose of the visit:

> That stupid birthday cake . . . is just another stupid cake; and you'll have all the cakes you want. But the candles are a fairy ring. And you will never again in your whole life have just that number to blow out. She was a sorceress. "You must puff hard," she said, "and you must blow out every one of them. And you must make a wish."

Welles continued:

> I puffed very hard. And suddenly the room was dark and my mother had vanished forever. Sometimes, in the dead watches of the night, it strikes me that of all my mistakes, the greatest was on that birthday just before my mother died, when I forgot to make a wish.[17]

Welles undoubtedly intended it as a pristine image; he was probably unaware that his portrait of Beatrice Welles strikes some readers as truly frightening.

It would be difficult to imagine a less exemplary role model than Richard Welles. But once again, expectations are reversed: his father served a role in his everyday adult life one might think his mother would occupy. Rather than suppressing information about his father, Welles delighted in proliferating it. He was especially fond of stories

[13] As, for instance, Preston Sturges does in his posthumously published memoir, *Preston Sturges*, adapted and edited by Sandy Sturges (New York: Simon and Schuster, 1990).

[14] Interview with William Alland, October 28, 1987.

[15] Powell, "The Life and Opinions of Orson Welles," p. 21.

[16] Leaming, *Orson Welles*, p. 13.

[17] Orson Welles, "A Brief Career as a Musical Prodigy," *Vogue* (Paris) December 1982, pp. 186–187.

involving them as companions—knowing fellows in the ways of the world, international travelers, and so on. This is undoubtedly related to his wish to be thought an adult, but there are other equally important considerations.

Just weeks before Welles's death in 1985, two extensive and ambitious biographies appeared. Welles granted Barbara Leaming virtually unlimited interview privileges for her *Orson Welles: A Biography*. She reciprocated by allowing practically everything he said to pass unchallenged, including obvious fabrications and more than a small amount of the most patent nonsense. Nevertheless, her work is indispensable as the fullest account on record of Welles's reminiscences and views. Charles Higham's *Orson Welles: The Rise and Fall of an American Genius* had an unusual provenance. In an earlier book, *The Films of Orson Welles*, Higham had aroused Welles's fury with his "fear of completion" theory, actually more a charge, that Welles was chronically self-destructive and that "all his blame of others for wrecking his work is an unconscious alibi" for his own recklessness and irresponsibility.[18] Welles retaliated by writing Higham into his uncompleted autobiographical film *The Other Side of the Wind* as a prissy critic whose name is emphatically mispronounced. In the new book, Higham displayed his own chronic inability to resist a salacious tidbit or to slant matters in the most insidious way possible, but his account of Welles's ancestry and childhood is exhaustively and masterfully researched, and this alone makes it one of the great contributions to Welles lore.

For all their fundamental differences, the two books open with the same phenomenon: Welles making up stories about his father. Welles says to Leaming that his father died at a "'great age.'" She interjects that, to the contrary, he was only fifty-eight. "No sooner do I blurt [that] out," Leaming continues, "than I realize that I certainly ought to have refrained from correcting Orson on so delicate a subject. Orson is perplexed. He has always thought of his father as being very old when he died" (p. 2). Higham begins with a quotation from the Paris *Vogue* memoir. Welles wrote that his father "lived to be a great age before setting himself on fire." Higham establishes that "there is not a word of truth in it"; not only did his father die at a relatively early age, but "the fire to which Welles refers was in fact caused by the servants in his father's hotel, who were testing a new flue by wafting the flames up it with newspapers." Welles describes the hotel as small; in fact, Higham asserts, it was very large. Welles says that the fire took place after "we'd just returned from China, and there was a nice Christmasy fall of snow on the ground the night of the fire. . . . The few old cronies my father had invited were yet to arrive, and most of the hotel staff had been given the night off to go to Dixon, six miles away, for the movie show." In fact, Higham establishes, the fire took place in the late spring of 1928, "almost exactly two years before Welles went to China and Japan with his father, and it was already unseasonably hot in that part of Illinois." The Grand Detour hotel was impressive but hardly "America's most exclusive," as Welles characterized it. Also, his father did not own other residences in Jamaica and Peking, as Welles claimed (p. 2). Welles continues in the same vein—around the time

---

[18]   Charles Higham, *The Films of Orson Welles* (Berkeley: University of California Press, 1970), p. 190.

of Kitty Hawk, his father invented an airplane of his own that flew while its engine remained on the ground, and so on—until he reaches what must be his all-time whopper: His father's mother was a practicing witch who performed sacrificial rites on a bloodstained altar in an upper story of her house and managed to insert diabolical lore into the text of the minister's funeral sermon for her son.[19]

Welles loved making up stories about his father and his father's relatives. There were the often-repeated tales of his father's nine great-aunts and their outlandish doings: one wore an enormous red wig on the streets of Kenosha and waved it at acquaintances, another exercised by tying herself to the back of her limousine and running along behind it, another fell out of a rickshaw in China and disappeared from the face of the earth, another was courted by a famous magician, another refused to be rescued from the Johnstown flood because of a party in progress, and another regularly bathed in ginger ale. Actually, there were only five aunts, one slightly eccentric, but all the rest is apparently untrue.[20] Perhaps the single image Welles most enthusiastically promoted was that of his father as world traveler accompanied by his young son to all sorts of exotic locales. Even though this characterization is taken almost universally at face value, there are grounds for serious doubt. Richard Welles's former Kenosha friends insisted that "he went abroad once" in his whole life and that his son's stories were pure fabrication.[21] After hearing Welles hold forth on the subject on a television talk show, Roger Hill once wrote in exasperation to another former Todd pupil that Welles had taken one single foreign trip with his father, to China, after his fourth year at Todd School.[22] Undoubtedly the Kenoshans understated the facts (it is unlikely they would have been in constant touch after Richard Welles left Kenosha) but it is also clear that Welles's account goes wildly to the opposite extreme. Is it possible that travel was a cover story used by the family for prolonged binges and periods of drying out in a hospital or sanitarium?[23]

He also promoted his father's reputation as a wastrel and philanderer. He told the *Post* authors how he used to sit up all night with his father absorbing his wisdom over a bottle of Holland gin.[24] He once told a youthful audience that he never used drugs himself, but his father had regularly smoked opium—"about once a month."[25] He often repeated the story, with a certain amount of ribald satisfaction it is said, that when he was still in short pants, his father used to take him along with him to brothels and "park him with the babes" while he conducted his business upstairs.[26]

Welles's tales of his father present him as a colorful, sometimes ribald Dickensian eccentric, a comic anachronism who continued to wear black spats even after light colors had come into fashion when automobiles eliminated horse droppings from the streets. But the comedic feature also clearly serves to screen out latent anxieties, as with the child in the brothel story. Or with this one: I once asked Welles how he first developed an interest in films. From his father, he replied, who saw everything that came

---

[19] For the record, Higham also discredits the grandmother story in every respect.

[20] See: "How to Raise a Child," October 20, 1940, p. 96; and Bates, "Kenosha Is Indignant," p. 3.

[21] Bates, "Kenosha Is Indignant," p. 2.

[22] Roger Hill to Dwight Whitney, undated [c. May 25, 1975], private collection.

[23] Lois Bader-Stein has searched the records of every likely institution within range of Kenosha and Chicago and found no evidence to support the conjecture, but someone—Doctor Bernstein, for instance—could have arranged for Richard Welles to be admitted under an assumed name.

[24] "How to Raise a Child," January 20, p. 96.

[25] Welles Press Conference at the Boston Opening of *F for Fake*, January 7, 1977.

[26] Interview with William Alland, October 28, 1987.

Beatrice Ives Welles, and actress Ruth Warrick as a young bride in *Citizen Kane*. Warrick told me she too was struck by the extraordinary resemblance between them the first time she saw a picture of Beatrice Welles. Warrick added that her personal relationship with Welles was motherly. She petted and consoled him, she said, when he went to pieces after the studio had a truckload of withered, rotting flowers delivered to the set with the message that they had been fresh when the picture was supposed to have started shooting. Warrick was the actress first considered for the role of Isabel Amberson.

out, at least until the advent of sound. When the first talking image appeared on the screen, Welles continued, his father rose at once, railed in abomination, pulled the startled child from his seat, stalked out with him in tow, and never entered a movie theater again in his life.[27] It is, of course, an often-told tale, to which Welles added his own special twist, the father-son companionship motif. In his telling, an ordinarily benign comic anecdote provides cover for a primal fable of discord—the eruption of an unbridgeable gulf between father and son, instigated by the father, over the thing the son values most. Although it too is apparently harmless, Welles's insistence on his father's superannuation may indicate a wish for his death. In fact, he raised this possibility himself in the "Black Spats" memoir, but in a teasing manner, remarking almost casually that he was convinced he had killed his father, promising to "try to write about this later," and never coming back to it.

In his baroque fantasy *Mister Arkadin* (1955), Welles's protagonist contrives to obliterate all traces of his past in order to guard the dark secret of his origins. Remove the sinister overtones, and Arkadin's story is not unlike Welles's own. Undoubtedly he was a prodigy, but his wildly exaggerated accounts of his accomplishments may be as significant for what they suppress as for what they reveal. Of his mother he said too little. Did the thought of her trigger associations too painful to contemplate? Of his father he said too much. Could the extreme ambivalence apparent in many of Welles's characterizations of him be symptomatic of a more deep-rooted conflict? Bazin attributed these idiosyncrasies to "egotistic fixation." In view of the foregoing account, "Oedipal" seems the more appropriate modifier, so long as this term is understood in the most general sense, as the entire bewildering complex of ambivalent and conflicting feelings toward the parents (including the sexual) with which an offspring struggles to come to terms throughout life.[28]

2

Citizen Kane has only one substantial scene of childhood, of course, but it is the center from which all else in the film radiates. Charles Foster Kane, age eight, is seen playing in the snow outside his mother's boarding house. A miraculous turn of events has occurred: a seemingly worthless piece of mining stock has become immensely valuable, and Kane's mother has determined to secure her son's prospects by making an arrangement which will place him and the assets in trust to one of the country's leading financial figures. (His father is allowed no say in the matter.) It will turn out to be the most significant event in Kane's life; although it guarantees his future financial success, he will (somewhat unaccountably) be separated from his mother for good. The trauma of his aborted childhood will leave a permanent emotional scar; it is symbolized by an object named at the beginning of the film but not identified until the end.

As we know, Welles also lost his mother at a tender age. (Nine. Intriguingly, he usually spoke of it—as in his deathbed memoir—as having occurred at Kane's age,

---

[27] Welles, interview with the author, August 9, 1979.

[28] In this essay I trace a generalized pattern of compulsive behavior originating in Welles's childhood which proved unsettling and destructive to his later creative efforts. While I make use of certain basic Freudian concepts, I have not cast this phenomenon in terms of Freudian theories of psychosexual development. My approach is derived from the transactional model of psychological development, which avoids specific, all-encompassing explanations originating in childhood and holds that behavior is modifiable across the life span. For a brief discussion, see: William McKinley Runyan, *Life Histories and Psychobiography: Explorations in Theory and Method* (New York: Oxford University Press, 1982), pp. 209–214. For a survey of work in developmental theory, see: David G. Perry and Kay Busey, *Social Development* (Englewood Cliffs, N.J.: Prentice-Hall, 1984).

eight.) There are numerous other parallels that give the scene an autobiographical dimension. Beatrice Welles was also headstrong and very much in charge of the family. (Kane Sr., an ineffectual dotterer, is modeled on Richard Welles.[29]) She insisted that her young son be raised her way and even dictated the terms of his guardianship after her death. (In both circumstances, like Mary Kane, she took special pains to see that the boy was kept at a distance from his father's influence.) Re-reading Welles's deathbed remembrance with the film's childhood separation sequence in mind will make abundantly clear how nearly Mary Kane resembles Beatrice Welles—in the icy stares by means of which she withers the elder Kane, for instance, but especially in her alternation between steely remoteness and loving solicitude in her relationship with her son. Mary Kane signs the boy over to a bank, without apparent remorse; minutes later she speaks to him lovingly and tenderly enfolds him in her arms. The most common interpretation of Rosebud—as the loss of a mother's love in the traditional sense (warm, total, unconditional)—simply does not square with the portrait of Mary Kane. Kane's immediate reaction to the news of the change in his status divulges his foremost concern. "You goin' Mom?" Whatever else it may represent, Rosebud stands first and foremost for a deep-seated fear of maternal rejection.

Was this fear what had been behind Welles's silence during all those years? If so, there can be no surprise that it would come to the fore so insistently in his first major original work. (Before *Citizen Kane*, Welles had been an adapter and producer of the work of others.) But unusual care had to be exercised—journalists and critics were a relentless lot, and there was no stigma that could be attached to a serious artist more devastating than "mother fixation." Not even a hint of an autobiographical implication could be allowed. It was in furtherance of this end that Welles discovered a special role for screenwriter Herman Mankiewicz, with whom he had grudgingly consented to share the writing credit on the film. He would use Mankiewicz as a cover and reserve the high road for himself. With uncharacteristic magnanimity Welles would proclaim, "Everything concerning Rosebud belongs to him," while maintaining that he himself originally had something more lofty in mind ("a line from a Romantic poem perhaps") but had allowed himself to be dissuaded.

Welles also disclosed crucial information about his feelings toward Richard Welles in the film, but for this he needed no special diversionary tactic because it was already in foolproof disguise. During the course of shooting, Welles was disturbed that some vital element was lacking in the story. In a move that was rash even for him, he feigned an illness, closed down production, and went into seclusion for three days. He emerged with a new scene he had written entirely by himself—the one in which Kane formally relinquishes control over his newspaper empire to his lifelong nemesis. The resultant symmetry is unerring—Kane's ascendancy and decline are both marked by formal ceremonies involving Thatcher and the signing of documents. But this was a byproduct; Welles's unease had been driven by something much stronger than concern for story structure. The following exchange early in the scene provides a vital clue:

[29] In the early drafts of the script he appeared again in Kane's later life, "a dandy as ever was," in the company of "a very obvious and very young tart" whom he has just married—allusions to Richard Welles's sartorial affectations and inclination toward certain types of women. First rough draft 4/16/40 and first draft continuity 5/9/40. See: Robert L. Carringer, "The Scripts of *Citizen Kane*," *Critical Inquiry* 5, no. 2 (Winter 1978), pp. 369–400.

THATCHER

You're too old to call me Mr. Thatcher, Charles.

KANE

You're too old to be called anything else. You were always too old.

Kane's first line is comic understatement: it is now fifty-eight years since Colorado and Thatcher has to be at least a hundred years old. But the followup line is puzzling: the antagonisms between these two have always involved matters of principle; age has never been at issue. The charge of perpetual superannuation only makes sense when it is understood as being directed at someone other than Thatcher: the person Welles always incorrectly remembered as being very old.

Richard Welles had recently been very much on Welles's mind. On May 15, 1940, just two weeks before the film went into the major phase of preproduction, Welles had come into his inheritance from his father. The event had been delayed for ten years by the terms of Richard Welles's will, and at this crucial time in the film's gestation, Welles would have been forced to confront the whole painful experience of his father's life all over again. The result of this psychological upheaval is crystallized in Welles's special scene. Since there had been no advance preparation, a standing set had to be used. Welles chose a courtroom and the scene as played suggests the reading of a will. Kane's retorts to Thatcher should be understood as in the "always too old" exchange— as asides to an absent antagonist.

THATCHER

There's always the chance that you'll die richer than I will.

KANE

It's a cinch I'll die richer than I was born.

"A *very* rich banker"—that, Welles confided late in his life, is what his father would have liked to have been. He "was born with more money than he had when he died," Welles went on, "and to him, I believe, that was a great *shame*."[30] Based on this information, Kane's line takes on a new dimension—it is Welles reproaching his father for his lifetime's failure and vowing to succeed where he had failed. The way it is put is unusually nasty, but not so much so as the *maledizione* with which the scene ends:

THATCHER

What would you like to have been?

KANE

Everything you hate.

[30] Leaming, pp. 5–6.

Transposed into the operative context, Kane's line becomes Welles saying to his father, "I hate everything you ever were."

Welles's Dickensian caricatures masked an overpowering animosity toward his father for the dismal mess he had made of his life. What appears to have galled him most was Richard Welles's betrayal of his remarkable talent. Welles would redeem the legacy: not only would he succeed, but he would succeed phenomenally at whatever he put his hand to.

In the decade after his father's death, Welles had a string of accomplishments that were truly extraordinary. After graduating from Todd School in the spring of 1931, he embarked on a walking tour of Ireland and, upon arriving in Dublin, presented himself at the celebrated Gate Theatre. There he talked his way into the role of the onerous Duke Karl Alexander in *Jud Süss* and was, at sixteen, a minor sensation. Back home, he was able to secure a coveted position in Katharine Cornell and Guthrie McClintic's touring repertory company for the 1933–1934 season. In 1935, at nineteen, he had his Broadway acting breakthrough in *Panic*, Archibald MacLeish's experimental free verse play about the Wall Street crash. In 1936 he directed the legendary "Voodoo *Macbeth*," and in 1937 Marc Blitzstein's leftist political opera *The Cradle Will Rock*. In 1937, when he and John Houseman founded their own repertory company, the Mercury Theatre, he had, at twenty-two, already established a reputation as the enfant terrible of American theater. His work in the fledgling medium of radio followed a similar trajectory. He was on the air as an actor as early as 1934. When the Mercury Theatre expanded into radio, it fundamentally altered the nature of broadcast drama. In 1938, it achieved international notoriety for what is undoubtedly the single most famous radio program ever aired. In 1939 Welles negotiated a Hollywood contract with unprecedented creative guarantees, and at twenty-four, he was at work on what would turn out to be the great American film.

Welles thrived on the marathon pace, the amphetamine highs, and the constant living on the edge that characterized these years. What excited him most was the sheer omnivorousness of it all. To those around him, he seemed driven. By what, John Houseman thought was obvious:

> Those of us who were close to Orson had long been aware of the obsessive part his father continued to play in his life. Much of what he had accomplished so precociously had been done out of a furious need to prove himself in the eyes of a man who was no longer there to see it. Now that success had come, in quantities and of a kind that his father had never dreamed of, this conflict, far from being assuaged, seemed to grow more intense and consuming.[31]

Apparently Houseman knew as little about Welles's childhood as Cotten. (This is also evident in the fact that the information about Welles's early years in Houseman's memoirs is taken from a 1938 *New Yorker* profile.) Rather than feeling compelled to live up to his father's legacy, Welles's real motivation seems to have been to *escape* it. Ironically,

[31] John Houseman, *Run-Through: A Memoir* (New York: Simon and Schuster, 1972), pp. 414–415.

his relentlessness and constant overreaching were curses of excess on the same scale as Richard Welles's, with predictable results. For every triumph in the remarkable decade after his father's death, there was a comparable failure. (The lows are conveniently banished from the authorized version of the boy genius.) Unable to capitalize on the Gate Theatre experience, Welles returned in ignominy to the refuge of Todd School. He tried his hand at playwrighting, with dismal results, and worked on amateur dramatic productions. A chance meeting got him an introduction that led to the Cornell tour, but nothing more came out of it than the promise of a minor role in *Romeo and Juliet* on Broadway the following season, and he returned once again to Todd, where he organized a summer festival with the Gate Theatre stars. *Romeo and Juliet* did bring him to the attention of Houseman. Except for *Doctor Faustus*, their collaborations under the auspices of the Federal Theater Project offered more spectacle than dramatic substance, and *Horse Eats Hat* was a resounding flop. For all its lofty ambitions, the Mercury Theatre stage operation survived scarcely more than a year, a victim of political differences with backers, chronic underfunding, and above all, Welles's reckless extravagance.[32] *Five Kings*, his grandiose Shakespearean adaptation sponsored by the Theatre Guild, was a colossal disaster in the making and it closed out of town, burying Welles's credibility as a stage entrepreneur in the wreckage. Welles spent his first four months in Hollywood on an ill-conceived adaptation of *Heart of Darkness* which finally had to be abandoned, and briefly on a second project that never got beyond the scripting stage. *Citizen Kane* and *The Magnificent Ambersons* constitute another episode in the alternating pattern of success and failure that Welles's career entailed.

3

Booth Tarkington was once considered the equal of his Midwestern contemporaries such as Sherwood Anderson and Sinclair Lewis. His literary mentor was William Dean Howells, and stylistically his work represents an amalgamation of the new realism of Howells and Dreiser and the older chronicle tradition of Thackeray and Trollope. *The Magnificent Ambersons* (1918) was the second novel in his so-called "Growth" trilogy, which dealt with the transformation of a fictionalized Indianapolis from its nineteenth-century agrarian and mercantile roots into a modern, smokestack metropolis. In this novel, the historical theme is embodied in the framework of a simultaneous decline and ascent: the patrician Ambersons, unable to adapt to new ways, lose their fortune and stature while the enterprising Eugene Morgan achieves distinction in the thriving new field of automobile manufacture. The story's emotional center is an interlinking of romantic relationships between the Ambersons and the Morgans.

The story begins in 1873. Isabel Amberson is the town beauty. Eugene Morgan, the foremost suitor for her hand, has too much to drink one night and loudly trips over the bass viol he has brought to serenade her. Regarding it as a mark of disrespect, Isabel henceforth spurns Eugene and marries a rival suitor, the feckless and dull Wilbur Minafer. Isabel and Wilbur have a single child, George, who is shamelessly indulged

---

[32] See Richard France's introduction to *Orson Welles on Shakespeare: The W.P.A. and Mercury Theatre Playscripts* (New York: Greenwood Press, 1990) for a revisionist view of Welles's accomplishments in theater.

Welles and Mercury Theatre business manager Jack Moss in October 1941, shortly before shooting began on *The Magnificent Ambersons.* Welles left Moss in charge while he was in South America.

and spoiled by his mother. Wilbur accepts the fact that his was a marriage of convenience, and keeps his place. Twenty years later Eugene Morgan returns, a widower with a marriageable daughter, Lucy. Isabel has maintained her exquisite beauty into middle age; Eugene is handsome, elegant, socially graceful, and self-possessed—the very opposite of Wilbur. Ancient passions are rekindled. George takes an instant disliking to Eugene. At the same time, he becomes romantically interested in Lucy. Wilbur has made a series of bad investments and his financial worries contribute to his early death. Eugene continues to call—on his spinster aunt Fanny Minafer's account, George thinks—but when George learns that Eugene's true interest is in his mother, he finds this situation unbearable. He begins to profess a deep reverence for his father that was never evident before, and he hypocritically invokes his father's memory to play on his mother's guilt. When Eugene calls to take Isabel for a drive, George orders him to stay away and slams the door in his face. After George rejects his mother's plea for reconciliation, she submits to his wishes, and the two of them go abroad alone. Isabel, always physically frail, falls ill. Shortly after their return, she worsens. Once again Eugene is prevented from seeing her. George is called to her bedside, and shortly afterward she dies. George, left penniless and with a spinster aunt to care for, forsakes a career in law to take a high-risk, high-pay job handling explosives. One day he is run down in the street by an automobile and has both legs broken. Lucy goes to him at the hospital and they are reconciled. After appropriate reflection, Eugene follows.

Tarkington openly acknowledges one of his primary story sources. Shortly after George has succeeded in forcing Isabel to give Eugene up, he is in his bedroom preparing to dress for dinner. He is wearing a long black velvet lounging robe. He catches a glimpse of himself in the mirror and lingers for a moment on his reflection. In an instant of realization, a literary quotation enters his head. He recites the lines to himself:

> 'Tis not alone my inky cloak, good mother,
> Nor customary suits of solemn black . . .
> But I have that within which passeth show;
> These but the trappings and the suits of Woe.

The central conflict in *The Magnificent Ambersons*—a son's almost pathological jealousy of his widowed mother's suitor—is borrowed from *Hamlet*. A number of incidental story elements also seem to have been suggested by Shakespeare's play, although Tarkington has freely transposed circumstances and characterizations—such things as the death of the hero's father, the widow's putting aside her mourning habits (so some think) all too soon, an Ophelia figure whose father opposes her courtship by the hero, the son's taunting of his mother and impertinence to her suitor, and the mother's emotional perplexity and untimely death. Tarkington has also changed the fundamental disposition of the story—from tragedy to a tragical romance with an affirmative outcome.

Continuity sketches for George's Hamlet scene, drawn by Joe St. Amon from Welles's first draft screenplay. The scene was deleted before shooting began.

With the arrival of Eugene, Isabel's loyalties become divided; for the first time in his life, George is faced with a lessening of his mother's unconditional devotion. What upsets him most is this implied maternal rejection. For Welles, the personal dimension of the situation was compounded:

> It has long been a family assumption that the author had my father in mind when he created the character which I will always think of as the Joseph Cotten role in *The Magnificent Ambersons*.[33]

Surely Welles had some idea of the potential danger this kind of subject matter held for him. Possibly the success of the radio version, in which he played George, bolstered his confidence. If so, it was a serious miscalculation. Radio adaptation as he practiced it was very largely a gathering of dramatically incandescent and exceptionally sonorous passages strung together with clever transitional devices. The production of a film would involve a relentlessly painstaking working through of the story material extending over several months' time. Welles's extreme personal investment in the dramatic issues involved virtually insured that the process would be psychically divisive.

In *Citizen Kane* Welles had toyed with the notion of a sexual component in the maternal relationship. In *The Magnificent Ambersons* Tarkington forced him to confront the issue directly. The occasion is the Amberson ball. George, his mother, and his grandfather are in the receiving line; Wilbur Minafer is inexplicably absent. George is about to meet Eugene for the first time.

> Standing beside his mother, George was disturbed by a sudden impression, coming upon him out of nowhere, so far as he could detect, that her eyes were brilliant, that she was graceful and youthful—in a word, that she was romantically lovely. He had one of those curious moments that seem to have neither a cause nor any connection with actual things. While it lasted, he was disquieted not by thoughts—for he had no definite thoughts—but by a slight emotion like that caused in a dream by the presence of something invisible, soundless, and yet fantastic. There was nothing different or new about his mother, except her new black and silver dress: she was standing there beside him, bending her head a little in her greetings, smiling the same smile she had worn for the half-hour that people had been passing the "receiving" group. Her face was flushed, but the room was warm; and shaking hands with so many people easily accounted for the pretty glow that was upon her. At any time she could have "passed" for twenty-five or twenty-six— a man of fifty would have honestly guessed her to be about thirty but possibly two or three years younger—and though extraordinary in this, she had been extraordinary in it for years. There was nothing in either her looks or her manner to explain George's uncomfortable feeling; and yet it increased, becoming suddenly a vague resentment, as if she had done something unmotherly to him.[34]

That Welles comprehended the import of this is clear from George's behavior once he learns that Eugene has a romantic interest in his mother. In the bathroom scene with Uncle Jack, George is hysterical at the prospect of their marriage; in lines cut from the

---

[33] "My Father Wore Black Spats," p. 185.

[34] Booth Tarkington, *The Magnificent Ambersons* (New York: Doubleday Page, 1918). Hill and Wang American Century Series, 1957, pp. 25–26. Freud's theory of an Oedipal subtext in *Hamlet* would have been available to Tarkington (Ernest Jones's famous elaboration of it was originally published in *American Journal of Psychology* in 1910), though there is no reason to believe he was familiar with it. Freud himself felt that writers had an instinctual understanding of this dynamic.

release version, he called it "unspeakable," "monstrous," "horrible."[35] "That you can sit there and speak of it!" he screams. "Your own sister!" Though he takes a somewhat gentler tone with his mother, he makes the same perfidious insinuation; in a scene also removed from the release version (George and Isabel are discussing Eugene's letter), George asks, "Do you suppose it ever occurs to him that I'm doing my simple duty? . . . That I'm doing what my father would do if he were here?"[36] In yet another scene removed from the release version, Isabel informs George by letter that she has acceded to his demands and given up Eugene. She writes, "My darling, my beloved. I think I shouldn't mind anything very much as long as I have you all to myself."[37] Shortly after, the two of them go abroad alone, almost as if on an extended honeymoon. On their return, George carries her in his arms to a waiting carriage. That there is an autobiographical implication in their relationship becomes evident in George's visit to Isabel on her deathbed, a scene that attempts the same aura of enchantment as in Welles's own maternal deathbed memoir.

The association of Eugene Morgan with Richard Welles posed an even more perplexing difficulty. Richard Welles had once been such a person—a dashing and stylish entrepreneur who, at age twenty-three, founded the Badger Brass Company of Kenosha and was its general manager when he met Beatrice Ives. He was, according to report, "largely responsible for its phenomenal success. The company grew from the original $25,000 capital to a concern worth $1,000,000" when it was sold in 1906.[38] But this was a different Richard Welles from the one his son knew. In his treatment of Eugene, Welles was coerced into an elaborate aesthetic fraudulence: he had to suspend his personal animus and, as it were, to reinvent his father as a double of his own exalted vision of himself. Adaptation necessities intensified the process. Tarkington's Eugene Morgan is a dimly realized and relatively minor character, an obligatory presence in a few showcase scenes functioning principally to deliver material of a homiletic nature. In casting a player of Joseph Cotten's stature as Eugene, Welles had made it obligatory to greatly expand the role. The Amberson ball provides a good illustration. In the novel, George and Lucy meet and engage straightaway and it is well into the evening before Eugene's identity is even revealed. In Welles's version, the action begins with an enraptured renewal of acquaintance between Eugene and Isabel as George, shut out for the moment, looks disdainfully on. Tarkington's ball ends with the general dancing in full swing. Welles's ends with Eugene and Isabel, oblivious to George and Lucy's presence, dancing alone like lovers after everyone else has gone. He added other new scenes for Eugene, such as the one in the arbor when Eugene urges Isabel to reveal their relationship to George. One effect of such changes is to intensify the Oedipal character of George's hatred for Eugene.

In *Hamlet*, in Freud's view, the continued presence of the Oedipal rival drove the young prince into a form of extreme self-abasement. A similar process occurred in Welles's adaptation: in the same way that he amplified Eugene's character, he diminished George's. Tarkington's George is much more rounded. For all his lofty arrogance, he has a number of redeeming virtues. He is brighter and cleverer by far than his peers.

[35] Cutting continuity, reel 4A, shots 31–32, 36–37.

[36] Cutting continuity, reel 5A, shots 11–12.

[37] Cutting continuity, reel 5A, shot 21.

[38] Kenosha *Evening News*, December 29, 1930, clipping in *HRC*.

His claims to superiority, while put forth in an offensive manner, are not without foundation. His refusal to pursue a career is motivated not by indolence or lassitude but by a sincere belief that he belongs to an aristocracy of privilege. He takes pride in the family and, within the family circle, is generous to a fault. He genuinely loves Lucy and reveals a tender and vulnerable side to her that he shows to no one else. Lucy is not the only one to recognize that George appears at his best when he is most transparent: her father observes that "in all my life, the most arrogant people I've known have been the most sensitive" (p. 73), and Uncle Jack (Uncle George in the novel) tells his nephew at their final parting, "the stuff of the old stock is in you. It'll come out and do something" (p. 208). George's most sympathetic moment is when he unflinchingly faces up to the truth: that he ruined his mother's life and hastened her death to no end; the gossip would have died down soon enough of its own accord, and besides, the town had ceased to care about the Ambersons and their doings anyway. Welles eliminated most of these subtleties and shadings in George's character, with the result that he comes off in the film as merely an arrogant, obnoxious snob.

Welles's original ending radically amplified his vilification of George and corresponding elevation of Eugene. In the novel, Eugene reads of George's accident as he is traveling east by train. When he arrives in New York, he visits a medium and through her establishes communication with the spirit of Isabel, who seems to be asking him to forgive her son. When he arrives home, he goes immediately to George's hospital room—Lucy is there already—and reconciliations abound. The supernatural element is not one of Tarkington's finer displays of creative imagination. When Welles was preparing the radio version of *The Magnificent Ambersons* in 1939, he wisely dispensed with it and had Eugene come around in a more conventional manner, as a result of Lucy's urging. He eliminated direct representation of the scene in George's hospital room, however, and instead had Eugene read an entry in his diary addressed to Isabel describing it to her. In the shooting script, Welles had the film ending in this same way. But just before shooting began he suddenly instituted an even more extreme departure from the novel. As originally shot, the film ended with Eugene visiting Fanny at the decrepit boarding house where she now resides. As Fanny rocks away and (a recurring motif) stares coldly into the distance, Eugene, oblivious to her feelings as always, rattles on about how he distinctly felt Isabel's presence in the hospital room.

Welles thought it "the best scene in the picture."[39] Even in the bland language of the cutting continuity, there are intimations of how powerful it must have been. Joseph Cotten, however, wondered if it might not be too Chekhovian for its own good. Preview audiences, accustomed as they were to upbeat and overwrought Hollywood endings, certainly found it so. In any case, the boardinghouse ending provided a means of eliminating George as a presence in the story. While this is a total reversal of expectations and an almost perverse denial of closure, it can nevertheless be seen as the ultimate culmination of Welles's reversal of stature of the two characters. The process itself can be seen as having an actual correspondence to Welles's life. For just as Welles methodically debased his alterego George, in the course of making *The Magnificent Ambersons*

---

[39] *The Orson Welles Story*, Arena (BBC television series), broadcast May 18 and 21, 1982.

he devalued himself artistically, often behaved in a manner that seems almost calculatedly detrimental, and eventually withdrew himself from direct participation in its realization.

For the only time in one of his major productions, Welles declined the leading role in *The Magnificent Ambersons*. The reason usually advanced is that he had grown up too much to be convincing as a college boy. This explanation has always been accepted at face value. Close scrutiny reveals its inadequacy. For one thing, Welles did not exhibit such fastidiousness with the other roles in the film. Early in the story, for instance, he asks us to accept Joseph Cotten, then in his middle thirties, as an ardent swain of twenty, and Dolores Costello, the same age as Cotten but showing it much more, as a girl of eighteen (a singularly ludicrous presentment in the shot of her puffy, middle-aged face in the window when Eugene trips over and smashes the bass viol). As the story progresses, he asks us further to accept that both could reappear twenty years later still looking almost the same. As George, Welles, who was then twenty-six, might have strained credulity somewhat in his younger scenes—a club meeting when he is supposed to be seventeen (a scene shot by Welles but later removed) and the Amberson ball and the snow ride, when he is supposed to be nineteen, but nowhere to the extent of Cotten or Costello earlier. Besides, Welles still had his baby face, and there were technical means of making him appear younger, such as makeup and lighting. (Makeup wizard Maurice Seiderman, who had performed virtual miracles with the age requirements on *Citizen Kane*, also worked on *The Magnificent Ambersons*.) Welles's height was not really a problem, since Tarkington's George is described as unusually tall. He is also exceedingly handsome, as Welles was in his twenties. As the story progressed and George aged, any perceived problem of this sort would have vanished of its own accord. When George returns from abroad with Isabel, he is only a year younger than Welles actually was, and at the time of his automobile accident he is a year older. Tim Holt has the sole advantage of a slightly more youthful appearance for the early scenes (he was then twenty-two), but for the most part the dramatic and physical requirements of the role are beyond his capabilities, and he comes off as something of a dunce. On the other hand, George Minafer could have been one of Welles's great roles. Welles seems to have been aware of this; "I was planning to play the part," he told an interviewer at the time, "but I decided [Holt] was the logical person for it. It wasn't an easy decision for me to make."[40] The conclusion seems inescapable that, rather than being extremely scrupulous in casting the role of George, Welles was deliberately avoiding it himself.

For the first month the film was in production, there were high spirits all around on the set. The ballroom scene, the film's great virtuosic tour de force, was completed, as well as two other key scenes, the dinner for Eugene and George's encounter with Fanny afterward on the stairs. But as shooting proceeded, the atmosphere changed. Welles himself grew increasingly moody and irritable. Those around him were accustomed to his flareups and constant swings in temper. But nothing before had persisted for so long or been as dark. Some detected what they thought a streak of outright meanness.[41] That Welles was more overextended than usual undoubtedly contributed, but a more

[40] Quoted by Cyril Vandour in "Holt & Sons," *Photoplay* 21, no. 6 (November 1942), p. 90.

[41] Richard Wilson and Amalia Kent, two of those who worked with him most closely on the production, recall the peculiarity of Welles's conduct at this time.

likely clue to his behavior is that the film's story elements that were personally most vexatious to Welles were being shot during this time. It was at this point, when Welles was at his most vulnerable, that the South American opportunity arose.

As part of an effort to foster hemispheric relations, the U.S. State Department section on Inter-American Affairs approached RKO with a proposal for a film to be shot on location in Brazil accentuating native customs and themes; the Department would partially underwrite the venture. With the concurrence of Nelson Rockefeller, Co-Ordinator of Inter-American Affairs, RKO President George Schaefer offered the assignment to Welles.[42] Welles accepted—out of genuine enthusiasm, unquestionably, but it was also a way of distancing himself from *The Magnificent Ambersons*. The centerpiece of the South American film was to be the Carnival in Rio. In order to be in place in Rio by Carnival time in mid-February, he would have to speed up shooting on *The Magnificent Ambersons* and would barely have time to complete it; postproduction would be left in the hands of others. In yet another display of moody ex–citability, he replaced cinematographer Stanley Cortez (who worked slowly but with scintillating results) with a reliable but totally commonplace RKO studio cameraman for the duration.

Robert Wise, the film's editor, was placed in charge of postproduction. He had edited *Citizen Kane* and enjoyed Welles's full confidence, although his ultimate accountability was to his employer, RKO. Jack Moss, business manager for the Mercury Theatre operation, was left behind as general overseer and liaison between Welles and the studio. Moss had no experience in film production and was never taken seriously by the studio hierarchy. Duplicate footage was to be sent to Welles in Rio and he would supervise the editing by cable, telephone, and shortwave radio. When the impracticability of this arrangement became evident, Welles asked for Wise to be sent to Rio, but this proved unworkable because of wartime travel restrictions. Wise proceeded according to the editing plan Welles had laid out just before leaving the country and subsequent instructions coming in from Rio. After he had completed a final cut and was readying a print for shipment to Rio, Welles suddenly ordered an extraordinary set of changes. All the footage between Isabel's receiving Eugene's letter and the family gathered in the hallway outside Isabel's room just before her death was to be removed. This would involve the following scenes: George and Isabel discussing Eugene's letter, Isabel's letter slipped under George's door telling him she will renounce Eugene, George's walk with Lucy on the street, the drugstore and poolroom, Fanny and the Major on the veranda one evening discussing their bad investments, Jack's visit to the Morgans, and Isabel's return.[43] In place of the cut would go a single new scene to be shot by Wise in which George enters his mother's room to find her unconscious. The new sequence of events would be: Isabel receives Eugene's letter, falls unconscious, and dies shortly after.

Wise's original cut was shipped to Welles on March 11 as scheduled. Meanwhile, Wise proceeded quickly with shooting of the new scene and the substitution was made in time for the first preview on March 17 in Pomona. As is well known, the Pomona

---

[42] Schaefer to Welles [?April 29, 1942], undated transcription in George Schaefer Collection, Western Heritage Center, Laramie, Wyoming.

[43] Cutting continuity, reel 5A shot 4 through reel 5B to second lap dissolve in shot 7, approximately 13 minutes 40 seconds.

preview was disastrous. A raucous, largely teenage audience had just been treated to a rousing wartime musical. Now they found themselves confronted with a complex, slow-paced, and generally downbeat period drama. Worse, its dramatic center was truncated. It is difficult to imagine how the impact of what Moss came to call Welles's "big cut" could have been anything other than devastating for the story. Having Isabel collapse and die as an immediate consequence of George's turning Eugene away is pure melodrama. The subtle Chekhovian quality Welles was said to be aiming for resided largely in the fragile emotional balance between Isabel and George: however reprehensible he was, Isabel partly bore the blame. She was freely complicitous in her fate; taking away this mitigating circumstance would leave George irredeemably venomous.

One likely explanation for an action so rash is that Welles was being driven by a private motive. The Oedipal character of George's relationship with his mother was most apparent—indeed, virtually explicit—in the deleted footage. Whether out of guilt, dread of personal self-exposure, or simply a generalized unease, Welles had second thoughts and wanted it taken out. That Welles's own reediting was partly to blame for the extreme hostility of the reaction at Pomona seems an inescapable conclusion.

Wise and Moss quickly restored all of Welles's big cut except for the scene of Fanny and the Major in time for a second preview in Pasadena on March 19. This time the audience reaction was much more favorable, not an unexpected outcome at an upscale location like Pasadena. But demographics are only part of the explanation. In his scene by scene account of the preview reactions, Wise emphasized that each of the restored scenes had been received favorably. George and Lucy's walk, he reported, had even played "beautifully."

Clearly, Schaefer had on his hands what the industry (usually with some derogation) called a "special" picture—one with appeal for only a limited segment of the filmgoing audience that stood no chance of recouping anywhere near its $1,000,000 cost. Schaefer forlornly delivered the bad news. Welles liked to depict Schaefer as something of a buffoon, as with the story that he had fallen asleep when *The Magnificent Ambersons* was first pitched to him. Perhaps he had, but Welles always neglected to mention that when Schaefer did give his assent for the film to proceed, it was with a major condition. Welles would give up the right of final cut which he had enjoyed in his original contract; after the first preview of *The Magnificent Ambersons*, the film could be edited at RKO's sole discretion. Schaefer avoided precipitous action for a time, perhaps a sign that he was considering some form of accommodation. But increasing signs of deep trouble on the South American venture, combined with lackluster box-office results on *Citizen Kane*, gradually eroded his confidence, and the order came: take whatever steps are necessary to make the film more attractive to a mass audience. Once again, Wise was put in charge. Instructions continued to flow in from Welles—he still wanted the big cut and other changes that may, to some, seem even more questionable—but Wise had been granted authority to act on his sole discretion; Schaefer himself would be final arbiter. The version cleared for release by Schaefer on June 8 ran eighty-eight minutes ten seconds, forty-three minutes shorter than the original version of March 11. It was test-marketed in July to spotty results and was in effect abandoned by the studio.

Welles's verdict: "*They* destroyed *Ambersons* and *it* destroyed me."[44] To the contrary, Welles himself must bear the ultimate responsibility for the affair's outcome. It was a string of questionable judgments and rash actions on his part that paved the way to the film's undoing. In adapting the story, he pitilessly denigrated the central character, forfeited the opportunity to appear in this role himself, and impulsively assigned it to an inferior performer. Welles himself might have redeemed the part, but preview audiences were unrelentingly hostile to Tim Holt. Regardless of how one views Welles's premature withdrawal from the film's production, the fact remains that he took no special precautions to safeguard its welfare in his absence. To the contrary, he entrusted the film's fate entirely to lower-level subordinates who would be powerless to defend his interests if the need arose. At the last minute, he had second thoughts and insisted on a drastic alteration that would almost certainly imperil the film's prospects with an audience. When serious difficulties did arise, there was no one to take charge on Welles's behalf, and his surrender of the right of final cut left the studio free to act as it chose. This is not to say that Welles acted irresponsibly; that he behaved *evasively* would be a more accurate characterization. Regarding each action, a vexatious personal involvement in the material was at play, and this factor overrode Welles's aesthetic judgment. He was divided against himself: engaged on one side of his nature in the creation of (judging from what does survive) one of the most visually brilliant films ever made in Hollywood, a formidable rival even to *Citizen Kane*, but on another side almost at the mercy of an elemental disquietude that impaired his artistic responsibility and detachment.

4

The South American project ended in disaster. Schaefer was deposed as studio head largely on account of Welles, and Welles's contract with RKO was terminated. Welles returned to Hollywood and remained visible through his involvement in entertaining troops but it soon became clear that he would never be entrusted with a major production again on his own terms. After directing and starring in two thrillers, the tedious *The Stranger* (1946) and the stylish but impenetrable *The Lady From Shanghai* (1948), he returned to Shakespeare and for the following decade committed his principal energies to Shakespearean tragedy.

Macbeth (1948), made for a studio that specialized in serials and B westerns, was an adaptation of a stage production put on at the Utah Centennial Festival the previous year; it is characterized by typically outrageous Wellesean interpolations and by touches of dazzling visual brilliance. *Othello* (1952) was the first of his international productions, released to widespread critical acclaim in Europe but generally ignored in the United States. During a hiatus in the shooting of the film, he appeared in a London stage version of the play produced by Laurence Olivier, to mixed reviews. In 1953, he

---

[44] *The Orson Welles Story.*

Welles at 30,
physically an ideal
specimen for Hamlet.

appeared on American television in a highly acclaimed *King Lear* directed by Peter Brook, and in 1956 he returned to New York in a controversial stage version of the play he directed himself, in which he was forced to perform from a wheelchair because of a leg injury sustained during rehearsals.

There is a conspicuous absence: Why is there no *Hamlet?* The omission is all the more puzzling when we recall what a formative role it had occupied in Welles's early career. In 1932, at age sixteen, he made his debut in classical theater at the Gate in Dublin as the ghost of Hamlet's father. The following year, when he took dramatic lessons in preparation for the road tour with the Katharine Cornell company, his primer was *Hamlet*—indeed, it was said, the personal signed copy of John Barrymore, who had studied with the same dramatic coach.[45] In 1934, his dual appearance as Claudius and his brother's ghost in the Todd School summer festival earned him a string of superlatives in a Chicago newspaper review.[46] His first directorial credit on network radio was for a two-part *Hamlet* in which he also starred for the Columbia Workshop series in the fall of 1936. A second *Hamlet* for radio to be produced, directed, adapted by, and to star Welles was announced for the Mercury Theatre "First Person Singular" series for August 18, 1938, but was dropped from the schedule without explanation.[47] After this, he never did the play again in any medium.

An explanation sometimes advanced is that Welles was too old and physically ungainly for Hamlet by the time of his major Shakespearean phase. Actually, in 1947 he was as trim and physically attractive as at any time in his adult life. Also, he was thirty-one—only one year older than Hamlet at the time of his father's death. (The current presumption that Hamlet is a younger man is probably most attributable to Laurence Olivier's interpretation in his 1948 film, the most widely seen of modern productions. Incidentally, Olivier was forty at the time.) I asked Welles's two closest associates (next to Houseman) in the heyday of the Mercury Theatre to comment on the anomaly. Richard Wilson said that Welles had spoken of doing *Hamlet* many times but just never got around to it.[48] William Alland conjectured that the explanation lay in the personal dimension of the material. Hamlet's "great scream," all his "anguish" about his parental relationships—"it's like Orson."

> Hamlet's a very disturbed young man. Very mixed up in his feelings. . . . I think that Orson understood Hamlet—I mean, there's many Hamlets you know, but I think Orson had a particular idea of *his* Hamlet, and I think it would be very similar—he would *look* very similar to Orson. . . . I think Orson could have played Hamlet, but I have a hunch he was intimidated inside. . . . I think it would expose . . . you know his childhood, don't you?[49]

In a sense, Welles did produce a vernacular version of *Hamlet* in *The Magnificent Ambersons*. One lesson he might have learned from the experience of that film was that parental relationships were too disruptive a force in his psychological life to be brought under creative control. Perhaps he did, and that is why there is no actual *Hamlet*. In any case, with *The Magnificent Ambersons* the egotistic, or Oedipal, fixation on childhood

[45] Charles Collins, "Eighteen Years Old, Scores Hit in Shakespeare" and June Provines, "Front Views and Profiles," unidentified newspaper columns, *HRC.*

[46] Herman Davies, Chicago *Daily News*, undated, *HRC.*

[47] For the radio information I am indebted to Professor Michael Ogden, author of a forthcoming book on Welles's career in radio.

[48] Interview with Richard Wilson, October 29, 1987.

[49] Interview with William Alland, October 28, 1987.

ceased to be a primary motivating force in his work. (Artifacts of it still occasionally appear, as in *Mr. Arkadin*, where the Welles character is excessively, almost incestuously protective of his daughter—played by Paola Mori, whom Welles would later marry—and extravagantly jealous of her potential lover.) In a rare moment of candor, Welles once told an interviewer that doing *The Magnificent Ambersons* had been a mistake. The reason he gave was that the film did nothing for his reputation as an actor. Instead, he said, "I should have gone back to New York and played Hamlet."[50]

[50] *The Orson Welles Story.*

A NOTE ON TEXTUAL PRACTICE

Cutting and *continuity* are film studio terms for *editing* and *story events.* A *cutting continuity* is a written transcription of the contents of the final edited version of a narrative film in the form in which it is intended for release to theaters. In general terms, it is an *alternative representation of a film's text in a variant medium.*

In the studio system, a cutting continuity was prepared for each film released. It provided the following information in the order indicated: number of the reel holding the contents indicated, duration of individual shots expressed in feet plus additional frames, sequential number of each shot, abbreviated descriptions of the images that appear on the screen and of noise effects or music on the soundtrack, and all dialogue or voiceover narration. The nature of the information suggests the primary use for which cutting continuities were intended: to allow discrete segments of the film to be easily located on the 35mm reels on which they were mounted. The cutting continuity was mimeographed and copies were included with prints of the film sent out to the regional distribution exchanges. If cuts were ordered after a film was put into release, or if replacement footage was needed for a damaged print, the cutting continuity was the basis for transactions with the exchanges. In any other circumstances requiring the perusal or manipulation of a portion of a film's contents (excerpting, for instance), the cutting continuity served as the point of reference. In the studio's day-to-day operations, a file copy of the cutting continuity would be used as a guide to the film's contents wherever possible to get around the cumbersome procedure of having to consult the film itself. Finally, in those days a *facsimile* such as a cutting continuity was usually deposited for copyright registration in place of an original copy of a film.

Cutting continuities were prepared by technical assistants in the studio's editorial department and sent to the typing pool, where different secretaries each worked on a single reel simultaneously. The procedure was usually handled with breakneck speed, since the time between completion of a finished cut of the film and its first showing requiring backup material (a sneak preview, for instance) might be as little as three days. The technical information in the continuities was flawlessly precise, since an error in a footage count could result in faulty instructions to the film laboratory and costly delays. The descriptions of the images were prepared with considerably less care. They were extremely sparse and written in a kind of staccato prose shorthand. These qualities reflected their primary function: to identify just the essential features of the shot (setting, camera and figure location and movement, sounds) without regard for stylistic values or story context. Following is the cutting continuity description of the shot in *The Magnificent Ambersons* of Eugene and Isabel dancing alone after the ball is over, perhaps the single most visually exhilarating moment in the film:

INT. HALL LS - Musicians standing around in FG by Xmas trees - Playing - Eugene and Isabel in BG dancing -

In fact, there is only *one* Christmas tree in the shot, and Eugene and Isabel are actually dancing in the *extreme* background. The transcriber is jotting down rough first impressions and letting it go at that. Working in this manner actually encouraged imprecision if not outright inaccuracy, and the more complex a film's narrative system, the higher the rate of misrepresentation. The cutting continuity of *The Magnificent Ambersons* is filled with incorrect or misleading information, such as factual errors concerning the images, faulty dialogue transcriptions, and attributions of dialogue to the wrong speaker. It also has a tendency to bypass situations that inhibit speed, giving a single phrase such as *talk indistinctly* for dialogue faintly heard (as when spoken at a distance from the camera) or *all talk at once* for overlapping (but nevertheless decipherable) dialogue. In addition, there is considerable variation among transcribers in spelling, punctuation, hyphenation, and grammatical usage, as well as in such matters as degree of familiarity with the story material and sometimes even standardized scripting conventions (for instance, in the designations given to shots in the range between medium shot and closeup). The secretaries in the RKO typing pool worked more scrupulously, proofreading the mimeographed masters aloud in teams and turning out highly accurate copies of the material as received, but they too displayed individual vagaries of usage. Indeed, one suspects it would have been possible to identify certain typists solely on the basis of their patterns of use of spaces, dashes, and periods. But minor errors and inconsistencies of these sorts rarely mattered. So long as the description was correctly matched with its corresponding shot number and footage count, the stripped down, first impression version adequately served the studio's purpose.

The only complete surviving record of an original, long version of *The Magnificent Ambersons* is the RKO cutting continuity of March 12, 1942. This version of the film was assembled by Robert Wise according to a precise set of instructions given him by Welles when the two screened a rough cut at the Fleischer Studios in Miami in early February as Welles was en route to South America. It ran 131 minutes, 45$^1/_3$ seconds. It is the text used for the reconstruction plan in this volume. Actually, the film was never shown publicly in this form. Welles ordered cuts and at least one major change before the first preview on March 17. Most of the cuts were restored by others for the second preview on March 19, but other scenes were left out. After the second preview, the massive reediting ordered by the studio began. Apparently no full transcription of the early changes by Welles was prepared, but even if one had been, the March 12 cutting continuity would in all likelihood still be the preferred master plan. After all, Welles had not yet seen the March 12 version when he ordered the changes, and his impulsive second guesses were not always improvements. Indeed, those of March 17 may even have contributed to the extremely negative reactions to that preview. The March 12 version is in close accord with the plan of shooting and is a full representation of Welles's original intention.

The aim of the reconstruction of *The Magnificent Ambersons* undertaken in this volume is to enable the reader to gain as clear an impression of the original film as is possible from the materials which survive. The first step toward achieving this goal was to provide a clear and consistent foundation text. In effect, this meant transforming the cutting continuity from a somewhat offputting technical-functional document into a reader-oriented one. Since the cutting continuity was prepared wholly by others and had no directorial authority, the necessary changes could legitimately be made so long as certain proprieties were observed.

Following is the cutting continuity treatment of the shot showing how Wilbur Minafer now has the upper hand over Eugene in the courtship of Isabel (reel 1A):

21-7 34.   EXT. STORE MS - Camera shooting up from street - Three standing before store - Isabel with huge dog on leash - Eugene at right - Music heard - Isabel turns coldly to left - Wilbur tipping his hat - The two go to left - Camera pans Eugene starts to follow them - They look coldly at him - Turn hurry down walk to BG - He looks after them - Voices heard -

Bronson   Wilbur Minafer! I never thought he'd get her. Well, what do you know....

Following is the revised treatment which appears in this volume:

Ext Shop MS - Camera shooting up from street - Three standing in front of ice cream parlor - Isabel with dog on leash - Eugene at right - Music heard - Wilbur tips his hat - Crosses in front of Eugene - Camera pans to follow - Isabel turns coldly away from Eugene toward background - Pan continues as she and Wilbur walk away - They hurry down walk as Eugene starts to follow - He stops - Looks after them -   **34** (21-7)

Bronson's Voice

Wilbur? Wilbur Minafer? I never thought he'd get her. Well, what do you know.

Following are explanations for the changes:

Giving footage count before shot number serves a film editor's needs; a reader typically refers to shot numbers much more often than to footage counts. Setting this technical information apart should make reading of the written text more congenial. So too should the substitution of a more familiar typeface.

Shot descriptions in cutting continuities are so formulaic that a reader adjusts to them without much effort. This one is unusually detailed, but the transcriber has fuzzied the sequence and logical relation of events. The material has been rewritten for clarity, specific details have been added, and run-on phrasing ("Turn hurry down walk") has been eliminated through rewording. Before changes of any sort were made in the cutting continuity descriptions of shots, however, the length of the corresponding shot in the release version was calculated on a Steenbeck viewing table to ensure that the two versions exactly matched. (Variations were treated on a case-to-case basis and are usually indicated in the footnotes.)

Although the writing has been considerably revised, the elemental syntactic features of the shot descriptions have been maintained. The first of these is the staccato prose rhythm. The second may not be immediately discernible. In the cutting continuity, when a shot opens with action in progress (as in the example above), participles are used to set the scene. After the final setting cue—here, "Music heard"—active verbs begin to be used. In a random selection with samples from all seven reels, twenty-two of twenty-four shots complied with this principle. Adhering to these two conventions—writing in staccato prose and setting the scene with participles—insured that the verbal style in the parts subjected to rewriting would be consistent with the verbal style in the sections deleted in the editing process, which had to remain as originally written.

In the final line of description, "voices" is incorrect since only *one* voice is heard. However, the cue is superfluous anyway, since the dialogue involved immediately follows. "Voice" is added after the speaker's name to indicate that the lines are heard as voiceover narration (the actor does not appear on the screen at this point).

The spatial arrangement of placing spoken lines in a single column along the right side of the page can make for a peculiar reading experience, especially when an unusually long speech leaves the other half of the page entirely blank.

The transcriber has missed the first "Wilbur" and has incorrectly characterized his intonation as emphatic rather than incredulous. The intent of the four periods at the end of Bronson's speech is unclear, since multiple periods (three to six) appear in passages of dialogue throughout the cutting continuity without apparent pattern. To eliminate this inconsistency of usage, the following guidelines have been applied: A line of dialogue is ordinarily followed by a single period, but in cases where there is a pause of three counts (one-two-three) or more after a spoken line, the pause is indicated by three unspaced periods (...). When a line of dialogue is interrupted, the break or continuation is indicated by three spaced periods (. . .). Since it is not possible to ascertain such nuances in the deleted scenes, the customary practice in them is a single period following a line of dialogue.

Throughout the cutting continuity generally, typographical and spelling errors have been corrected, inconsistent spelling, punctuation, and grammatical usage have been regularized, and obvious omissions have been added. Also for clarity in reading, a single shot location heading is used consistently for a scene, as in "Dining Room" (reel 4A, shots 2 through 25), where the original also gave "Room" and "Table," or "Bathroom" (reel 4A, shots 28 through 47), where the original also gave "Room," "Bathtub," and "Tub."

Perhaps the single most troublesome matter in the cutting continuity was inconsistent identification of shots according to the distance between the camera and the person or object being filmed.

Seven shot labels are used in *The Magnificent Ambersons* cutting continuity: LS (Long Shot), MLS (Medium Long Shot), MS (Medium Shot), CS (Close Shot), MCS (Medium Close Shot), MCU (Medium Closeup), and CU (Closeup).

ELS (extreme long shot) is not used, although it should be—for the camera setup in which the camera is so far away that the surroundings dominate the characters: the shots of the exterior of the Amberson mansion, for instance, or of Pendennis seen racing home alone in the snow scene (reel 2B shot 38), or of the automobile seen receding into the distance across an expanse of snow (reel 2B shot 85). This is distinctly different from **LS** (long shot), which is characteristically a middle distance camera setup which maintains human figures and environment in complementary scale, as with the several occasions on which George is seen riding through the town. **MLS** (medium long shot) is used mainly for interior shots encompassing, say, a stretch of hallway, as when George is seen crossing to his mother's room after he has seen Eugene's letter (reel 5A shot 3) or an entire large room, as when George is seen kneeling at his mother's bed begging for forgiveness (reel 6B, in the continuation after the lap dissolve in shot 3), but there are inconsistencies—as in the dinner scene (reel 4A), where MLS is used for a full shot of the Amberson dining room in shot 23 but LS is used in shot 2.

MS (medium shot) *is* used consistently, most typically for full-figure shots of a character group occupying the middle foreground.

But there were chronic difficulties with the close-range setups. In the cutting continuity: a **MCS** (medium close shot) is typically a character group filling the frame and appearing to be about six feet from the camera; a **MCU** (medium closeup) is typically a single figure loosely framed or a group tightly framed and appearing to be about four feet from the camera; a **CU** (closeup) is typically a single figure filling the frame or a group dominating it and appearing to be about two to three feet from the camera. However, these three shot designations were often interchanged. Moreover, CS (close shot) is often used indeterminately for all three. Finally, there is yet another camera setup which is not differentiated—an **ECU** (extreme closeup), showing an object such as the groaning spigot in the bathroom scene (reel 4A shot 28) or part of a face in exaggerated perspective (reel 4A shot 29) which appear to be about one foot from the camera; such shots are subsumed under CU (closeup). A segment from the snow ride (reel 2B) provides a good illustration of this pattern of incongruency in the cutting continuity. The car stalls, George gets behind and pushes, the ride resumes amid talking and singing: of the twenty-seven shots depicting this action (numbers 45 through 71), thirteen are inconsistently designated.

The following measures were taken to regularize shot usage: ELS and ECU were added; CS was eliminated because it had no precise meaning. This left a total of eight shot designations: **ELS, LS, MLS, MS, MCS, MCU, CU,** and **ECU**. On the basis of this revised scheme, shots in the release version were individually checked and appropriate corrections were made in the corresponding shots in the cutting continuity. For consistency, one change was made in the deleted sections: MCS was substituted in place of CS.

All of the foregoing changes have been made without the use of brackets [ ] or other indicating signs: an all-inclusive identifying practice would not only have overwhelmed the text, but it would also have interfered with an already daunting notational system that is necessary for more substantive matters. I call attention to other changes of a special nature in footnotes.

3

AN AMBERSON FAMILY CHRONOLOGY

The chronology is reconstructed from Welles's shooting script, the only source that gives precise dates for all the events. For consistency, the order of events is also as given in the shooting script. (Material shot but later deleted is indicated within brackets.) The ages of most of the characters are not specified in the script and have had to be deduced from internal evidence or, in the absence of such information, by inference from Tarkington's novel. Quotations, unless otherwise indicated, are from Welles's script.

1873

Major Amberson made a great fortune (in the Panic of 1873, Tarkington implies) and the "magnificence" of the Ambersons began. "Their splendor lasted throughout all the years that saw their Midland town spread and darken into a city."

1885

Eugene Morgan, inebriated, trips over his bass viol outside the Amberson mansion, where he has come to serenade Isabel. Isabel, taking it as a mark of disrespect, begins to spurn Eugene and favor a rival suitor, the bland but dependable Wilbur Minafer, whom she eventually marries. Isabel at this point, according to Tarkington, is "eighteen or maybe nineteen"; Eugene, Isabel's brother Jack, and Wilbur are all probably one or two years older. (Note: Welles later added the touch of having Eugene drive a primitive steamcar in the would-be courtship scenes. He cheated slightly on technological accuracy; according to the studio factsheet, it was an authentic model actually built in 1893.)

1894

George, age nine, "a princely terror," rides imperiously through the town in his pony cart. He harasses a laborer working in a sandpile.

1895

George, riding through town again, has a fight with Elijah, a boy who taunts him about his "girly curls." When Elijah's father intercedes, George, in a fit of anger over an allusion to his mother, tells him to "go to—" (the scene ends just before the forbidden word). An unrepentant George is interrogated by his parents about the incident as the Major heartily laughs it off.

1902

George, seventeen, home from school, rides through town again in his customary manner, cracking the hardware store man's behind with his whip. [George goes to a meeting of a boys' club, "Friends of the Ace." When he learns another president has been elected while he was away at school, he blackmails the others into immediately reinstalling him by reminding them the clubroom belongs to his grandfather.]

1904

The Amberson ball, "the last of the great long-remembered dances." Among the guests are Eugene, recently returned to the town a widower, and his daughter, Lucy, near the same age as George, now nineteen. Eugene's reappearance begins to stir "ancient passions," as Uncle Jack puts it. Afterwards George is intensely curious about Eugene's intentions. Isabel tells George of her worries over the state of Wilbur's health. On an outing the following day, George's sleigh overturns in the snow and he and Lucy ride home with Eugene, Isabel, Jack, and Aunt Fanny Minafer in Eugene's horseless carriage. Wilbur dies; the viewing is in the library at the Amberson mansion. (Note: In Welles's script the date given on Wilbur's headstone is 1904. Therefore, he would have died within days after the Christmas ball. In the novel, Wilbur dies the following September.)

1905

On his return home from college graduation, Fanny treats George to strawberry shortcake in the Amberson kitchen. When George and Jack begin to tease her about Eugene she becomes hysterical and bolts from the room. [George looks out the window and sees unsightly excavations all over the lawn. Jack explains that the Major is building rental houses, probably in a desperate effort to increase his income.] George, Isabel, and Fanny are escorted through the Morgan automobile works by Lucy and Eugene. Afterwards, Isabel and Fanny go for a ride with Eugene in his newest model while George takes Lucy out in his little horsedrawn buggy. George begins to propose, obviously not for the first time. Lucy resists; she is disturbed because George has no productive goals for his life. (George correctly surmises that she reflects her father's attitude.) [That evening, George, Isabel, and Fanny sit and talk on the Amberson verandah. Later, Fanny insinuates to George that Isabel may be prematurely forsaking her mourning responsibilities. When he is alone, George conjures up a vision in which Lucy begs his forgiveness and renounces her father.] Eugene and Isabel talk alone in the arbor; their courtship has in fact resumed and they are semi-engaged, although Isabel postpones telling George. While Lucy is briefly away, Eugene is invited to the Ambersons' for dinner. When the subject turns to automobiles, George openly insults Eugene. After Eugene leaves, Fanny reveals Eugene and Isabel's relationship to George, saying it's widely known and talked about. George rushes across the street and confronts the gossipy Mrs. Johnson about a "scandal" involving his mother's name. Next day when Eugene calls to take Isabel for a ride, George turns him away. Eugene sends a plaintive letter to Isabel, which George rejects outright, forcing Isabel to break with Eugene. Next day, on a long walk through the town, Lucy breaks with George, not because of what he has done to her father but for his apparent aimlessness. George takes Isabel on an extended trip abroad.

1910

[The Major and Fanny talk on the verandah one evening. The town is changing; the Major's resources are dwindling; Fanny is contemplating investing in an automobile headlight venture.] On a visit to Eugene and Lucy at *their* new mansion, Jack reveals the precarious state of Isabel's health. George returns with Isabel, so frail she has to be carried. Eugene calls to see her and starts to force his way past George but Jack and Fanny dissuade him on doctor's advice. Isabel dies. The Major dies not long after, leaving a virtually depleted estate. Jack and Fanny have also lost *their* means through the failure of the headlight venture. (Note: In Tarkington, the Major dies almost a year later than Isabel, but in Welles's version the two events occur much closer together in time.)

1911

George has been counting on Fanny's help to see them through, but she now confesses she too is broke. She collapses against the water boiler, which is "not hot, it's cold," she shrieks, because the plumbers have disconnected it. In order to support Fanny, George forgoes his plans for a career in law and takes a high-paying job handling explosives. Jack uses his influence as a former congressman to obtain a consulship and George sees him off at the train. George pays his last visit to the Amberson mansion, kneeling at his mother's bed to beg forgiveness.

1912

Eugene and Lucy walk in their garden. Lucy is reconciled to her fate. She recites a fable of an Indian tribe who once lived here, and its overbearing chief, "Vendonah," or "Rides-Down-Everything"—George, obviously, as Eugene recognizes. One day George is struck by a passing automobile. Eugene reads a newspaper account of the accident and after pained reflection decides to visit him in the hospital. (His driver tells him Lucy is already there.) That evening he writes a letter to Isabel telling her of the scene in the hospital and of feeling her strong presence in the room. (Note: In the shooting, Welles changed the ending to a scene at Fanny's boardinghouse where Eugene makes the report to her. In the release version, Lucy and Eugene are together when they learn the news. Lucy leaves immediately to go to George; Eugene eventually follows. In the final scene Eugene walks with Fanny in the hospital corridor.)

THE MAGNIFICENT AMBERSONS

Production #340
Certificate #7800

Cutting Continuity
March 12, 1942
No. of reels: 14
Footage: 11,858 feet
Running Time: 131 minutes 45$^1/_3$ seconds

1 (28-8)[2] FADE IN TITLE #1 - To sound of radio broadcasting waves -

AN RKO RADIO PICTURE

LAP DISSOLVE

[TITLE #2 -

A MERCURY PRODUCTION

FADE OUT][3]

2 (132-10) BLACK SCREEN -

NARRATOR'S VOICE

The magnificence of the Ambersons began in 1873.

Music heard[4] -

NARRATOR'S VOICE

Their splendor lasted throughout all the years that saw their Midland town spread and darken into a city. In that town in those days . . .

FADE IN EXT HOUSE LS[5] - Camera shooting across street to house in background - Women converging before gate on walk - Carriages pass - Women move off in opposite directions - White horse comes on at left pulling streetcar, "Western-Midland Transit Co. No. 1" -

NARRATOR'S VOICE

. . . all the women who wore silk or velvet knew all the other women who wore silk or velvet, and everybody knew everybody else's family horse-and-carriage. The only public conveyance was the streetcar.

Woman leans out upper window in house, waves, calls -

WOMAN

Yoohoo!

Driver stops car - It goes off track - Passengers get off car - Men lift car onto track - Women get back on car - Woman running from house gets on car - Men push car - Climb onto it as horse pulls it to right -

---

[1] The film was mounted on double reels and the individual reels were called sections A and B rather than being consecutively numbered.

[2] Length of shot expressed in feet plus additional frames. 90 feet equals one minute of running time; "1 (28-8)" means that shot 1 runs 28 feet plus 8 frames.

[3] Welles intended for *The Magnificent Ambersons* to open in the same way he had originally intended for *Citizen Kane* to open, without credits and going directly from the logo to a black screen. The release version changes logo to "A MERCURY PRODUCTION by ORSON WELLES" and adds Title #3: "THE MAGNIFICENT AMBERSONS From The Novel by BOOTH TARKINGTON."

[4] First statement of *Toujours ou jamais*, a waltz by Emil Waldteufel (a lesser-known contemporary of Johann Strauss) which composer Bernard Herrmann uses here to signify the vanishing past to which the Ambersons cling. He uses *Toujours ou jamais* thematically throughout the film to track their decline; all but three musical cues of his original score quoted from it.
   (A *cue* is any passage of music intended to accompany a film's images. This usage derives from the silent era, when pianists or organists selected the music for a scene from books of generic musical passages cued for such things as mood or tempo.)

[5] Long Shot. For an explanation of shot abbreviations, see "A Note on Textual Practice," pp. 37–38.

NARRATOR'S VOICE

A lady could whistle to it from an upstairs window, and the car would halt at once, and wait for her, while she shut the window, put on her hat and coat, went downstairs, found an umbrella, told the "girl" what to have for dinner, and came forth from the house. Too slow for us nowadays, because the faster we're carried the less time we have to spare.[6] But in those days they had time for everything . . .

LAP DISSOLVE[7]

EXT HOUSE LS - Snow over everything - Sleighs coming on at left - Go to right - Boys throwing snowballs - Music heard - People passing on walk -

NARRATOR'S VOICE

. . . time for sleigh rides, and balls, and assemblies, and cotillions, and open house on New Years . . .

LAP DISSOLVE

NIGHT SEQUENCE

EXT HOUSE LS - Camera shooting across to house in background - Moon shining - Lanterns strung along yard - Lights shining from windows of house - Couples milling - Music heard -

NARRATOR'S VOICE

. . . and all day picnics in the woods, and even that prettiest of all vanished customs, the serenade.

LAP DISSOLVE

EXT STREET LS - House in background dark - Street light at left burning - Eugene and boys running on from right background - Run to foreground with instruments - Eugene trips in foreground - Camera pans to follow as Eugene rolls over on bass fiddle in extreme foreground - He sits up - Looks upward anxiously -

NARRATOR'S VOICE

Of a summer night, young men would bring an orchestra under a pretty girl's window, and flute, harp, fiddle, 'cello, cornet and bass viol would presently release their melodies to the dulcet stars.

[EXT WINDOW CU - Isabel looking out window to foreground - Frowning - Music heard   **3 (2-5)]**[8]

EXT HOUSE MCS - Camera shooting up to window - Isabel standing in window - Turns - Exits - Light shining through window -   **4 (4-9)**[9]

[NARRATOR'S VOICE

During the earlier years of this period . . .

---

[6] In the release version (hereafter *RV*) "dress customs of the time" sequence (from narrator's line in shot 4 through end of shot 13) is inserted here.

[7] The cutting continuity (hereafter *CC*) does not assign a new shot number after a lap dissolve. (A *lap dissolve* is a transitional device in which the end of one shot is optically superimposed over the beginning of the next; the first shot slowly "dissolves" out.)

[8] *RV* holds shot 3 longer (20-6) to include action of Isabel closing curtains and turning away from window and eliminates shot 4.

[9] Shaded vertical bar designates material that was deleted in *RV*.

5 (7-15) | Ext Saloon Door MS - Door in foreground swinging - Men in silk hats inside - Music heard -

NARRATOR'S VOICE

. . . while bangs and bustles were having their way with women, there were seen men of all ages . . .

DAY SEQUENCE

6 (7-10) | Ext Lake MS - Camera shooting down to boat on water - Wilbur rowing - Isabel with parasol - Music heard - He turns boat around -

NARRATOR'S VOICE

. . . to whom a hat meant only that rigid, tall silk thing known to impudence as a . . .

7 (5-7) | Ext Street ECU - Camera shooting up to Major Amberson with top hat on - Snowball hits it - Knocks it off - He turns to foreground - Smiles - Music heard -

NARRATOR'S VOICE

. . . "stove-pipe"...[10] But the long contagion of the . . .

8 (9-7) | Int Room MCU - Reflection of Eugene in mirror in long underwear wearing derby - Music heard - He takes it off - Puts on another -

NARRATOR'S VOICE

. . . "Derby" had arrived: one season the crown of this hat would be a bucket, next it would be a spoon.

9 (6-1) | Int Room MCU - Eugene's feet pulling off boots on bootjack - Music heard - He kicks boot, then bootjack to right -

NARRATOR'S VOICE

Every house still kept its bootjack, but high-topped boots gave way . . .

10 (11-8) | Int Room CU - Eugene's hands putting shoes on his feet - Music heard -

NARRATOR'S VOICE

. . . to shoes and "Congress gaiters"; and these were played through fashions that shaped them now with toes like box-ends and now with toes . . .

11 (14-7) | Int Room CU - Eugene's feet with pointed shoes on - Toes wiggling - Music heard - He pulls on trousers - Camera pans slightly upward as he gets into them - He moves partly off left struggling with trousers - Mirror shows his reflection -

---

[10] Three unspaced periods (...) indicate a pause in speaking of three counts (one-two-three) or more.

NARRATOR'S VOICE

. . . like the prows of racing shells. Trousers with a crease were considered plebeian; the crease proved that the garment had lain upon a shelf, and hence was "ready-made."

INT ROOM MS - Reflection in mirror of Eugene walking to foreground - Wearing short coat over evening clothes - Then he comes on left foreground - Looks at himself in mirror - Exits left foreground - Reflection exits in background -[11] Comes on again in mirror reflection wearing long overcoat - Then he comes on again left foreground - Looks at himself in mirror - Camera tilts slightly upward - Eugene exits left foreground - Reflection exits background -

12 (23-1)

NARRATOR'S VOICE

With evening dress a gentleman wore a tan overcoat, so short that his black coat-tails hung visible five inches below the overcoat. But after a season or two he lengthened his overcoat till it touched his heels...and he passed out of his tight trousers . . .

EXT DOOR MCS - Camera shooting down to threshold of open door - Eugene's legs come out wearing baggy trousers - Music heard - Camera tilts upward showing Eugene standing holding big candy box and cane - Smoking cigar - He starts to foreground -

13 (9-5)

NARRATOR'S VOICE

. . . into trousers like great bags.][12]

EXT HOUSE LS - Camera shooting across street to house - Eugene coming from house in background - Others passing on walk - Music[13] and Narrator heard - Eugene crosses on walk to left - Camera following - Children running on in foreground - Run down street to left background - Camera panning - Eugene going to left background - Tips his hat as carriage passes -

14 (20-15)

NARRATOR'S VOICE

The people were thrifty in that Midland town because they were the sons or grandsons of the "early settlers," who had opened the wilderness with wagons and axes and guns, but with no money at all. The pioneers . . .

EXT TOWN LS - Man coming on in foreground with bicycle - Carriage going to background - General activity - Music and Narrator heard - Eugene and others walking across street - Children running in street - Camera panning to left following Eugene - He tips hat to women - Comes to foreground - Camera pans following him to left passing fountain - Tips hat to woman - Man drinking - Tips his hat - Eugene goes to background - Couple watching -

15 (44-0)

NARRATOR'S VOICE

. . . were thrifty or they would have perished; they had to store away food for the winter, or goods to trade for food, and they often feared they hadn't stored enough. They left traces of that fear in their sons and grandsons. In the minds of most of these, indeed, their thrift was next to their religion. To save, even for the sake of saving, was their earliest lesson and discipline. No matter how prosperous they were, they could not spend money either upon "art" . . .

---

[11] An almost imperceptible match cut not noted either in *CC* or *RV* occurs at this point.

[12] In *RV* material beginning with narration in shot 4 to end of shot 13 ("customs of dress" sequence) is moved forward and inserted at shot 2.

[13] Herrmann's music cue *Varation 3* (on the Waldteufel waltz), a coronet solo referring to Gay Nineties ragtime music, chided Eugene's dandy dress.

Herrmann's score was subjected to the same treatment as the film's images. (RKO President George Schaefer had complained that Herrman's score was too "somber.") RKO's Music Director, Constantin Bakaleinikoff, assumed charge of the rerecording, ordered the removal of a number of Herrman's cues, and assigned the task of rescoring to RKO studio composer Roy Webb (*I Walked with a Zombie, The Spiral Staircase, Notorious*).

Magnificent Ambersons continuity sketches by Joe St. Amon. These were found in the notebook containing Welles's personal copy of the shooting script.

EXT STREET MCS - Camera shooting upward following Eugene going to left background - Crossing street - Tips his hat to ladies passing - General activity - He goes toward building in background -

16 (27-0)

NARRATOR'S VOICE

. . . or upon mere luxury and entertainment, without a sense of sin.

LAP DISSOLVE

EXT STREET MLS - Sign "Amberson Boulevard" - Boy on bicycle riding past right to left - Eugene on walk at right crossing to left - Tips hat at townspeople offscreen - Stone marker "Amberson" in front of mansion - Eugene turns through gate toward mansion - Another bicycle passes left to right -

NARRATOR'S VOICE

Against so homespun a background, the magnificence of the Ambersons was as conspicuous as a brass band at a funeral.

Voices heard -

JEROME'S VOICE[14]

There it is!

HOLMES'S VOICE

The Amberson mansion!

EXT STREET MS - Chorus of townspeople standing looking across right to Amberson mansion -

17 (3-15)

AUGUST

The pride of the town!

BAXLEY

Well, well.

EXT MANSION MS - Camera shooting through statues in foreground - Eugene coming on at right on walk approaching mansion entrance -

18 (4-15)

HUMPHREY'S VOICE

Sixty thousand dollars for the woodwork alone!

EXT STREET ECU - Camera shooting up to faces of two women -

19 (4-2)

GEORGIA

Hot and cold running water . . .

[14] In the chorus of townspeople, Jerome, Holmes, August, Baxley, Humphrey, and Georgia are the real names of the bit players in these roles. Only Mrs. Foster, Mrs. Johnson, and Fanny are character names. See cast list, p. 301.

MRS. FOSTER

. . . upstairs and down!

20 (5-7)   EXT STREET ECU - Camera shooting up to man -

AUGUST

And stationary washstands in every last bedroom in the place!

21 (11-7)   EXT STREET MCU - Camera shooting upward - Man at left foreground - Humphrey coming to him - Talking - Others in background -

HUMPHREY

Well, sir, I presume the President of the United States'd be tickled to swap the White House for the new Amberson Mansion if the Major'd give him the chance.

22 (5-10)   EXT STREET CU - Camera shooting up by August talking -

AUGUST

But by the Almighty Dollar, you can bet your sweet life the Major wouldn't.

BAXLEY

Well, well.

23 (26-3)   EXT DOOR MCS - Eugene's gloved hand ringing bell - He approaches door with box of candy - Camera pans to follow - He waits - Sam the butler opens door -

EUGENE

Is Miss Amberson at home?

SAM

No, suh, Mist' Mo'gan. Mis' Ambuhson's not home.

EUGENE

Well thanks, Sam.

Sam closes door in Eugene's face - Music starts -

FADE OUT

24 (20-13)   FADE IN EXT DOORS MCS - Eugene's gloved hand ringing bell - He approaches door with flowers - Camera pans to follow - He waits - Sam opens door - Says sharply before Eugene can speak -

SAM

No, suh. Mis' Ambuhson ain't at home to you, Mist' Mo'gan.

EUGENE

Thanks.

Eugene turns away -

EXT STREET MCS - Camera shooting up at group of townspeople looking off to left - Fanny at far left - **25** (4-2)

FANNY

I guess she's still mad at him.

MAN'S VOICE

Who?

EXT STREET CU - Camera shooting up to Fanny and Mrs. Johnson looking to right fore-ground - **26** (4-5)

MRS. JOHNSON

Isabel.

FANNY

Major Amberson's daughter.

EXT STREET MCS - Mansion in background - Eugene climbing onto steam car - Sits down - Starts it - Drives to left - Camera pans to follow - **27** (16-5)

HUMPHREY'S VOICE

Eugene Morgan's her best beau. Took a bit too much to drink the other night right out here, and stepped clean through the bass fiddle serenadin' her.

Crowd heard laughing -

MAN'S VOICE

Well, well.

EXT STREET ELS - Eugene on steam car driving to left foreground away from mansion - Towns-people enter in extreme right background - **28** (4-12)

MAN'S VOICE

I haven't seen her since she got back from abroad.

MAN'S VOICE

Isabel?

29 (10-12) | EXT STREET CU - Camera shooting up at three men - Bronson, in center, looks to man at right -

BRONSON

Well, sir, I don't know as I know just how to put it...but she's—she's kind of a . . .

30 (6-3) | EXT SHOP MCS - Ice cream parlor door opening -

BRONSON'S VOICE

. . . delightful looking young lady.

Isabel coming out with a Saint Bernard on leash - Wilbur following her - Music heard - Isabel moves to left foreground - Camera pans to follow - Steam car heard -

31 (3-12) | EXT STREET MCS - Eugene on steam car - Stopping it - Blows whistle - Music heard -

32 (2-1) | EXT SHOP MCU - Wilbur and Isabel in foreground - Smiling - Whistle heard - They look to right - Music heard -

33 (4-13) | EXT SIDEWALK MCS - Eugene taking bouquet from steam car - Music heard - He approaches them - Takes off his hat -

34 (21-7) | EXT SHOP MS - Camera shooting up from street - Three standing in front of ice cream parlor - Isabel with dog on leash - Eugene at right - Music heard - Wilbur tips his hat - Crosses in front of Eugene - Camera pans to follow - Isabel turns coldly away from Eugene toward background - Pan continues as she and Wilbur walk away - They hurry down walk as Eugene starts to follow - He stops - Looks after them -

BRONSON'S VOICE

Wilbur? Wilbur Minafer? I never thought he'd get her. Well, what do you know.

35 (7-9) | INT BARBER SHOP MCS - Uncle Jack in barber chair with lather on face - Turns as barber exits left - Jack looking into camera - Addresses group of men seen behind him in reflection in mirror -

JACK

Well, Wilbur may not be any Apollo, as it were, but he's a steady young business-man.

36 (107-11) | INT SEWING ROOM MS - Camera shooting up through sewing machine and dress form in foreground - Women around room - One at left talking surprised - Mrs. Foster in background in corset and bustle -

FIRST WOMAN

Wilbur Minafer!

Mrs. Johnson stooped over at right - Raises up to address others -

MRS. JOHNSON

Looks like Isabel's pretty sensible for such a showy girl.

FIRST WOMAN

To think of her taking him.

SECOND WOMAN

Yes, just because a man any woman would like a thousand times better was a little wild one night at a serenade!

MRS. FOSTER

What she minds was his makin' a clown of himself in her own front yard. Made her think he didn't care much about her.

Mrs. Foster steps down - Comes to foreground - Others gather around her as Mrs. Johnson helps her on with kimono -

MRS. FOSTER

She's probably mistaken, but it's too late for her to think anything else now. The wedding'll be a big Amberson-style thing—raw oysters floating in scooped-out blocks of ice . . .

She sits down by sewing machine as she talks - First woman comes partly on in extreme foreground - Hands coffee cup to Mrs. Foster -

MRS. FOSTER

. . . and a band from out of town. And then Wilbur'll take Isabel on the carefullest little wedding trip he can manage, and she'll be a good wife to him, but they'll have the worst spoiled lot of children this town will ever see.

FIRST WOMAN

How on earth do you figure that out, Mrs. Foster?

MRS. FOSTER

She couldn't love Wilbur, could she?...Well, it'll all go to her children and she'll ruin them!

LAP DISSOLVE

EXT STREET LS - People moving around at left on walk - Pony and cart coming forward from background - Young George driving - Music heard -

NARRATOR'S VOICE

The prophetess proved to be mistaken in a single detail, merely...Wilbur and Isabel did not have children; they had only one.

George steadily moving toward foreground -

MRS. FOSTER'S VOICE

Only one! But I'd like to know if he isn't spoiled enough for a whole carload!

NARRATOR'S VOICE

Again she found none to challenge her. George Amberson Minafer, the Major's one grandchild, was a princely terror.

George in cart exits extreme left foreground -

37 (7-15)   EXT STREET MS - Laborer leaning over pile of sand - George driving from background - Turning corner sharply - Laborer leaps out of way yelling -

LABORER

Hey! By . . .

Cart exits left foreground - Laborer rushes forward - Angrily throwing down tool -

LABORER

. . . golly! I guess you think you own this town!

[GEORGE'S VOICE

I will when I grow up.

38 (16-2)   EXT STREET MCS - Laborer in right foreground running after George - George in cart yelling back over shoulder - Laborer moves to left and stops - George races to background in cart - Music heard -

GEORGE

I guess my grandpa owns it now, you bet!

LABORER

Aw, pull down your vest!

GEORGE

Don't haf' to! Doctor says it ain't healthy!

He drives to left background - Man moves to right - Camera pans - George yells back at man -

GEORGE

But I'll tell you what I'll do . . .

Man runs after cart - George yelling -

GEORGE

. . . I'll pull down my vest if you'll wipe off your chin!

He races to background in cart - Music heard -

EXT STREET MS - Camera shooting across street - People in front of buildings in background - George driving on at right background - Drives pony to extreme left foreground and exits - Music heard -]¹⁵	**39** (10-0)

EXT STREET MLS - Camera shooting past cannon monument at left foreground - Buildings in background - George races on in cart - Exits left - Music heard -	**40** (3-14)

NARRATOR'S VOICE

They <u>did</u> hope to live to see the day, they said . . .

EXT STREET MLS - Man in front of building in background - George riding on right background - Passes lamppost - He turns corner rapidly - Camera pans to follow - Rides to extreme left foreground - Music heard -	**41** (4-10)

NARRATOR'S VOICE

. . . when that boy would get his comeuppance!

EXT SIDEWALK MCU - Camera shooting up to woman and Bronson - She asks - Surprised - Music stops -	**42** (11-13)

WOMAN

His what?

BRONSON

His comeuppance. Something's bound to take him down, some day, and I only want to be there.

EXT YARD CU - Camera shooting up to boy looking left - Yelling derisively -	**43** (2-12)

ELIJAH

Enh, look at the girly-curleys . . .

EXT YARD MLS - Boy watching street from behind gate in yard - George riding on from right -	**44** (27-8)

ELIJAH

. . . enh, look at the girly-curleys.

George stops -

---

¹⁵ *RV* eliminates all of the foregoing dialogue within brackets. Shots 38 and 39 are shortened and Welles's narration is dubbed in: "There were people—grown people they were" (38) "who expressed themselves longingly" (39). The child actor's lips can still be seen moving but the change is almost imperceptible because he is advancing rapidly into the background and the laborer has his back to the camera.

ELIJAH

Say, Bub, where'd you steal your mother's ole sash!

George stands up in cart -

GEORGE

Your sister stoled it for me! She stoled it off our old clo'es line an' gave it to me.

ELIJAH

You go get your hair cut! Yah! And I haven't got any sister!

GEORGE

Yeah, I know you haven't at home. I mean the one that's in jail.

ELIJAH

I dare ya to git down outta that pony cart!

George starts to get out of cart -

45 (4-5)   EXT STREET MCS - Camera shooting upward past boy standing by gate at right foreground - George in background jumping down from cart -

GEORGE

I dare ya outside that gate!

46 (4-14)   EXT YARD MLS - Boy by gate to George standing on other side of fence -

ELIJAH

I dare ya half way here! I dare ya!

George runs to gate - Yelling -

GEORGE

Here I come!

He starts to leap over gate -

47 (1-12)   EXT GATE MCU - Camera shooting up over gate - George in foreground leaping onto boy in yard -

48 (4-12)   EXT YARD MCS - Two boys fighting - Struggling - Yelling indistinctly -

49 (2-1)   EXT WINDOW CU - Curtains parting - Bronson looks out - Boys still heard fighting -

50 (1-14)   EXT YARD MCS - George wrestling Elijah to ground - Camera pans to follow -

EXT WINDOW CU - Bronson inside yelling at George - Knocks on glass - Boys heard yelling -   **51** (4-5)

BOY'S VOICE

Mother! Mother!

BRONSON

Boy! Boy!

Bronson turns away from window -

EXT HOUSE MS - Camera panning left to front porch -   **52** (9-7)

GEORGE'S VOICE

Pick on someone your own size, you big bully!

Bronson opens door and rushes out - Claps hands and shouts -

BRONSON

Hey! Boy!

He runs down to left foreground -

EXT YARD MCS - Boys fighting on ground in foreground - George sitting on Elijah - Holding   **53** (3-10)
him down - Bronson running from background to them -

ELIJAH

Mother!

Bronson grabs George -

EXT YARD MCU - Bronson dragging George off Elijah -   **54** (3-1)

ELIJAH

Mother!

Camera pans up to Bronson tugging -

BRONSON

Boy! Boy!

EXT YARD MCS - Bronson continuing to pull George away - George hits Bronson in stomach -   **55** (5-10)

BRONSON

That'll be enough of that! Oof!

Elijah runs off to background -

GEORGE

You stop that, you!

56 (2-2) | EXT YARD CU - Camera shooting up at George hitting out to left -

57 (1-10) | EXT YARD CU - Camera shooting up at Bronson groaning and doubling up -

58 (2-0) | EXT YARD CU - Camera shooting up at George looking up to left -

GEORGE

I guess you don't know who I am!

59 (3-10) | EXT YARD CU - Camera shooting up at Bronson looking down to foreground -

BRONSON

Yes, I do! And you're a disgrace to your mother!

60 (2-4) | EXT YARD CU - Camera shooting up at George looking up to left -

GEORGE

You shut up about my mother!

He hits out to left again -

61 (4-7) | EXT YARD CU - Camera shooting up at Bronson groaning and doubling up again as fists hit him -

BRONSON

She ought to be ashamed to let a bad little boy like you . . .

62 (9-4) | EXT YARD CU - Camera shooting up at George punching left -

GEORGE

You pull down your vest, you ole billygoat, you! Pull down your vest, an' wipe off your chin, an'—an' go ta . . .

63 (1-2) | EXT YARD ECU - Bronson, shocked, shouts -

BRONSON

<u>WHAT!</u>

FADE OUT

DAY SEQUENCE

FADE IN EXT ARBOR MS - Mansion exterior in extreme background - George standing defiantly near foreground with back to others - Major sitting at left - Isabel and Wilbur sitting at right - Wilbur reading letter -

64 (87-10)

WILBUR

"This was heard not only by myself but by my wife and the lady who lives next door."

GEORGE

He's an ole liar!

MAJOR

Georgie! You mustn't say "liar."

ISABEL

Dear, did you say what he says you did?

GEORGE

Welllll—Grandpa wouldn't wipe his shoe on that ole story teller.

ISABEL

Georgie, you mustn't . . .

GEORGE

I mean, none of us Ambersons wouldn't have anything to do with him.

ISABEL

That's not what we're talking about.

GEORGE

I bet if he wanted to see any of us, he'd have to go 'round to the side door!

Major laughs loudly -

ISABEL

No, Georgie.

WILBUR

Please! Father!

Major still laughing -

ISABEL

From his letter he doesn't seem a very tactful person, but . . .

GEORGE

He's just riffraff.

ISABEL

Oh, you mustn't say so.

George turns - Goes to mother -

ISABEL

And you must promise me never to use those bad words again.

GEORGE

I promise not to...

He crosses to left and behind Major -

GEORGE

. . . unless I get mad at somebody.

He exits left - Music heard -

LAP DISSOLVE

EXT STREET CU - Camera shooting up to three men - Bronson at left talks to others -

BRONSON

Wait 'til they send him away to school—then he'll get it. They'll knock the stuffing out of him.

LAP DISSOLVE

EXT STREET LS - Camera shooting from shadows near intersection - Men idling in sunshine along side street in background - Older George racing on in buggy along side street - Turns corner rapidly - Proceeds up street to background - Music heard -

NARRATOR'S VOICE

But George returned with the same stuffing.

65 (10-11) EXT STREET MCU - Man in apron bending over in extreme foreground - George racing on from right - Crosses behind man - Cracks man with whip - Camera pans to follow as man runs after George yelling - George looks back - Rides around corner in background and exits -

MAN

    Got any sense? See here, Bub, does your mother know you're out? Turn down your pants, you would-be dude!

EXT STREET MS - Camera shooting up from ground - George racing to foreground - Camera panning to follow - Music heard - Man leaps out of way - Exits left foreground -   **66** (9-10)

[MAN'S VOICE

    Rainin' in dear ole Lunnon!

Camera makes 180° pan to right following George - Buggy wheel fills screen as it passes - Man heard yelling -

MAN'S VOICE

    Git off the earth!

George races to background - People watching - He cuts in front of team of horses - They rear up - Making noises - He turns corner -

EXT STREET MLS - Camera shooting up from ground - George races on from right - Camera pans to follow - George proceeds down street to left background - Music heard -][16]   **67** (10-5)

LAP DISSOLVE

INT CLUB ROOM MCS - Letters and club sign on door - George's shadow comes on outside - He knocks on glass -

INT CLUB ROOM MCS - Camera shooting past Fred sitting in foreground at desk - Others in background - George's shadow seen on door in background - Boy at right background raps on glass with knife -   **68** (3-14)

INT CLUB ROOM MCU - Boy at right with knife - George outside door raps signal - Another boy comes on at left foreground - Opens door - One at right folds arms - Exits as George comes in opening door in front of him - Boy in foreground - Folds arms -   **69** (11-0)

SECOND BOY

    Welcome, Friend of the Ace.

GEORGE

    Welcome, Friend of the Ace.

INT CLUB ROOM MLS - Boys around room - Greet George standing in doorway at left background with others -   **70** (8-0)

BOYS

    Welcome, Friend of the Ace.

---

[16] *RV* eliminates dialogue of shot 66 and transposes first line of Welles's narration in shot 7 of reel 1B to become narration of shots 66 ("When Mr. George Amberson Minafer came home for the holidays in his sophomore year nothing about him") and 67 ("encouraged any hope that he had received his comeuppance").

Boy talks to George - George looking at Fred at desk -

                              BOY

    Hi, George.

Fred talks - George talking to other boy -

                             FRED

    Take your seat in the secret semicircle.

                            GEORGE

    Look here, Charlie Johnson . . .

                             FRED

    We will now proceed to the business in hand.

INT CLUB ROOM MCS - Fred sitting at desk in foreground - George and others in back-   **71 (9-5)**
ground - He motions to Fred - Talks to Bill at left -

                            GEORGE

    . . . what's Fred Kinney doing in the president's chair?

Fred raps on desk - George turns -

                            GEORGE

    Didn't you all agree I was to be president just the same, even if I was away at
    school?

INT CLUB ROOM MCU - Three in foreground - Look at Fred behind desk in background rap-   **72 (6-4)**
ping on desk - Talking -

                             FRED

    All Friends of the Ace will take their seats! I'm president of the F.O.T.A. now,
    George Minafer.

INT CLUB ROOM LS - Boys around desk in background - Fred pounding on desk -   **73 (11-11)**

                             FRED

    This meeting will now come to order.

George shouts angrily -

                            GEORGE

    No it won't. You put down that gavel.

Fred pounds on desk - George grabs gavel away from him -

> GEORGE

It belongs to my grandfather. Give it to me.

> FRED

I was legally elected here.

> GEORGE

All right.

INT CLUB ROOM MCU - Fred sitting in foreground - George facing him - Boys around George -   **74** (4-0)

> GEORGE

You're president.

He turns to boys -

> GEORGE

Now we'll hold another election.

INT CLUB ROOM MCU - George and boys in foreground - Fred leaps up behind desk in background talking angrily -   **75** (10-6)

> FRED

We will not!

Fred talks sitting down at desk -

> FRED

We'll have our regular meeting, and then we'll play euchre, a nickel a corner just what we're here for. This meeting will now come to order.

He pounds on desk with gavel - George leans over - Grabs gavel -

REEL 1 SECTION B

DAY SEQUENCE

1 (8-9) INT CLUB ROOM MCS - Fred in foreground - George on other side of desk trying to take gavel from him - Boys on other side in background - George takes it from him - Puts it on desk -

GEORGE

That belongs to my grandfather. Who's the founder of the F.O.T.A. if you please?

He looks around at other boys in background belligerently -

2 (15-10) INT CLUB ROOM MS - Camera shooting up at group of boys around George - Fred sitting at desk in background - George talking belligerently -

GEORGE

Who got the janitor to let us have most of this furniture? You think you could keep this clubroom a minute if I told my grandfather I didn't need it for a literary club any more? And another thing . . .

3 (15-14) INT CLUB ROOM MCU - Boy at left foreground - George on other side of him looking around talking - Boy at right - Fred in background at desk -

GEORGE

. . . I want to say something on how you men been acting, too! If that's what you want, you can have it. I was going to bring some port wine down here and we'd have a little celebration some night like we do in our crowd at school.

4 (32-7) INT CLUB ROOM MS - Camera shooting up past Fred sitting at desk right foreground - To George turning from boys in background -

GEORGE

But, you men got a new president now!

He goes to door in background -

GEORGE

I guess all I better do is resign!

He stops in background by door as Charlie looks around - Talks quickly -

CHARLIE

All those in favor of holding a new election say, "Aye."

Boys raise hands -

ALL

Aye!

Fred leaps up in foreground -

FRED

That's unfair!

George in background turns -

GEORGE

All those in favor of me being president instead of Fred Kinney say, "Aye!"

ALL

Aye!

GEORGE

The "Ayes" have it.

George comes to foreground - Grinning - Fred hurries down around desk at left - Hurries to door in background -

FRED

I resign!

He rushes out door in background - Exits slamming door -

INT CLUB ROOM MS - Boys looking to foreground laughing - George goes around behind desk in background - Taking off his hat -   **5 (11-6)**

GEORGE

Old red-head Fred'll be around next week. He'll be around bootlickin' to get us to take him back in again.

INT CLUB ROOM MCU - Camera shooting up to George looking around smiling - Talking - Taking cigar from pocket - Smelling it -   **6 (10-7)**

GEORGE

Well, fellows, I suppose you'd like to hear from your president. I don't imagine there's any more business before the meeting.

INT CLUB ROOM MLS - Boys sitting and standing around room - George in background pounds on desk -   **7 (81-7)**

GEORGE

Meeting adjourned.

Boys laugh - Rise - Move around - Camera pans - They go to left - George talking to them -

GEORGE

I had a pretty good time at the old school, back East.

They gather around card table - Listening as George talks boastingly -

GEORGE

Had a little trouble with the faculty and had to come home. But the family stood by me as well as I could ask. Anybody that's game for a little quarter-limit poker or any limit they say, why I'd like to have 'em sit at the president's card-table.

Boys all sit down around table in foreground -

LAP DISSOLVE

NIGHT SEQUENCE

EXT AMBERSON MANSION ELS - Camera shooting over grounds to lighted house in background - Sleighs and carriages along fence - Others passing in foreground - Music heard -

NARRATOR'S VOICE

[When Mr. George Amberson Minafer came home for the holidays in his sophomore year nothing about him encouraged any hope that he had received his come-uppance.][17] Cards were out for a ball in his honor, and this pageant of the tenantry was the last of the . . .

LAP DISSOLVE

EXT DOORS MCS - Lucy and Eugene advancing from extreme foreground toward background - Camera moving to follow them - Eugene holding hat on - Servants open doors - Sound of wind and music heard -

NARRATOR'S VOICE

. . . great, long-remembered dances that "everybody talked about."

Camera continues to follow them across vestibule and inside - Sam greets them - Crosses right after they pass - Lucy looks to left -

LUCY

Hello, there!

She runs to left - Exits - Sam takes Eugene's hat -

[17] Moved in *RV* to become narration of shots 66 and 67 in reel 1A.

8 (42-10) | INT ROOM MLS - People around Christmas tree at left foreground - Crowd moving around in background talking - General activity - Eugene in extreme background removing coat and scarf - Music heard - Camera moving slowly to background - Guests crossing in front of camera - Camera gradually moving in toward receiving line - Uncle John speaking to Major - Isabel and George looking on at left -

> JOHN

> I suppose that's where they'll put the Major when his time comes. Now don't you look at me like that, Major.

Camera moves closer - John comes to George extending his hand -

> JOHN

> Georgie!

> MAJOR

> Sam!

Major comes to right foreground - Exits - John shakes George's hand - Laughs - George frowns - Eugene approaches receiving line - Camera moving closer -

> JOHN

> You look fine. Ha! Ha! There wuz a time though, in your fourth month, that you were so puny nobody thought you'd live.

George looks embarrassed - John turns to foreground -

> JOHN

> Where's Fanny?

> GEORGE

> 'Member you very well indeed.

John exits right foreground - Eugene takes Isabel's hand - Greets her -

> EUGENE

> Isabel.

9 (3-3) | INT ROOM CU - Isabel smiling up at Eugene partly on right foreground - George behind her frowning - Music heard -

> ISABEL

> Eugene!

INT ROOM CU - Isabel partly on left foreground - Eugene facing her smiling - Looks up to foreground - Music heard -

10 (4-2)

EUGENE

This your boy, Isabel?

INT ROOM MCU - Isabel in center turning left to George to present Eugene - George frowning - Eugene lets go of her hand -

11 (11-15)

ISABEL

George, this is Mr. Morgan.

George shakes Eugene's hand - Responds curtly -

GEORGE

Remember you very well indeed!

Isabel laughs embarrassed - Eugene smiles -

EUGENE

George, you never saw me before in your life. But from now on you're going to see a lot of me . . .

INT ROOM CU - Isabel partly on left foreground - Eugene at right looks at her - Smiling -

12 (6-11)

EUGENE

. . . I hope.

She smiles - Music heard[18] -

ISABEL

I hope so too, Eugene.

EUGENE

Where's Wilbur?

INT ROOM MCU - Eugene partly on right foreground - Isabel facing him smiling - George at left behind her frowning in disapproval - Music heard -

13 (8-2)

ISABEL

You'll find him in the game room with some of the others...He never was much for parties, remember?

INT ROOM CU - Isabel partly on left foreground - Eugene facing her at right nodding - Smiling -

14 (6-0)

---

[18] In *RV* Boccherini's *Minuet*, arranged by Webb.

EUGENE

Yes, I remember.

He turns slightly to right - Smiling -

EUGENE

I'll come back for a dance.

15 (85-0) INT ROOM MCS - Eugene at right foreground - Isabel smiling up at him - George behind her at left frowning - Music heard -

ISABEL

Please do.

Eugene looks to left holding out his hand -

EUGENE

Eugene Morgan, Major Amberson.

Major comes on at left - Grips his hand -

MAJOR

Well, well, well!

The two men exit right - Couple coming on in foreground - Greeting George and Isabel - Lucy coming on in foreground -

GEORGE

Remember you very well, indeed. Remember you very well, indeed.

Major heard talking indistinctly - Jack coming on in background - Lucy coming on in foreground greeting Isabel and George -

LUCY

Miss Morgan.

EUGENE'S VOICE

Jack!

JACK

Gene!

Jack exits right - Lucy takes George's hand - He smiles -

Remember you very well, indeed!

He smiles holding onto Lucy's hand - Isabel smiles -

ISABEL

You don't remember her either, Georgie, but of course you will. Miss Morgan's from out of town...You might take her up to the dancing, I think you've pretty well done your duty here.

GEORGE

Be delighted.

He holds out his arm - She takes it - They turn - Come to foreground - Isabel watching after the two - Camera moving back - Showing people around - George talks to Lucy -

GEORGE

What did you say your name was?

LUCY

Morgan.

GEORGE

Oh.

Jack and Eugene come on passing camera in extreme foreground - Jack with arm around Eugene -

JACK

Well, I'm certainly glad you're back.

EUGENE

It's nice to be back, too, Jack. Been a long time.

Eugene and Jack cross in front of George and Lucy - Go to background - Continue talking - Lucy glances at Jack - Says to George -

LUCY

Who's that?

He glances back at Eugene - Answers - As they walk to foreground -

GEORGE

Oh I didn't catch his name when my mother presented him to me. You mean the queer-looking duck?

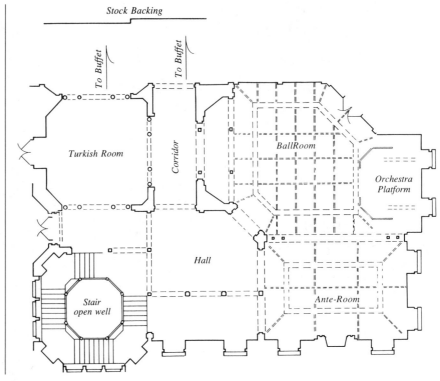

General Plan
Amberson Mansion
Third Floor—redrawn
from original blue-
prints, in the John
Mansbridge Collection
at UCLA, which are
of too poor quality
to copy.

Stock Backing

To Buffet

To Buffet

Turkish Room

Corridor

BallRoom

Orchestra
Platform

Hall

Stair
open well

Ante-Room

LUCY

The who?

GEORGE

The queer-looking duck.

LUCY

Oh, I wouldn't say that.

They start up steps at right - Camera pans to follow - Pan continues past musicians playing in foreground - Camera moves to follow them up steps as they talk -

GEORGE

The one with him's my Uncle Jack. Honorable Jack Amberson. I thought everybody knew him.

LUCY

He looks as though everybody ought to know him. It seems to run in your family.

GEORGE

Well I suppose most everybody does know him . . .

They exit at right -

INT BALCONY MCS - George and Lucy coming up steps from left background - Camera pans to follow - Music heard - Others following - George and Lucy come to foreground -   **16 (30-9)**

GEORGE

. . . out in this part of the country especially. Uncle Jack's pretty well known.

They come up to extreme foreground past camera to left foreground -

GEORGE

He's a congressman, you know.

LUCY

Oh, really?

Camera pans following them up toward right background -

GEORGE

Oh, yes.

They continue to background - People around -

GEORGE

The family always liked to have someone in Congress.

They go through crowd to right - Camera pans to follow - They exit - Music heard - George talking indistinctly - People around talking -

GEORGE

It's sort of a good thing in one way.

Camera pans up to right - Showing crowd of couples going up steps and balcony above to background - Much talking and confusion -[19]

INT STAIRCASE MLS - Camera shooting up to balcony - Crowd moving up to background - John heard talking - Music heard - General talking and noises -

17 (21-13)[20]

JOHN

Solid black walnut every inch of it—balustrades and all.

John stops up at right background slapping railing - Talking over music and crowd -

JOHN

Sixty thousand dollars worth o' carved woodwork in the house! Like water! Spent money like water! Always did! Still do! Like water!

Fanny comes on behind him - He turns as he talks -

JOHN

Gosh knows where it all comes from!

He sees her -

JOHN

Hello . . .

INT BALCONY MCU - John turning to Fanny above at right by railing - Crowd passing - Music heard - General confusion - John talking to her -

18 (14-10)

JOHN

. . . Fanny!

---

[19] The entire ballroom sequence is cut into severely in *RV*. Surviving evidence suggests that this sequence may truly have been "the greatest tour de force of my career" that Welles called it (in Leaming, *Orson Welles*, p. 241). His shooting plan involved a series of backward-moving camera shots that traversed the third floor of the Amberson mansion, where the ballroom was located, along a circular course, twice. The *RV* not only destroyed the rhythm of this plan but also rendered the physical layout of the space incomprehensible.

Certain documents make it possible to recover precise details concerning the shooting of the sequence. Welles's own copy of the shooting script for the film, on which continuity supervisor Amalia Kent made extensive cutting notes during the shooting, is in the Welles Collection at Lilly Library. The blueprint of the third-floor set is in the John Mansbridge Collection in the Theater Arts Library, UCLA. The information in the footnotes throughout the sequence identifying precise camera placements and movements is from the cutting notes. This information should be used in connection with the floor plan of the set, a reconstruction of which appears on p. 74.

Incidentally, Welles's emphatic claim to Leaming that the entire ballroom sequence was originally "*one* reel without a single cut" (p. 241) is not borne out either by such documentary evidence or by the testimony of participants in the shooting.

[20] George and Lucy climbed *two* circular sets of stairs. A crane followed the action up to the third-floor balcony.

FANNY

Hello, Uncle John.

Lucy and George come on at left - George talks to Fanny -

GEORGE

Aunt Fanny.

She goes to them talking surprised - The two stopping -

FANNY

Well . . .

JOHN

Hello.

FANNY

. . . is this Lucy Morgan?

GEORGE

Miss Morgan, Miss Minafer.

FANNY

You must favor your mother, my dear. I never knew her.

John grabs Fanny -

JOHN

Come on . . .

INT HALL MCS - George, Lucy, Fanny, and Uncle John in foreground - Others moving around on staircases in background - Music heard - John holding onto Fanny talking - Bringing her to near foreground - John and Fanny smiling -

JOHN

. . . there's dancing going on. Hoopla!

He continues bringing her to foreground - Camera moving back - Lucy and George following them - John talking loudly -

JOHN

Le's push through an' go see those young womenfolks crack their heels! Start the circus! Hoopse-daisy! Ha-ha-ha.

19 (43-9)[21]

---

[21] Reverse angle shot from the hall. The camera has been removed from the crane and placed on a camera dolly, a wheeled platform. The camera moves backward across the ballroom and stops to the left of the orchestra platform.

(Dance music plays throughout the ball sequence, but there was so much rescoring for *RV* that it is impossible to determine Herrmann's original plan. Records indicate that he did use *Toujours ou jamais* and *At a Georgia Camp Meeting*.)

John and Fanny start dancing - Dance to right foreground - Exit - George and Lucy dancing to foreground - Others dancing around - Music stops - People applaud - George coming to foreground with Lucy - Camera moving back through ballroom -

GEORGE

Give me the next one and the one after that, and every third one the rest of the evening.

LUCY

Are you asking?

INT BALLROOM MCU - Camera shooting up at Fanny and John letting their breaths out - People moving around in background -

20 (107-15)[22]

JOHN

Well, I don' want any more o' that!

He turns to Fanny at left as she moves to background - Wilbur coming on behind John - General noises heard -

JOHN

Jus' slidin' 'round!

She talks to Wilbur -

FANNY

Wilbur . . .

John passes them to left background - Talking loudly - Fanny and Wilbur whispering - He follows John to left background passing behind George and Lucy -

JOHN

Call that dancin'?

Wilbur grabbing him trying to quiet him - He stops - Talks loudly to Lucy and George -

WILBUR

John! John!

JOHN

Rather see a jig any day in the world! Hello, young lady.

He nudges her - Winks - Laughs - She laughs - Speaks -

LUCY

Hello.

---

[22] Reverse angle facing orchestra platform. Camera moves backwards across the ballroom and through corridor towards Turkish room. (In late Victorian mansions, culturally motival rooms were commonplace; this one is probably a sitting room.)

Wilbur brings John to foreground - Talking to George -

WILBUR

I'll send Uncle John home.

GEORGE

All right, Father.

John looks around laughing - Talking loudly - Wilbur nodding - Murmuring - Bringing him to foreground - Camera moving back - George and Lucy following - People around ballroom -

JOHN

Ain't very modest some of 'em. I don't mind that, though. Not me.

Wilbur exits left with John -

LAP DISSOLVE

Camera moving back - George and Lucy following - Activity in ballroom in background - Group of boys come on in foreground - All smiling - Greeting Lucy - George looking around jealously -

FIRST BOY

Hello, Lucy.

LUCY

Hello.

SECOND BOY

Hello, Lucy.

LUCY

Hello, Argyle.

THIRD BOY

Hello, Lucy.

LUCY

Hello.

She sniffs bouquet as they come to foreground - Boys going to background - Camera moving back - George talks jealously -

GEORGE

How'd all these ducks get to know you so quick?

Music changes - She smiles -

LUCY

Oh, I've been here a week.

GEORGE

Seems to me you've been pretty busy! Most of these . . .

Another group of boys comes on - Greeting her with smiles -

BOY

Hello, Lucy.

LUCY

Hello.

George and Lucy continue to foreground - Camera moving back - George speaks disgustedly -

GEORGE

. . . most of these ducks, I don't know what my mother wanted to invite 'em here for, anyway.

LUCY

Don't you like them?

GEORGE

Oh, I used to be president of a club that we had here, and some of 'em belonged to it. But I don't care much for that sort of thing any more. I really don't see why my mother invited 'em.

They stop in foreground - Camera stops -

LUCY

Maybe she didn't want to offend their fathers and mothers.

GEORGE

I hardly think that my mother need worry about offending <u>anybody</u> in this old town.

LUCY

It must be wonderful, Mr. Amberson—Mr. Minafer, I mean.

GEORGE

What must be wonderful?

LUCY

To be so important as that!

GEORGE

Oh, that isn't important.

Couple coming on at right foreground - Pass them - George greets them disinterestedly -

MAN

Good evening.

GEORGE

Good evening.

He continues talking to Lucy -

GEORGE

Anybody that really is anybody ought to be able to do about as they like in their own town, I should think.

He looks off left - Lucy looks off left -

INT BALLROOM[23] MLS - Eugene and Fanny dancing between columns - Couples dancing in background - Music heard - Eugene waves to right - Calls out

21 (86-8)

EUGENE

Hello.

The two dance toward background - George coming on at right - George staring at Eugene - Turns to Lucy as she comes on at right -

GEORGE

Well!...how's that for a bit of freshness!

LUCY

What was?

She crosses in front of him and joins him -

GEORGE

That queer-looking duck waving his hand at me like that.

LUCY

He meant me.

[23] Actually, Eugene and Fanny seem to be dancing in the passageway to the buffet area outside the Turkish room. Camera moves laterally alongside Lucy and George as they walk from Turkish room to stairwell.

She waves at Eugene - George talks jealously again as they cross to left foreground - Camera pans to follow them -

GEORGE

Oh, he did? Everybody seems to mean you.

She smells flowers - Camera moves left to follow them - Music heard - They pass people -

GEORGE

See here! Are you engaged to anybody?

LUCY

No.

GEORGE

You certainly seem to know a good many people!

LUCY

Papa does. He used to live here in this town before I was born.

GEORGE

Where do you live now?

LUCY

We've lived all over.

Camera moves to follow them to left foreground as they talk -

GEORGE

What do you keep moving around so for? Is he a—promoter?

LUCY

No, he's an inventor.

GEORGE

Oh? What's he invented?

Major comes on at left foreground - Speaks to George -

MAJOR

Georgie.

GEORGE

Grandfather.

The two continue to foreground - Camera follows as they go up steps to left -

LUCY

Just lately he's been working on a new kind of horseless carriage.

GEORGE

Horseless carriage? Ottomobiles? Well, well.

Lucy turns to face him - Continuing up steps -

LUCY

Don't you approve of them, Mr. Minafer?

GEORGE

Oh, yes, they're all right.

She sits on steps at left background -

LUCY

You know, I'm just beginning to understand.

INT HALL MLS - Camera shooting from above on steps - Lucy sitting on steps at right with back to camera - George at left facing her - People seen dancing in ballroom in extreme background - Eugene and Fanny seen dancing together - Other guests moving around in hall - Music heard -

22 (111-8)[24]

GEORGE

Understand what?

George sits at left - Looks down at her -

GEORGE

What?

She looks up at him -

LUCY

What it means to be a real Amberson in this town. Papa told me something about it before we came, but I see he didn't say half enough.

GEORGE

Did your father say he knew the family before he left here?

LUCY

I don't think he meant to boast of it. He spoke of it quite calmly.

---

[24] Reverse angle from behind stairwell as Lucy and George sit on *third* set of stairs leading up to tower.

GEORGE

Most girls are usually pretty fresh.

She smells her flowers as he continues impatiently - Music stops - Eugene and Fanny approach from ballroom in background -

GEORGE

They ought to go to a man's college for about a year. They'd get taught a few things about freshness. Look here. Who sent you those flowers you keep making such a fuss over?

Eugene calls to Lucy -

EUGENE

Lucy!

Lucy glances at Eugene and continues -

LUCY

He did.

GEORGE

Who's "he"?

LUCY

"The queer-looking duck."

EUGENE

I've come for that dance.

George talks derisively to Lucy - Eugene and Fanny come to steps and start up -

GEORGE

Oh, him? I s'pose he's some old widower. Heh—some old widower.

LUCY

Yes, he is a widower. I ought to have told you before; he's my father.

George embarrassed -

GEORGE

Oh, well that's a horse on me. If I'd known he was your . . .

Eugene comes up stairs - Isabel follows him - Eugene speaks to Lucy -[25]

---

[25] Isabel and Jack have emerged from corridor alongside Turkish room and come to join them.

EUGENE

This is our dance...but I guess I won't insist on it.

ISABEL

George, dear, are you enjoying the party?

GEORGE

Yes, Mother, very much. Will you please excuse us? Miss Morgan?

Lucy takes George's arm - They go down steps - Camera moving down to Isabel and Eugene -

Others in background - Jack stepping up in background - Music heard - Isabel talks proudly - Jack watching the two exit down steps in background -

ISABEL

It's charming, isn't it?

EUGENE

Hm?

ISABEL

Those children. It's touching. But of course they don't . . . it's touching.

Jack talks - Two in foreground turning to him - Start down to him -

JACK

Do you know what I think whenever I see these smooth triumphal young faces?

INT HALL MS - Fanny below at left of steps - Isabel, Eugene, and Jack turning on steps - Start down - Jack talking - Music heard -   **23** (239-13)[26]

JACK

I always think . . .

They come down -

JACK

. . . oh, how you're going to catch it.

Isabel smiling - Talks to Jack -

ISABEL

Jack.

---

[26] Reverse angle toward stairs. Group forms at bottom of stairs and camera advances ahead of them as they walk to and cross Turkish room toward buffet area. Action resumes in *RV* with WIPE/DISSOLVE as they approach punch bowl.

They come down to foreground - People passing - Camera moving back - Jack talking - Others coming down steps behind them -

JACK

Oh, yes. Life's got a special walloping for every mother's son of 'em.

ISABEL

Maybe some of the mothers can take the walloping for them.

They cross to right foreground - Camera pans following them - Jack laughing -

JACK

Not any more than she can take on her own face the lines that are bound to come on her son's.

The four stop in foreground - Jack at right talking - People passing -

JACK

I suppose you know that all these young faces have got to get lines on 'em?

ISABEL

Maybe they won't. Maybe times will change and nobody will have to wear lines.

EUGENE

Times have changed like that for only one person I know.

Eugene laughs at Isabel - The four come to foreground - Following camera as they talk -

JACK

What puts the lines on faces? Age or trouble? Ha, we can't say that wisdom does it. We must be polite to Isabel.

They all laugh - Eugene talks as they come to foreground -

EUGENE

Age puts some, and trouble puts some, and work puts some . . .

They stop as Eugene talks - People moving around in background -

EUGENE

. . . but the deepest wrinkles are carved by lack of faith. The serenest brow is the one that believes the most.

ISABEL

In what?

EUGENE

In everything. Oh, yes, you do.

ISABEL

Why, I believe—I believe I do.

Jack laughs - Talks as they follow camera through arch to foreground -

JACK

Isabel. There're times when you look exactly fourteen years old.

Camera moves back over table in foreground - Major standing at left of table by punch bowl - Fanny, Eugene, Isabel, Jack approach -

MAJOR

Eggnog, anybody?

EUGENE

Not for me, Sir.

MAJOR

I see you kept your promise, Gene.

Wilbur approaches behind them - Major in foreground - Addressing Isabel - Jack at right pouring punch -

MAJOR

Isabel, I remember the last drink Gene ever had. Fact is, I believe if he hadn't broken that bass fiddle, Isabel never would have taken Wilbur.

Major laughs -

MAJOR

What do you think, Wilbur?

WILBUR

I shouldn't be surprised. If your notion's right, I'm glad Gene broke the fiddle.

Major moves around Eugene to Isabel - Rests hand under her chin -

MAJOR

What do you say about it, Isabel? By jingo. She's blushing.

ISABEL

Who wouldn't blush.

They all laugh - Major moves right - Camera pans to follow - Eugene goes to Fanny - Leads her to right following Major - Others turn right -

FANNY

    The important thing is that Wilbur did get her . . .

Sam crosses with tray from right to left in foreground - Eugene gazing off to right -

FANNY

    . . . and not only got her but kept her.

EUGENE

    There's another important thing—that is, for me. In fact it's the only thing that makes me forgive that bass viol for getting in my way.

George and Lucy come on right foreground - Cross to left -

JACK

    Well, what's that?

EUGENE

    Lucy.

George and Lucy stop in extreme foreground - Lucy makes half-turn right in response - Camera moves back -

JACK

    You havin' a good time?

Major comes on right - Holds Eugene's arm - Group moves left - Camera pans to follow -

MAJOR

    I don't suppose you ever gave up smoking.

EUGENE

    No, sir.

MAJOR

    Well, I've got some Havanas.

Group continues to background - Camera moves to follow - Stops at table -

JACK

    Do your ears burn, young lady?

Lucy laughs - George and Lucy come forward to table in foreground -

GEORGE

Would you care for some refreshments, Miss Morgan?

LUCY

Yes, thanks.

George serves her - Eugene and Jack in background lighting cigars -

GEORGE

What did you say your name was?

LUCY

Morgan.

GEORGE

Funny name.

Eugene approaching behind them -

LUCY

Everybody else's name always is.

GEORGE

I didn't mean it was really funny.

Jack advancing to join Eugene -

GEORGE

That's just one of the crowd's bits of horsing at college.

Lucy laughs - Eating olive - Eugene moves behind and between them -

GEORGE

I knew your last name was Morgan. I meant your first name.

Eugene interjects to George -

EUGENE

Lucy.

Eugene and Jack exit right - George looks after Eugene indignantly -

GEORGE

Well!

LUCY

Is "Lucy" a funny name, too?

Woman leading man and Mrs. Johnson from room in background to foreground[27] -

GEORGE

No, Lucy's very much all right.

LUCY

Thanks.

Woman and man stop at table - Mrs. Johnson exits right - Woman indicating olives -

WOMAN

Here they are. Here they are, Henry.

HENRY

Are they?

GEORGE

Thanks for what?

LUCY

Thanks about letting my name be Lucy.

She takes George's arm - They turn to background -

They go to background - Mrs. Johnson comes on at right -

WOMAN

No, they're not.

MRS. JOHNSON

No?

WOMAN

No.

Henry and the two women turn to right background -

---

[27] They enter the buffet area from the ballroom. The wall along the upper edge of the ballroom set is "wild"—that is, removable.

REEL 2 SECTION A

NIGHT SEQUENCE

INT BALLROOM MS - Lucy and George coming to foreground - Others around - Man going to background - George bumps into one - Ignores him - The two exit right foreground - Man turns - Talks angrily - Jack and Eugene by table in background - Crowd noise heard - Man moving to foreground - Two in background coming to him -

1 (376-8)[28]

> MAN

Look at that! Look at that boy! Sorry, your highness.

Man exits right - Jack and Eugene come to foreground - Camera moving back - Music heard - They stop in foreground -

> JACK

I can't see why Isabel doesn't see the truth about that boy!

> EUGENE

Hm?

> JACK

Georgie.

> EUGENE

What's the matter with him?

> JACK

Huh, too much Amberson, I guess for one thing. Yes, and for another, his mother just fell down and worshipped him from the day he was born. Oh, I don't have to tell you what Isabel Amberson is, Gene. Oh, she's got a touch of the Amberson high stuff about her, but you can't get anybody who ever knew her to deny that she's just about the finest woman in the world.

> EUGENE

No, you can't get anybody to deny that.

They come to foreground talking following camera - Through doorway - Crowd noise heard - Jack talking - Others around -

> JACK

Well, she thinks he's a little tin god on wheels. Why, she actually sits and worships him! You can hear it in her voice when she speaks to him. See it in her eyes when she looks at him. My gosh! What does she see when she looks at him?

---

[28] Perhaps the most lamented of all the lost footage: most of a four-minute, single-take, horseshoe-shaped tracking shot. Reverse angle from preceding shot, camera facing punch bowl. (Setting is still the buffet area, not the ballroom.) After business of George's rudeness, camera moves ahead of Eugene and Jack as they walk slowly through corridor between Turkish room and ballroom and into hall, diverts to new business with olives, picks up Eugene and Jack again, follows them into anteroom, backs into ballroom ahead of them and pauses on their conversation in front of a mirror. Only tail end of shot survives, beginning at end of Eugene's and Jack's conversation. Camera moves backward across ballroom as Eugene and Isabel dance, pauses on Lucy and George, resumes backward move as Lucy and George dance away and Isabel and Eugene dance to foreground. Camera comes to a stop at upper end of ballroom, completing the horseshoe.

Cinematographer Stanley Cortez has always implied that the idea for this shot came from him (see, for instance, "American Film Institute Seminar," *American Cinematographer,* November 1976, pp. 1242–1243). Continuity supervisor Amalia Kent claims she suggested it to Welles (interview with Robert Carringer, October 25, 1987).

REEL 2A   97

They stop by woman at left before mirror -

                          EUGENE

Huh, she sees something that we don't see.

                            JACK

What's that?

                          EUGENE

An angel.

                            JACK

Angel!

Little man hurries on - Talks to woman -

                          HENRY[29]

There they are.

                          EUGENE

I'll take one of these.

Eugene and Jack exit right - Two[30] hurrying to foreground - Woman talking - Camera moving back -

                       MRS. JOHNSON

The olives.

                       MISS GILBERT

Roger.

                       JACK'S VOICE

Angel.

                       MISS GILBERT

Come over here and look at the olives.

The two[31] stop by group around butler holding tray of olives - General talking and activity as people gather around him - Looking at olives as picking them up - Talking -

                          HENRY

You're supposed to eat them.

---

[29] Character names for bit roles in this deleted sequence are from the cutting notes.

[30] Reference unclear.

[31] Reference unclear.

MRS. JOHNSON

Green things they are, something like a hard plum.

ROGER

A friend of mine told me they tasted a good deal like a bad hickory nut.

MRS. JOHNSON

I hear you gotta eat nine . . .

HENRY

And then you get to like them.

ELLIOT

Well, I wouldn't eat nine bad hickory nuts to get to like <u>them</u>.

ROGER

Kind of a woman's dish, anyway, I suspect.

MRS. JOHNSON

Well, I reckon most everybody'll be makin' a stagger to worm through nine of 'em, now Amberson's brought 'em to town.

People laugh - Put olives back on tray - Go to background - Some exit - Butler coming to foreground with tray - Mrs. Johnson watching him -

JACK'S VOICE

All mothers are like that.

EUGENE'S VOICE

Um-hum.

Mrs. Johnson reaches around behind butler - Grabs olives from tray - Eugene and Jack coming on at right - Butler exits - She bumps into Eugene -

MRS. JOHNSON

Excuse me.

She rushes to background - Servant coming on with tray - Eugene puts glass down on tray -

EUGENE

Here you are.

The two cross to left - Butler crossing - Camera pans - Jack talks surprised as Eugene goes to butler -

EUGENE

Here, take this.

The two men come to foreground - Camera moving back through room - Men talking -

EUGENE

That's what she sees.

JACK

Angel? My nephew? Look at him. Do you see an angel?

EUGENE

No. All I see is a remarkably good-looking young fool-boy with the pride of Satan and a set of nice drawing-room manners.

JACK

What do you mean?

They stop - The two men talk -

EUGENE

Mothers are right. Mothers see the angel in us because the angel is there.

JACK

A-ha. You mean Georgie's mother is always right.

EUGENE

I'm afraid she always has been.

Eugene crosses to left - Jack following talking - Camera following them to fireplace at left background - Fire burning - Mirror over fireplace showing crowd dancing -

JACK

Yes, well, wait till you get to know young Georgie a little better.

EUGENE

Jack, if you were a painter, you'd paint mothers with angels' eyes holding little devils on their laps.

Jack laughs - Eugene comes to foreground -

EUGENE

Me, I'll stick to the Old Masters and the cherubs.

Music stops - People in mirror seen applauding -

JACK

Well, somebody's eyes must have been pretty angelic if they've been persuading you that Georgie Minafer is a cherub.

EUGENE

They are. They're more angelic than ever.

Music heard - Eugene turns to Jack -

EUGENE

Good-bye, I've got this dance with her.

They begin moving to foreground - Camera moves back -

JACK

With whom?

EUGENE

With Isabel, of course.

JACK

Eighteen years have passed—but have they? Tell me, have you danced with poor old Fanny too, this evening?

EUGENE

Twice! Wilbur . . .

Wilbur and Isabel come on right foreground - Eugene takes Isabel's hand - Jack takes her other hand - They lead her forward with Wilbur following behind - Camera continues to move back -

JACK

My gosh! Old times certainly are starting all over again.

EUGENE

Old times? Not a bit! There aren't any old times. When times are gone, they're not old, they're dead! There aren't any times but new times.

Eugene takes Isabel in his arms - They dance forward as camera moves back - Others dancing around - Lucy and George come on at left - Follow Eugene and Isabel - Lucy and George smile - Eugene and Isabel dancing exit left - Lucy and George continue forward - Stop - Face each other in extreme foreground -

LUCY

What are you studying in school?

GEORGE

I beg your pardon?

LUCY

What are you studying in school?

GEORGE

College!

LUCY

College.

GEORGE

Oh, lots o' useless guff!

LUCY

Why don't you study some useful guff?

GEORGE

What do you mean, "useful"?

LUCY

Something you'd use later, in your business or profession.

GEORGE

I don't intend to go into any business or profession.

LUCY

No?

GEORGE

No.

LUCY

Why not?

GEORGE

Well, just look at them...that's a fine career for a man, isn't it! Lawyers, bankers, politicians! What do they ever get out of life, I'd like to know. What do they know about real things? Where do they ever get?

LUCY

What do you want to be?

GEORGE

A yachtsman.

Lucy and George dance into background - Other couples dancing around - Music swells - Camera moves back - Stops - Eugene and Isabel come on from left - Dance to foreground -

LAP DISSOLVE

INT HALL LS - Musicians in foreground by Xmas tree - Playing - Eugene and Isabel in far background dancing -

INT HALL MS - Eugene and Isabel dancing in foreground - Lucy and George coming down steps from above in background - Talking faintly heard - She sits down near foot of stairs - **2 (12-9)**

GEORGE

What good are they? They always break down.

LUCY

They do <u>not</u> always break down.

GEORGE

Of course they do!

INT HALL MCS - Lucy on steps - George sits down at left by her - Music heard - Camera slowly moving closer to them as they talk - **3 (52-8)**

GEORGE

Horseless carriages! Ottomobiles!

LUCY

Hmh?

GEORGE

People aren't going to spend their lives lying on their backs in the road letting grease drip in their faces. No, I think your father'd better forget about 'em.

LUCY

Papa'd be so grateful if he could have your advice.

GEORGE

I don't know that I've done anything to be insulted for!

LUCY

You know, I don't mind your being such a lofty person at all. I think it's ever so interesting. But Papa's a great man!

GEORGE

Is he? Well, let us hope so. I hope so, I'm sure.

He looks to foreground - She looks at him frowning - Both look to foreground offscreen -

4 (5-15) INT HALL MS - Isabel and Eugene dancing - She smiles up at him -

LUCY'S VOICE

How lovely your mother is!

5 (12-4) INT STEPS CU - Two sitting on steps -

GEORGE

I think she is.

LUCY

She's the gracefullest woman! She dances like a girl of sixteen.

GEORGE

Most girls of sixteen are pretty bad[32] dancers.

6 (154-4) INT HALL MCS - George rising helps Lucy up - Takes her arm - They cross hall to left - Camera moves back and pans to follow -

GEORGE

Anyhow, I wouldn't dance with one of them unless I had to...Uh—the snow's fine for sleighing; I'll be by for you in a cutter at ten minutes after two.

Isabel and Eugene dancing on right foreground - Music stops - They stop - Smile at each other - George and Lucy stop -

LUCY

Tomorrow? I can't possibly go.

EUGENE

Thank you, Isabel.

Applause heard - Eugene and Isabel look to foreground -

JACK'S VOICE

Bravo! Bravissimo!

---

[32] On the screen the word Tim Holt says is clearly "bum," as called for in the shooting script; the new reading was likely dubbed in as a gesture of deference to the Production Code office.

Lucy moves toward them from background -

> LUCY

Papa.

Eugene and Isabel in foreground turn to face Lucy and George in background -

> EUGENE

Lucy...I'll get your things.

Eugene goes to left background - Camera pans to follow - Moves forward toward George and Lucy -

> GEORGE

If you don't, I'm going to sit in a cutter at your front gate and if you try to go out with anybody else he has to whip me before he gets to you.

She laughs - Goes to Eugene in left background - Camera pans to follow -

> JACK'S VOICE

Hey, you two—I think you ought to take this in case you break down in that . . .

Jack comes on right with coat and robe - Goes to Lucy and Eugene in background - All talking at once -

> JACK'S VOICE

. . . horseless carriage.

Fanny rushes on from right - Goes to Lucy -

> FANNY

You better take this scarf, Lucy dear.

George calls to Jack -

> GEORGE

Uncle Jack?

> JACK

What is it?

Isabel runs on in foreground - Goes to group in background - Jack coming to George in foreground -

> EUGENE

Good-night, Isabel.

  GEORGE

Come here.

                                                        ISABEL

Fanny, where are you going?

                                                        FANNY

Oh, just out to look.

                                                        ISABEL

Do you think you'll be warm enough, Lucy?

Camera moves in to Jack and George -

                                                        JACK

Well?

                                                        GEORGE

Oh, nothing.

                                                        JACK

Here, hold this.

Jack hands fur blanket to George - Puts on coat as they talk - Others in background continue
talking indistinctly -

                                                        GEORGE

Who is this fellow Morgan?

                                                        JACK

Why, he's a man with a pretty daughter, Georgie.

                                                        GEORGE

He certainly seems to feel awfully at home here, the way he was dancing with
Mother and Aunt Fanny.

                                                        JACK

Well...I'm afraid your Aunt Fanny's heart was stirred by—ancient recollections,
Georgie.

                                                        GEORGE

You mean she used to be silly about him?

                            JACK

Oh, she wasn't considered, uh—singular. He was, uh—he was popular.

                          GEORGE

Ohhh.

George hands blanket back to Jack -

                            JACK

Do you take this same passionate interest in the parents of every girl you dance with?

                          GEORGE

Oh, dry up! I only wanted to know.

They go to background - Camera moves after them -

                          GEORGE

Lucy—about that sleigh ride.

                            JACK

I want to look at that, uh, automobile carriage of yours, Gene.

Lucy comes on at left - Others gather in darkened entryway - All talking at once -

                       FANNY'S VOICE

I'm coming out, too.

                          ISABEL

Fanny, you'll catch cold.

                            JACK

If we're going to ride in that thing tomorrow, I want to see if it's safe.

                          EUGENE

Good-night, Isabel.

                          ISABEL

Good-night, Eugene.

Eugene exits left - Isabel in dark profile looks after him - Lucy behind her in reverse profile faces George - George talks sternly -

GEORGE

You be ready at ten minutes after two.

LUCY

No, I won't.

GEORGE

Yes, you will. Ten minutes after two.

People heard talking indistinctly - Lucy smiles -

LUCY

Yes, I will.

She exits left -

JACK'S VOICE

C'mon, Gene! Show us how it works!

EUGENE'S VOICE

If it does work.

7 (11-4) EXT STREET MS - Camera shooting through fence - Group running through snow to auto in background - Camera pans to follow - They laugh - Shivering -

FANNY

I suppose you'll break down.

EUGENE

Come on, Lucy.

LUCY'S VOICE

I'm coming, Papa.

FANNY

I hope you're gonna be warm enough!

Eugene and Lucy get up on car - Motor starts - Jack tosses blanket to Eugene -

JACK

Here's a blanket for you, Eugene. Catch!

EXT STREET MCS - Eugene and Lucy settling down on seat - Pulling blanket over their laps -
Motor heard - Car shaking -

                                EUGENE

'Night!

Several Voices

'Night! Bye!

Car moving - Wind blowing - Lucy shivers making noises - Calls out over noise -

                                 LUCY

Papa?

                                EUGENE

Huh?

                                 LUCY

Papa, do you think George is terribly arrogant and domineering?

                                EUGENE

Oh, he's still only a boy...Plenty of fine stuff in him...Can't help but be, he's—
Isabel Amberson's son.

                                 LUCY

You liked her pretty well once, I guess, Papa.

                                EUGENE

Do still.

                                 LUCY

She's lovely. Lovely! Papa, I wonder sometimes . . .

                                EUGENE

What?

                                 LUCY

. . . I wonder just how she happened to marry Mr. Minafer.

He laughs -

                                EUGENE

Ha-ha. Oh, Wilbur's all right.

                                              LAP DISSOLVE

INT HALL MS - George and Isabel come on climbing steps at right - Walk down hallway - Camera moves to follow -

GEORGE'S VOICE

I know that isn't all that's worrying you.

ISABEL

Well, several things. I've been a little bothered about your father, too.

GEORGE

Why?

ISABEL

It seems to me he looks so badly.

GEORGE

He isn't any different from the way he's looked all his life, that I can see.

ISABEL

He's been worried about some investments he made last year. I think the worry's affected his health.

GEORGE

What investments? See here—he isn't going into Morgan's ottomobile concern, is he?

ISABEL

Oh, no. The automobile concern is all Eugene's.

Door heard opening - Light shines on Isabel and George - They stop - Camera stops - They look to left -

ISABEL

No, your father's rolling mills . . .

REEL 2 SECTION B

INT DOORWAY CU - Wilbur coming to foreground -

1 (3-1)

ISABEL'S VOICE

Hello, dear.

INT HALL MCS - Isabel and George in foreground - Looking off left - Jack and Fanny coming from background -

2 (4-11)

ISABEL

Have you had trouble sleeping?

GEORGE

Look here, Father . . .

INT DOORWAY CU - Wilbur looking to foreground - George comes on right foreground - Back to camera -

3 (3-15)

GEORGE

. . . about this man Morgan and his old sewing machine?

INT HALL CU - Wilbur partly on left foreground - Facing George -

4 (7-15)

GEORGE

Doesn't he want to get Grandfather to put some money into it? Isn't that what he's up to?

George looks to right as he hears -

FANNY'S VOICE

You little silly.

INT HALL MCS - Isabel standing in foreground - Fanny in background talking - Jack exiting right background -

5 (14-10)

FANNY

What on earth are you talking about? Eugene Morgan's perfectly able to finance his own inventions these days.

Fanny crosses to right behind Isabel -

GEORGE'S VOICE

I'll bet he borrows money from Uncle Jack.

Isabel speaks reprovingly -

ISABEL

Georgie, why do you say such a thing?

6 (17-15) INT HALL CU - George looking over his shoulder to foreground - Wilbur on left facing him -

GEORGE

He just strikes me as that sort of a man.

George looks back at Wilbur -

GEORGE

Isn't he, Father?

WILBUR

He was a fairly wild young fellow twenty years ago. He was like you in one thing, Georgie. He spent too much money. Only he didn't have any mother . . .

7 (2-13) INT HALL MCS - Isabel standing looking to foreground - Fanny in background - Listening -

WILBUR'S VOICE

. . . to get money out of a grandfather for him.

8 (11-2) INT HALL MCS - George at right foreground - Facing Wilbur - Wilbur turning to doorway in left background as he talks -

WILBUR

But I believe he's done fairly well of late years . . .

Wilbur exits in background as he talks -

WILBUR

. . . and I doubt if he needs anybody else's money to back his horseless carriages.

Isabel comes on in foreground - Crosses in front of George toward doorway -

9 (6-5) GEORGE

Well, what's he brought the old thing here for then?

People that own elephants don't take their elephants with 'em when they go visiting.[33]

10 (17-11) INT HALL MCS - George at right foreground - Isabel standing in doorway in background looking at him -

---

[33] A line from Tarkington's novel, probably deleted because it sounded strange to a 1940s audience.

GEORGE

What's he got it here for anyway?[34]

WILBUR'S VOICE

I'm sure I don't know. You might ask him.

Isabel looks at George -

ISABEL

I'll be in to say good-night, dear.

She closes door behind her - Hall darkens - George turns to foreground - Calls in whisper -

GEORGE

Aunt Fanny!

INT HALL MLS - Fanny standing at right background - George comes on left foreground -   **11 (14-3)**

FANNY

What in the world's the matter with you?

George goes to her -

GEORGE

I suppose <u>you</u> don't know why Father doesn't want to go on that horseless carriage trip tomorrow.

They walk together into background -

FANNY

What do you mean?

INT HALL LS - Fanny and George in background coming toward foreground - Sam in extreme   **12 (248-14)**
background putting out lights - George talks sarcastically -

GEORGE

You're his only sister and yet you don't know.

FANNY

Why, he—he—he never wants to go anywhere that I ever heard of. What <u>is</u> the matter with you?

GEORGE

He doesn't want to go because he doesn't like this man Morgan.

---

[34] Undoubtedly deleted because it was unnecessarily repetitive after deletion of the preceding line.

Awwh. Good gracious.

Door opens at left - Jack comes out -

                              FANNY

Eugene Morgan isn't in your father's thoughts at all, one way or the other.

                              JACK

Good-night.

                              FANNY

Why should he be?

                              GEORGE

Good-night.

                              FANNY

Good-night.

                              GEORGE

Hey!

                              JACK

Are you two at it again?

She starts to foreground - Stops and turns toward George -

                              GEORGE

What makes you and everybody so excited over this man Morgan?

Jack speaks disparagingly -

                              JACK

This man Morgan.

                              FANNY

Excited!

                              JACK

Oh, shut up.

Fanny turns to Jack -

                              FANNY

Can't . . .

Jack exits in doorway - Fanny continues impatiently -

                              FANNY

. . . can't people be glad to see . . .

She turns to left foreground - Moves down hallway - George follows her - Camera pans to follow
them -

                              FANNY

. . . an old friend, without silly children like you having to make a to-do about it?

They stop by door at left foreground - Peacock statue in background - George crosses in front of
her - Steps to left foreground -

                              FANNY

I've just been suggesting to your mother that she might give a little dinner for
them.

                             GEORGE

For who?

                              FANNY

For whom, Georgie.

He mimics her -

                             GEORGE

"For whom, Georgie."

Fanny hesitates -

                              FANNY

For Mr. Morgan and his daughter.

                             GEORGE

Oh, look here, don't do that—Mother mustn't do that.

Fanny speaks mockingly -

                              FANNY

"Mother mustn't do that."

GEORGE

It wouldn't look well.

FANNY

"Wouldn't look w—."...See here, Georgie Minafer! I suggest...that you just march straight on into your room! Sometimes you say things that show you have a pretty mean little mind.

She opens door - Goes inside - Slams it after her -

GEORGE

What upsets you this much?

JACK'S VOICE

Shut up!

FANNY'S VOICE

I know what you mean.

Door flies open - Fanny bursts out angrily -

FANNY

You're trying to insinuate that I'd get your mother to invite Eugene Morgan here on my account . . .

JACK'S VOICE

I'm going to move to a hotel!

FANNY

. . . because he's a widower.

GEORGE

What?

FANNY

What!

He laughs - She laughs derisively - Glares at him - He continues in surprise -

GEORGE

I'm trying to insinuate that you're setting your cap for him, and getting Mother to help you?

FANNY

Oohhhh!

She goes inside room -

GEORGE

Is that what you mean?

She slams door in his face - He smiles - Turns right - Moves down hallway - Camera pans to follow - Jack comes out door at left -

FANNY'S VOICE

You attend to your own affairs!

George turns - Looks back toward Fanny's room amazed -

GEORGE

Well, I will be shot!

He turns to Jack -

GEORGE

I will! I certainly will be shot!

Fanny heard raving -

FANNY'S VOICE

Ohh!

JACK

Oohh!

Jack exits through doorway - George walks into background - Laughing - Door heard slamming -

LAP DISSOLVE

INT STABLE MCS - Doors opening - Lucy runs inside - Horses heard neighing - Eugene driving auto to foreground - Yelling indistinctly -

EUGENE

Look out, Lucy. Look out, dear.

LUCY

Right.

She follows him to right foreground - He drives in - Stops - Horses heard - She comes to car - Talks as he climbs out - Noises heard -

LUCY

You know, I wish George wasn't so conceited and bad-tempered. He's really quite nice.

He talks to her - Stamping and neighing heard -

EUGENE

What's that, dear?

LUCY

George! Maybe I shouldn't call him exactly bad-tempered.

EUGENE

Of course not. Only when he's cross about something.

He crosses to right - Talking - Camera panning -

EUGENE

Whoa—whoa—whoa.

He goes around auto - She laughs - He fixes light -

EUGENE

You know, dear, you need only three things to explain all that's good and bad about George.

LUCY

What?

EUGENE

Whoa—whoa—whoa.

They come to right foreground - He kneels fixing light - Two horses stamping and rearing in stalls in background - Eugene talking -

EUGENE

Well, he's Isabel's only child. He's an Amberson. He's a boy.

LUCY

Well, Mr. Bones, of these three things, which are the good ones and which are the bad ones?

EUGENE

    All of them.

He blows out light -

FADE OUT

FADE IN EXT STREAM MS - Camera shooting down to stream - Snow on both banks - Reflections in water of sleigh moving - Musical bell motif -   **13** (9-10)[35]

EXT ROAD MS - Horseless carriage stalled in road in foreground - Eugene at right cranking - Jack by him - Isabel and Fanny in left background jumping up and down in snow -   **14** (7-6)

FANNY

    Do you think you'll get it to start?

They jump up and down squealing -

EXT COUNTRY LS - Camera shooting through woods - Sleigh in background circling around to left foreground - Camera pans to follow - Bells heard - George driving - Lucy at his side -   **15** (6-13)

EXT ROAD MCS - Camera shooting from below under car - Eugene trying to crank it -   **16** (3-13)

JACK'S VOICE

    What's wrong with it, Gene?

EXT ROAD MCU - Camera shooting through Eugene's legs - Eugene cranking car -   **17** (5-8)

EUGENE'S VOICE

    I wish I knew.

EXT COUNTRY LS - Camera shooting up slope - Sleigh races on from right - Crosses to left - Exits -   **18** (4-3)

EXT ROAD MCS - Camera shooting from above - Eugene with back to camera - Cranking car -   **19** (4-4)

EXT SLOPE MLS - Camera shooting through woods - Sleigh races on from right - Circles around bend to left foreground - Camera pans to follow - Bells heard - They nearly exit left -   **20** (10-10)

EXT ROAD MCU - Camera shooting through Eugene's legs - Eugene cranking car rapidly - Motor catches with terrific noise -   **21** (5-10)

EXT ROAD MS - Eugene beside car at right - Jack behind him - Eugene leaps onto car - Isabel and Fanny in left background come to car - Motor knocking - Much noise and confusion as they all talk at once - Jack, Isabel, and Fanny push car to right - Camera pans to follow - Jack falls into snow - Car stops - Laughter -   **22** (19-1)

---

[35] The snow ride sequence was shot on location at an icemaking plant. The spatial restrictions necessitated the 180° pans (as when shooting the moving sleigh) and the unusual lighting (viewers will note that the performers' shadows are sometimes thrown in inconsistent directions).

23 (4-14)	EXT ROAD MCS - Camera shooting up through branches to road - Horse and sleigh race from right foreground into background -
24 (9-3)	EXT ROAD MS - Eugene on stalled car - Motions and yells to others to push -

EUGENE

> C'mon, push! Push, Jack!

Car starts moving - Sleigh comes on at left background - Lucy laughing - Rises - Waves - George gestures mockingly -

GEORGE

> Git a horse! Git a horse!

Sleigh passes car -

25 (6-14)	EXT ROAD MS - Camera shooting over fence - Car partly on left - Sleigh continues past car - Circles to right background - Camera pans to follow -

GEORGE

> Git a horse.

LUCY

> Git a horse.

26 (5-9)	EXT SLOPE LS - Camera shooting up snow bank - Sleigh coming on above at left background - Crosses to right - Camera pans to follow - Runner breaks -

GEORGE

> Look out, Lucy!

Couple tumble into snow - Roll down embankment - Horse and sleigh exit right -

27 (3-7)	EXT CAR MCU - Camera shooting over Eugene's shoulder - Runaway sleigh in extreme background crossing right to left - Lucy heard crying out - Eugene leaps down off car -

FANNY'S VOICE

> What's happened to them?

ISABEL'S VOICE

> Oh, Georgie!

Eugene runs to background -

28 (3-3)	EXT ROAD MS - Camera shooting down - Four running from car in background to extreme foreground - All talking at once -

EXT SLOPE MCS - Camera shooting up slope - George holding onto Lucy as they roll down to foreground - They stop in extreme foreground lying on ground - Harp glissando -	**29** (4-2)
EXT SLOPE MS - Camera shooting up - Eugene running to foreground - Stops - Music heard - Looks down to foreground - Sees -	**30** (2-7)
EXT GROUND CU - Camera shooting down - Two lying on ground - George holding Lucy in his arms - Music heard - She smiles up at him - He kisses her - She tries to pull away -	**31** (4-1)

EXT COUNTRY MCU - Eugene looking down to foreground - Smiles -   **32** (3-6)

EUGENE

Are you all right?

EXT GROUND CU - Camera shooting down - George holding Lucy in his arms - They sit up - Look to foreground -   **33** (2-7)

ISABEL'S VOICE

Georgie!

EXT COUNTRY MCU - Camera shooting up - Eugene in foreground - Turns to left -   **34** (4-5)

EUGENE

They're all right, Isabel. This snowbank's a feather bed.

He runs to left foreground - Exits -

EXT COUNTRY MS - Eugene running from extreme foreground to background - George and Lucy on snow in background by fence - Music heard -   **35** (19-11)

ISABEL

Georgie!

Jack, Isabel, and Fanny run on - Isabel terrified -

EUGENE

Lucy, dear?

LUCY

I'm fine, Papa.

Eugene helps Lucy and George up -

EUGENE

Nothing the matter with them at all.

ISABEL

Oh Georgie!

JACK

They're all right, Isabel.

Eugene helps Lucy to left foreground - Fanny crosses extreme foreground to them -

FANNY

Are you sure you're not hurt, Lucy, dear?

George moves up bank right - Camera pans to follow - Jack in background - Isabel moves from extreme right foreground to George -

ISABEL

Georgie?

GEORGE

Don't make a fuss, Mother.

Eugene, Lucy, and Fanny come on extreme right foreground - Follow Isabel and George to background - Camera pans to follow -

ISABEL

George, that terrible fall!

GEORGE

Please, Mother, please.

Eugene starts to jump over fence -

36 (24-4) EXT COUNTRY MS - Camera shooting through branches - Pans to follow group climbing over fence - Music heard -

GEORGE

I'm all right!

ISABEL

Are you sure, Georgie? Sometimes one doesn't realize the shock.

They hurry through woods to right foreground -

JACK

Oh, Isabel.

ISABEL

I've just got to be sure, dear.

Pan continues as they move to background -

GEORGE

I'm all right, Mother. Nothing's the matter.

ISABEL

Let me brush you off, dear.

EUGENE

You look pretty spry, Lucy. All that snow becomes you.

JACK

That's right, it does.

All laugh -

EXT COUNTRY MS - Camera shooting up - Group coming down through snow to foreground -
Music heard -   **37** (3-7)

GEORGE

That darn horse.

EXT COUNTRY ELS - Horse racing to background with overturned sleigh -   **38** (4-0)

JACK'S VOICE

Pendennis will be home long before we will. All we've got to depend on . . .

EXT COUNTRY MS - Camera shooting through car in foreground - Group coming from background in snow - Car shaking - Sound of car heard - Music heard -   **39** (11-12)

JACK

. . . is Gene Morgan's broken-down chafing-dish yonder.

Laughter - Explosion in foreground heard - They all groan - Run to car -

EUGENE

She'll go. All aboard!

EXT ROAD MS - Group climbing up into car - All laughing talking - Music heard -   **40** (6-9)

JACK

You'll have to sit on my lap, Lucy!

LUCY

All right.

41 (16-11)   EXT ROAD MCS - Camera shooting through car - Isabel brushing snow off George - Eugene at left - Music heard - George embarrassed -

ISABEL

Then stamp the snow off. You mustn't ride with wet feet.

GEORGE

They're not wet. For goodness sakes, get in. You're standing in the snow yourself. Get <u>in</u>, Mother!

The two lift Isabel up into car - Eugene tucks her in -

EUGENE

You're the same Isabel I used to know. You're a divinely ridiculous woman.

42 (13-5)   EXT CAR CU - Eugene in foreground - Turning to George at right beside him - Music heard -

EUGENE

George, you'll push till we get started, won't you? Push?

George stares at Eugene - Surprised -

ISABEL'S VOICE

Divinely and ridiculous just counterbalance each other, don't they?

43 (7-11)   EXT CAR MCU - Eugene partly on in foreground - Isabel facing him - Lucy and Jack behind her -

ISABEL

Plus one and minus one equal nothing. So you mean I'm nothing in particular?

44 (13-15)   EXT ROAD MCS - Isabel in foreground on car - Eugene and George standing on other side - Eugene laughs - George glares at Eugene -

EUGENE

No, that doesn't seem to be precisely what I meant.

He cranks car - Explosions heard - Car begins moving left - All yell and talk indistinctly - Car goes to left - Camera tilts down to show George pushing car - Car stops again -

128   THE MAGNIFICENT AMBERSONS

EXT CAR MCS - Eugene and Isabel on front seat - Three behind laughing - Car shaking - Explosions heard -   **45** (3-8)

EXT ROAD MCU - Camera shooting down to George behind car - Fumes from exhaust blowing in his face - He coughs - Group heard laughing - Explosions heard -   **46** (8-7)

EXT CAR CU - Lucy, Jack, and Fanny before camera - Jack calls -   **47** (2-8)

JACK

Come on, Georgie, push!

EXT ROAD MCU - Camera shooting down to George behind car - He looks up to foreground - Shouts -   **48** (2-8)

GEORGE

I'm pushing!

EXT CAR CU - Jack, Lucy, and Fanny laughing - Car shaking - Noises heard -   **49** (2-14)

JACK

Push harder.

EXT ROAD MCU - Camera shooting down to George behind car - Pushing - Noises heard -   **50** (3-2)

EXT CAR MCU - Camera shooting up - Group on car in foreground - Eugene pulls back on steering rod - Explosions heard - Group laughing - Car moves forward -   **51** (1-7)

EXT ROAD MS - Camera shooting through tree branch - Car moving to left - George pushing - Mechanical sounds - General laughter - George leaps up on back of car - Car stalls again - All groan - He jumps down -   **52** (8-11)

EXT ROAD CU - George standing behind car - Fumes rising - He grimaces - Gasps - Groans - Pushes -   **53** (8-5)

EXT CAR MCS - Group in car - Jack climbs down - Eugene pulls back on steering rod - Laughter heard - Motor heard -   **54** (6-1)

EXT ROAD MS - Camera shooting through tree branch - Eugene, Isabel, Fanny, and Lucy on car - Jack comes around beside George - They push - Wheels spin in snow - Jack calls -   **55** (5-10)

JACK

Come on, Georgie, push!

EXT CAR CU - George pushing - Straining -   **56** (7-8)

GEORGE

What do you think I'm doing?

He waves fumes away - Gasps for air -

57 (5-11) EXT CAR MCS - Isabel and Eugene in foreground - Fanny and Lucy in back seat - Eugene climbs down - Fanny talks to Lucy -

> FANNY
>
> Your father wanted to prove that his horseless carriage would run, even in the snow.

58 (6-3) EXT CAR MCS - Jack standing in foreground - Fanny and Lucy sitting above in car - Jack starts to sing -

> JACK
>
> "As-s-s-s I walked along the Boy de Boolong . . ."

> FANNY
>
> It really does, too.

> LUCY
>
> Of course.

> FANNY
>
> It's so interesting.

59 (10-13) EXT CAR MCU - Fanny talking to Lucy - Jack heard singing -

> FANNY
>
> He says he's going to have wheels all made of rubber and blown up with air. I should think they'd explode.

Jack continues singing as Isabel joins in -

> SINGING
>
> "With an independent air
>
> You can hear the girls declare
>
> He must be a millionaire
>
> You can . . ."

60 (3-5) EXT CAR CU - George behind car - Coughing at fumes - Pushing -

> FANNY'S VOICE
>
> But Eugene seems very confident.

SINGING

". . . hear them sigh"

EXT CAR CU - Fanny talking rapidly to Lucy -   **61** (10-9)

SINGING

"And wish to die"

FANNY

Oh, it seems so like old times to hear him talk.

SINGING

"You can see them wink the other eye

At the man who . . ."

Fanny starts to sing with others -

SINGING

". . . broke the bank at Monte Carlo."

JACK'S VOICE

Here we go!

EXT ROAD MCS - Car coming to foreground - Jack leaps onto back seat - George leaps onto   **62** (4-12)
back runner -

GROUP

Hooray!

JACK

We're off!

Car moves to extreme foreground -

EXT ROAD MS - Camera shooting through tree branch - Whole group on car - Car moving to   **63** (7-7)
background - George standing on back - All continue singing -

SINGING

"As I walked along the Boy de Boolong"

EXT CAR MCS - Car moving to right foreground -   **64** (4-6)

"With an independent air

Hear the girls declare"

65 (11-13) EXT CAR MCS - Fanny and Jack sitting in back seat - Facing Lucy - Singing - George leaning over from back between Fanny and Jack - Car going to right -

SINGING

"Be a millionaire"

JACK

"Be a millionaire"

Lucy talks to George as others continue singing -

SINGING

"As I walked along the Boy de . . ."

LUCY

George, you tried to swing . . .

66 (3-15) INT CAR CU - Jack in foreground - Singing - George leaning over behind him -

SINGING

"Boolong"

LUCY'S VOICE

. . . underneath me and break the fall for me when we went over.

SINGING

"With an independent air"

67 (3-7) EXT CAR CU - Lucy smiling to foreground -

LUCY

I knew you were doing that. It was nice of you.

SINGING

"You can hear the girls declare

Be a millionaire"

EXT CAR CU - Jack in foreground - Singing - George on right -   **68 (5-4)**

GEORGE

Wasn't much of a fall to speak of. How 'bout that kiss?

SINGING

"OHHHHHHHH . . . You can . . ."

EXT CAR ECU - Lucy joins the singing -   **69 (3-13)**

LUCY WITH OTHERS

"Can hear them sigh and wish to die"

EXT CAR ECU - George grins - Smirks - Joins singing -   **70 (3-13)**

GEORGE WITH OTHERS

"You can see them wink the other eye"

EXT CAR MCU - Fanny left foreground - Jack and George at right - All singing loudly -   **71 (10-15)**

SINGING

"At the man who broke the bank at Monte Carlo."

George off key - Jack looks at him - Fanny starts again - Jack joining -

FANNY SINGS

"As I . . ."

". . . walk along the Boy de . . ."[36]

EXT CAR MCU - Eugene and Isabel in foreground - Others in background singing - Isabel talks to him -   **72 (20-4)**

FANNY SINGS

". . . Boolong . . . ."

ISABEL

When we get this far out you can see there's quite a little smoke hanging over town.

Singing stops - Jack talks -

JACK

Yes, that's because the town's growing.

---

[36] The following deletion exemplifies a recurring pattern: Virtually everything involving the fundamental changes taking place in the town as its feudal and agrarian character gives way to the rise of industrialism and the growth of an urban working class is eliminated in *RV.*

EUGENE

Yes, and as it grows bigger it seems to get ashamed of itself so it makes that big cloud and hides in it.

ISABEL

Oh, Eugene.

73 (22-11) EXT CAR CU - Isabel in foreground - Eugene on other side of her - Car shaking -

EUGENE

You know, Isabel, I think it used to be nicer.

ISABEL

That's because we were young.

EUGENE

Maybe. It always used to be sunshiny, and the air wasn't like the air anywhere else. As I remember it, there always seemed to be gold dust in the air.

74 (48-14) EXT CAR CU - Lucy partly on right foreground - Sitting on Jack's lap - He talks to her - George leaning in behind them disgusted -

JACK

How about it, young folks? You notice any gold dust?

Lucy laughs - George talks derisively -

GEORGE

Gold dust?

They talk - Car shaking -

LUCY

I wonder if we really do enjoy it as much as we'll look back and think we did?

JACK

Of course not.

LUCY

I feel as if I must be missing something about it, somehow, because I don't ever seem to be thinking about what's happening at the present moment. I'm always looking forward to something. Thinking about things that will happen when I'm older.

George talks to Lucy - Jack whistling -

> GEORGE
>
> You're a funny girl. But your voice sounds pretty nice when you talk along together like that.

George looks off to left - Yells -

> GEORGE
>
> Hey, look at those fences all smeared.

EXT CAR CU - Fanny at right whistling - George at left holding on frowning - Car shaking violently -   **75** (21-9)

> LUCY'S VOICE
>
> That must be from soot.

Fanny talks to him -

> FANNY
>
> Yes. There're so many houses around here now.

> GEORGE
>
> Grandfather owns a good many of them, I guess—for renting.

> FANNY
>
> He sold most of the lots, Georgie.

> GEORGE
>
> He ought to keep things up better. It's getting all too much built up. Riffraff!

EXT CAR CU - Lucy laughing - Whistling heard -   **76** (2-10)

> GEORGE'S VOICE
>
> He lets . . .

EXT CAR CU - George talking indignantly - Whistling heard -   **77** (5-2)

> GEORGE
>
> . . . these people take too many liberties. They do anything they want to.

EXT CAR CU - Lucy whistling -   **78** (3-14)

EXT CAR CU - George looking to foreground - Car shaking -   **79** (3-11)

GEORGE

You know, you've got that way of seeming quietly . . .

He exits right -

EXT CAR CU - Lucy partly on right foreground whistling - Jack at left whistling - George behind them - Talking angrily -

80 (30-2)

GEORGE

. . . superior to everybody else. I don't believe in that kind of thing.

LUCY

You don't?

GEORGE

No. Not with me. I think the world's like this.

Lucy gestures - Starts singing loudly -

LUCY

"La, la, la."

George glares - Continues talking as she and Jack sing loudly -

GEORGE

There's a few. There's a few people that from their birth and position and so on, puts them on top, and they ought to treat each other entirely as equals. I wouldn't speak like this to everybody.

EXT CAR CU - George looking to foreground - Exasperated - Talks angrily - Lucy and Jack heard singing -

81 (7-1)

GEORGE

Oh, I had a notion before I came for you today that we were going to quarrel.

EXT CAR CU - Lucy singing - Talks -

82 (6-6)

LUCY

No we won't. Takes two!

She continues to sing - Smiling -

LUCY

"La, la, la."

She starts singing -

LUCY SINGS

"As I walked . . ."

83 (6-0) EXT CAR MCS - Eugene and Isabel in front seat singing - Others behind them singing - Car shaking -

SINGING

". . . walked along the Boy de Boolong

With an independent air"

84 (2-12) EXT CAR CU - George looking exasperated as singing is heard -

85 (20-7) EXT COUNTRY ELS - Camera shooting over embankment in foreground - Town seen in far background - Group in car going along through snow to right background -

SINGING HEARD

"Hear the girls declare

He must be a millionaire

You can hear them sigh

And wish to die . . ."

Singing and motor sound recede into distance as car moves to extreme background[37] -

IRIS OUT[38]

---

[37] The background of this shot is a painting done in the style of Currier and Ives.

[38] The shot closes down to darkness in a contracting circle. Welles used this technique from silent film to signify the closing of an era and the end of "the magnificence of the Ambersons."

REEL 3 SECTION A

DAY SEQUENCE

FADE IN EXT DOORS MCU - Crepe hanging on door - Music heard - Shadow of Eugene appears on door - Seen removing hat - Ringing bell - Sam opens door from inside -

1 (39-4)

SAM

Mr. Morgan.

Lucy comes on from right foreground with Eugene - They go inside - Sam closes door -

INT ROOM MS - Camera shooting up as if from point of view of coffin - Townspeople coming on at left passing by looking into coffin - Eugene in group in background shaking hands with Major - Eugene comes to foreground with Lucy as people continue filing past - Eugene and Lucy pause to look - Move left as camera pans to follow them - Flowers in extreme foreground come into view - Eugene and Lucy pass behind George - George staring to foreground - Fanny standing beside George - Eugene goes to Isabel standing at left - Camera continues pan - Eugene and Isabel exit left - Fanny follows and moves to extreme left foreground -

2 (78-14)

INT ROOM ECU - Camera shooting up to Fanny staring to left foreground - Watching tensely - Music picks up again -

3 (19-1)

[LAP DISSOLVE

EXT CEMETERY MS - Camera shooting up to tombstones of Amberson family - One at right with Wilbur's name on it - Music heard[39] -

FADE OUT][40]

FADE IN INSERT #1 - College diploma in Latin - Camera Matte effect showing George's name[41] -

4 (438-4)

GEORGIUM AMBERSON MINAFER

Camera moves back from diploma -

LAP DISSOLVE

NIGHT SEQUENCE[42]

FADE IN - EXT AMBERSON MANSION ELS - Camera shooting across to house in background - Lights in windows - Rain heard pouring down - Thunder - Lightning flash -

LAP DISSOLVE

---

[39] Herrmann's music cue "Death and Youth" originally accompanied shots 3 and 4: Wilbur's funeral music, followed by *Gaudeamus igitur*, a joyful student song, over the shot of George's diploma.

[40] Replaced in *RV* by MCU of camera shooting up to Bronson and August looking down as if at tombstone. Bronson says: "Wilbur Minafer...a quiet man...Town'll hardly know he's gone."

[41] The phrasing is unclear but may mean that the periphery of the image is masked by a device in the camera (an "in-camera matte effect") so that George's name would stand out prominently.

[42] The first of the radically disjunctive transitions in *RV*. With the allusion to George's graduation eliminated, the kitchen sequence seems at first to be a continuation of matters involving Wilbur's death. The fact that George and Fanny are both dressed in mourning black reinforces the association. Only through their conversation is it revealed that several months have passed and the occasion is George's return home after his graduation.

INT KITCHEN MS - George sitting at table in foreground - Eating - Gulping down his food -
Fanny standing by sink at window in left background - Rain pouring down - Thunder heard -
She comes to George with cake as she talks - Camera pans to right to follow -

                              FANNY

    Where did Isabel go to?

                              GEORGE

    She was tired.

She crosses behind George -

                              FANNY

    Never was becoming to her to look pale...Look out.

She puts cake down before him - He talks delightedly with mouth full -

                              GEORGE

    Oh boy, strawberry shortcake.

                              FANNY

    It's first of the season. Hope it's big enough.

She sits down at right beside him -

                              GEORGE

    You must have known I was coming home.

                              FANNY

    Hm.

                              GEORGE

    What'd you say?

                              FANNY

    Nothing.

He takes huge bite of cake - Makes approving sound -

                              GEORGE

    Umh!

                              FANNY

    Sweet enough?

GEORGE

Fine.

George gulps down cake as Fanny questions him - Pumping him for information -

FANNY

Suppose your mother's been—pretty gay at the commencement?...Going a lot?

GEORGE

How could she in mourning? All she could do was sit around and look on. That's all Lucy could do either, for that matter.

FANNY

How did Lucy get home?

GEORGE

On the train with the rest of us.

FANNY

Quit bolting your food!

George continues gulping food vigorously -

FANNY

Did you drive out to their house with her before you came here?

GEORGE

No. She went home with her father.

FANNY

Oh, I see...Don't eat so fast, George!

Loud thunder -

FANNY

So, uh...Eugene came to the station to meet you?

GEORGE

To meet us?...How could he?

FANNY

I don't know what you mean...Want some more milk?

GEORGE

No thanks.

FANNY

I haven't seen him while your mother's been away.

GEORGE

Naturally. He's been East himself.

FANNY

Did you see him?

GEORGE

Naturally, since he made the trip home with us.

FANNY

He did? He was with you all the time?

GEORGE

Unh-unhh. Only on the train, on the last three days before we left. Uncle Jack got him to come along.

FANNY

You're going to get fat.

GEORGE

I can't help that—you're such a wonderful housekeeper. You certainly know how to make things taste good.

FANNY

Mmmmm.

GEORGE

I don't think you'd stay single very long if some of these bachelors or widowers around town should just want . . .

FANNY

It's a little odd.

Thunder heard -

GEORGE

What's odd?

Jack comes on above in background - George glancing back at him as Fanny talks - Jack walks down steps -

> FANNY
>
> Your mother's not mentioning that—Mr. Morgan had been with you.

Jack comes forward toward them - Stands behind them as they talk - George continues eating cake -

> GEORGE
>
> Didn't think of it, I suppose.

George casts mischievous glance at Fanny -

> GEORGE
>
> But I'll tell you something in confidence.

> FANNY
>
> What?

> GEORGE
>
> Well, it struck me that Mr. Morgan was looking pretty absent-minded most of the time. And he certainly is dressing better than he used to.

Jack enters the conversation - Talks teasingly - George eating and drinking - Fanny looking down stonily -

> JACK
>
> Oh, he—isn't dressing better, he's dressing up...Fanny, you ought to be a little encouraging when a—prize bachelor begins to show by his haberdashery...what he wants you to think about him.

> GEORGE
>
> Uncle Jack tells me the factory's been doing quite well.

> JACK
>
> Quite well?

> GEORGE
>
> Honestly, Aunt Fanny . . .

> JACK
>
> Why listen! Eugene's got . . .

GEORGE

. . . I shouldn't be a bit surprised to have him request an interview and declare that his intentions are honorable, and ask my permission to pay his addresses to you. What had I better tell him?

Fanny begins to sob - Both men look concerned -

GEORGE

Oh, Aunt Fanny!

JACK

Oh, Fanny, we were only teasing.

FANNY

Oh, let me alone!

JACK

Please, Fanny!

GEORGE

We didn't mean anything.

She leaps up - Brushes Jack aside - Rushes to background - George leaps up following her - Trying to console her - She cries out through her sobs -

FANNY

Let go of me! Please, please let me alone!

GEORGE

We didn't know you got so sensitive as all this.

She runs up steps in background - Exits through door - Slams it after her - George turns slowly to Jack -

GEORGE

It's getting so you can't joke with her about anything any more.

Jack comes to table in foreground - Sits down - George standing in background talks to him -

GEORGE

It all began when we found out father's estate was all washed up and he didn't leave anything...I thought she'd feel better when we turned over his insurance to her. Gave it to her absolutely without any strings to it. But now—mmmh.

Jack talks thoughtfully -

> JACK
>
> Yeah...Think maybe we've been...teasing her about the wrong things.

George crossing to left to window -

> JACK
>
> Fanny hasn't got much in her life...You know, George, just being an aunt isn't...really the great career it may sometimes seem to be...I really don't know of anything much Fanny has got...

George leans over sink - Looks out window staring - Rain pouring down -

> JACK
>
> . . . except her feeling about Eugene.

> JACK
>
> You know, I think perhaps we ought to . . .

George shouts dumbfounded -

> GEORGE
>
> Holy cats!

George runs to background - Jack turning - Talking surprised -

> JACK
>
> What's wrong, Georgie?

George runs out door in background - Jack leaping up calling after him -

> JACK
>
> Why, Georgie!

Jack runs to background - Stops - Grabs up coat and umbrella - Hurries to background putting on coat - Calling -

> JACK
>
> Georgie! Georgie!

He starts out door -

EXT HOUSE MS - Rain pouring down - George running from door in background to foreground - Jack running out after him - Putting on coat - Yelling as George exits right foreground -   **5** (4-7)

JACK

Georgie.

Jack raising umbrella hurries to foreground -

EXT EXCAVATIONS MLS - Buildings partly erected in background - Storm raging - Rain falling - George runs on left foreground - Turns to foreground - Yelling -

6 (5-3)

GEORGE

What is this?

EXT HOUSE MS - Rain pouring down - Storm heard - Jack running to foreground with umbrella - Waving -

7 (2-12)

GEORGE'S VOICE

Looks like excavations.

Jack exits right foreground -

EXT EXCAVATIONS MCU - George standing at left foreground - Jack running on with umbrella - Rain pouring down - George yelling over noise of storm -

8 (15-14)

GEORGE

Looks like the foundations for a lot of houses! Just what does Grandfather mean by this?

He rushes to background toward partly constructed buildings - Jack following - Talking -

JACK

My private opinion is he wants to increase his income by building these houses to rent. For gosh sakes come in . . .

EXT STRUCTURES MCS - Framework of buildings in background - George running on in foreground - Storm raging -

9 (8-0)

JACK'S VOICE

. . . out of the rain!

George runs to buildings in background - Yelling - Jack running on at right foreground with umbrella - Goes to him -

GEORGE

Can't he increase his income any other way but this?

JACK

It would appear he couldn't. I wanted him to put up . . .

EXT BLDG MCU - Two standing - Storm raging - Jack at right yelling - Trying to hold umbrella over both of them -

10 (9-1)

> JACK
>
> . . . an apartment building instead of these houses.

The two shout at each other -

> GEORGE
>
> An apartment building! Here?

> JACK
>
> Yes, that was my idea.

> GEORGE
>
> An apartment house!

EXT RAIN CU - George looking to right - Water streaming down his face - He yells - Shocked -

11 (3-12)

> GEORGE
>
> Oh, my gosh!

Jack heard -

> JACK'S VOICE
>
> Don't worry!

EXT UMBRELLA CU - Jack looking to left foreground - Shouting over noise of storm -

12 (5-9)

> JACK
>
> Your grandfather wouldn't listen to me, but he'll wish he had, some day.

EXT RAIN CU - George looking to right shouting - Rain pouring down his face -

13 (4-11)

> GEORGE
>
> But why didn't he sell something or other, rather than do a thing like this?

EXT UMBRELLA CU - Jack shouting to left foreground -

14 (4-11)

> JACK
>
> I believe he has sold something or other, from time to time.

EXT RAIN CU - George shouting to right -

15 (3-9)

Ray Collins and Tim Holt between takes for the scene in the rain on the Amberson lawn.

GEORGE

Well, in heaven's name, what did he do this for?

EXT UMBRELLA CU - Jack shouting to left -

16 (3-11)

JACK

In heaven's name, to get money. That's my deduction.

EXT RAIN CU - George shouting to right -

17 (4-4)

GEORGE

I suppose you're joking—or trying to.

EXT UMBRELLA CU - Jack shakes his head - Storm heard -

18 (3-13)

JACK

That's the best way to look at it.

FADE OUT

DAY SEQUENCE

FADE IN INT FACTORY MS - Pounding anvil heard - Camera shooting over sparks in extreme foreground - Fanny, Isabel, Lucy, Eugene, and George gathered around watching - Worker comes on left foreground with white hot steel bar - Pounds bar on anvil - Sparks flying - Women scream - Men laugh - Workman exits left - Lucy talks to others amid general noises and confusion -

19 (155-1)

LUCY

And we're now turning out a car and a quarter a day.

Worker crosses in extreme foreground right to left - Pushing partly assembled car - Camera pans to follow - Worker exits left - Fanny, Isabel, and Eugene come to left foreground - Camera moves with them as they proceed down assembly line - Loud factory noises - Laughing - Talking -[43]

ISABEL

Isn't that marvelous.

FANNY

What's marvelous?

Men in extreme foreground hoisting up part of car -

ISABEL

They're turning out a car and a quarter a day.

---

[43] Studio records suggest that Herrmann's "Toccata," a percussion piece imitating the sounds of the factory, was recorded for this sequence. It was apparently never used, however, presumably because the loud factory sound effects made it superfluous.

FANNY

Oh!

Camera continues to follow them through factory -

GEORGE'S VOICE

Mother! Mother!

George comes on at right -

EUGENE

Fanny!

Eugene crosses to Fanny in background -

GEORGE

All this noise and smell seems to be good for you. I think you ought to come here
every time you get the blues.

FANNY

Oh, she never gets the blues, George. I never knew a person of a more even disposition.

They stop by Eugene's old steam car in which he tried to court Isabel - Eugene, Isabel, and Fanny
in foreground - George and Lucy in left background in shadows behind old car -

ISABEL

No, it's this place.

FANNY

I wish I could be more like that.

ISABEL

Wouldn't anybody be delighted to see an old friend take an idea out of the air like
that—an idea most people laughed at him for . . .

Fanny turns her back to them - Moves a few steps to background -

ISABEL

. . . and turn it into such a splendid humming thing as this factory.

Fanny turns to face Isabel - Eugene moves toward car -

EUGENE

D'ya remember this?...Our first machine. The Original Morgan Invincible.

ISABEL

I remember.

FANNY

How quaint.

Isabel turns - Takes Eugene's arm - All resume walking left - Camera continues moving with them -

ISABEL

Of course I'm happy. So very, very happy.

LUCY

Just look at the Morgan now, Mrs. Minafer.

ISABEL

It's beautiful—just beautiful.

They pause by model of new car at left - Eugene and Isabel exit in background - George inspects car - Lucy addresses Fanny -

LUCY

Did you ever see anything so lovely?

GEORGE

As what?

LUCY

As your mother!

George, Lucy, and Fanny resume walking - Move to foreground in front of car - Camera moving back -

LUCY

She's a darling!

Lucy takes George's arm - They come to right foreground - Eugene and Isabel come on at left as she talks -

LUCY

And Papa looks as if he were going to either explode, or utter loud sobs!

George and Lucy exit right - Isabel leads Eugene left - Fanny coming after - They pass photograph of Morgan car with caption "Ideal for the Professional Man" - Camera moves and pans to follow -

ISABEL

It's just glorious...It makes us all happy, Eugene. Give him your hand, Fanny.

Eugene holds Fanny's hand - Three come together in tight shot -

ISABEL

There. If Brother Jack were here, Eugene would have his three oldest and best friends congratulating him all at once. We know what Brother Jack thinks about it, though.

Eugene looks to left foreground and smiles - Isabel looks up at him -

EUGENE

I used to write verse about twenty years ago. Remember that?

ISABEL

I remember that, too.

Fanny stares off left grimly -

EUGENE

I'm almost thinking I could do it again...to thank you for making a factory visit into such a kind celebration.

FADE OUT

EXT FACTORY ENTRANCE MS - Camera shooting over buggy to entrance in background - General noises heard - Lucy and George coming from entrance - At left - He helps her up onto buggy -

20 (23-2)

LUCY

Gracious! Aren't they sentimental.

She sits down - Camera pans - He climbs in beside her - Amused -

GEORGE

People that age are always sentimental. They get sentimental over anything at all.

He picks up reins - Drives to left - Exits - Car comes out of factory in background - Eugene driving - Isabel and Fanny in back seat - Camera pans following them to left - They go down street to left background -

REEL 3 SECTION B[44]

DAY SEQUENCE

EXT TOWN LS - Auto in background racing down street to foreground - People on both sides of street watching - Dust rising - Eugene driving Isabel and Fanny - Turns corner in right foreground and exits - Dust clears - George and Lucy following same path in buggy -

1 (14-14)

EXT STREET MCS - George and Lucy riding in buggy to right - Dust clearing - Music heard - Camera moves with them throughout entire shot - They ride through town -

2 (204-8)

GEORGE

I'll still take a horse, any day.

Lucy laughs - They ride on silently -

GEORGE

Whoa.

LUCY

Oh, don't.

GEORGE

Why? Do you want him to trot his legs off?

LUCY

No, but . . .

GEORGE

"No, but" what?

LUCY

. . . I know when you make him walk it's so you can give all your attention to proposing to me again. George, do let Pendennis trot again.

GEORGE

I won't.

LUCY

Get up, Pendennis. Go on! Trot! Commence!

GEORGE

Ha! Ha! Lucy, if you aren't the prettiest thing in this world! When are you going to say we're really engaged?

---

[44] Another violent disruption of continuity occurs at this point in *RV*. The foregoing shot clearly establishes that after the factory visit everyone goes for a ride—Isabel and Fanny in Eugene's newest model automobile, Lucy in, characteristically, George's horse and buggy. *RV* eliminates the shot and inserts next, as the beginning of reel 3B, the scene under a tree on the Amberson lawn in which Isabel and Eugene agree that George ought to be told about their relationship (reel 4A, shot 1 and shot 2 to first lap dissolve). This is premature since at this point it is not yet clear that their courtship has formally resumed. In *CC* George's blow-up at the dinner table comes just after the scene on the lawn (reel 4A, shots 9 to 16): hence there was a buildup in intensity in his rivalry with Eugene and ground was prepared for his termination of his mother's romance. *RV* continues with the shot originally intended to come next, the start of the rides. Eugene and the women can be glimpsed briefly as they speed past throwing up dust, but the basis for connecting the shot to the earlier action has been lost.

LUCY

Not for years. So there's the answer.

GEORGE

Lucy! Dear, what's the matter? You look as if you were going to cry...You always do that whenever I can get you to talk about marrying me.

LUCY

I know it.

GEORGE

Well, why do you?

LUCY

One reason's because—I have a feeling it's never going to be.

GEORGE

You haven't any reason or . . .

LUCY

It's just a feeling. I don't know—everything's so unsettled.

GEORGE

If you aren't the queerest girl! What's unsettled?

LUCY

Well, for one thing, George, you haven't decided on anything to do yet. Or at least if you have, you've never spoken of it.

GEORGE

Lucy, haven't you perfectly well understood that I don't intend to go into a business or adopt a profession?

LUCY

What are you going to do, George?

GEORGE

Why, I expect to lead an honorable life. I expect to contribute my share to charities, and take part in—well, in movements.

LUCY

What kind?

GEORGE

Whatever appeals to me. I should like to revert to the questions I was asking you, if you don't mind.

LUCY

No, George, I think we'd better . . .

GEORGE

Your father's a businessman.

LUCY

He's a mechanical genius . . .

GEORGE

It's your father's idea.

LUCY

. . . or he's both!

GEORGE

Isn't it your father's idea that I ought to go into a business and that you oughtn't to be engaged to me until I do?

Camera speeds up - Begins to move in front of them - Entire street now stretches into distance -

LUCY

No, I've never once spoken to him about it.

GEORGE

But you know that's the way he does feel about it.

LUCY

Yes.

Camera now directly in front of them - Streetcar tracks come into view at left -

GEORGE

Do you think that I'd be very much of a man if I let any other man dictate to me my own way of life?

LUCY

George! Who's dictating your way of life?

GEORGE

I don't believe in the whole world—scrubbing dishes or selling potatoes or trying law cases.

Camera slows down - They move alongside it again - Go to right foreground -

GEORGE

No, I dare say I don't care any more for your father's ideals than he does for mine!

LUCY

George!

GEORGE

Giddap, Pendennis!

They exit right - Camera still moving - Enclosed carriage comes on from left behind them - Races across screen -

3 (531-12)[45]   INT CARRIAGE CU - Major and Jack seated in moving carriage - Conversing - Squeaking of carriage and hoofbeats heard - Music heard[46] -

JACK

Well—seems to have recovered...Looks in the highest good spirits.

MAJOR

I beg pardon?

JACK

Your grandson. Last night he seemed inclined to melancholy.

MAJOR

What about?...Not getting remorseful about all the money he's spent at college, is he?...I wonder what he thinks I'm made of?

JACK

Gold...and he's right about that part of you, Father.

MAJOR

What part?

JACK

Your heart.

---

[45] In *RV* a lap dissolve joins the two shots.

[46] Herrmann's musical cue "Major and Jack" (also called "Prelude") originally accompanied the carriage ride. Scored for low winds, brass, and strings, it developed the elegiac theme of the dialogue. It has been eliminated from *RV*.

MAJOR

I suppose that may account for how heavy it feels, nowadays, sometimes...This town seems to be rolling right over that old heart you mentioned just now, Jack...Rolling over it and burying it under!

When I think of those devilish workmen yelling around my house and digging up my lawn . . .

JACK

Never mind, Father. Don't think of it. When things are a nuisance, it's a good idea not to keep remembering 'em.

MAJOR

I try not to. I try to keep remembering that I won't be remembering anything now very long. Not so very long now, my boy. Not so very long now, huh. Not so very long!

LAP DISSOLVE

NIGHT SEQUENCE

EXT MANSION LS - Camera shooting over barren yard - Mansion at right - Traffic lights passing on street in background -

LAP DISSOLVE

EXT PORCH MS - Music heard[47] - George sitting at left at top of steps - Fanny sitting in left background rocking in creaking chair - Isabel sitting at right - Her silhouette showing against lit window -

FANNY

I don't believe we'll see as many of those ottomobiles next summer.

Isabel and Fanny talk - George looks off glumly -

ISABEL

Why?

FANNY

I've begun to agree with George about their being a fad more than anything else. Like roller skates. Besides, people just won't stand for them after a while. I shouldn't be surprised to see a law passed forbidding the sale of ottomobiles the way there is with concealed weapons.

---

[47] Herrmann's "First Nocturne," scored for solo violin and small orchestra, played during most of this sequence (through shot 5). It lasted more than five minutes and was the longest musical passage he ever wrote for a film score.

"I won't be
remembering
anything now
very long."

ISABEL

You're not in earnest, Fanny.

FANNY

I am, though!

ISABEL

Then you didn't mean it when you told Eugene you'd enjoyed the drive this afternoon.

FANNY

I didn't say it so very enthusiastically, did I?

ISABEL

Perhaps not, but he certainly thought he'd pleased you.

FANNY

I don't think I gave him any right to think he'd pleased me.

ISABEL

Why not, Fanny? Why shouldn't you?

FANNY

I hardly think I'd want anyone to get the notion he'd pleased me just now. It hardly seems time yet to me.

Isabel whistles - Fanny stops rocking -

FANNY

Is that you, George?

GEORGE

Is that me what?

FANNY

Whistling "On Yonder Rock Reclining"?

Isabel talks amused -

ISABEL

Oh, it's I.

FANNY

Oh.

ISABEL

Does it disturb you?

FANNY

No, not at all, just had an idea that George was depressed about something—
wondered if he could be making such a cheerful sound.

ISABEL

Troubled about anything, Georgie?

GEORGE

No.

Isabel laughs - Fanny talks to her -

FANNY

Are you laughing about something?

ISABEL

Pardon?

FANNY

I asked: Were you laughing at something?

ISABEL

Yes, I was. It's that funny, fat old Mrs. Johnson across the street.

Isabel rises - Goes behind George as she talks -

ISABEL

She has a habit of looking out her bedroom window with a pair of opera glasses.

FANNY

Really!

ISABEL

Really. She looks up and down the street, but mostly over here. Sometimes she
forgets to turn out the light in her room, and there she is, spying for all the world
to see. Can you see her, Georgie?

GEORGE

Hm? Oh, pardon me, I didn't hear what you were saying.

ISABEL

It's nothing. Just a funny old lady—she's gone now. I'm going too . . .

George rises - Isabel goes to right background -

ISABEL

. . . at least, I'm going indoors to read.

She exits talking -

ISABEL

It's cooler in the house, though it's really not warm anywhere, since nightfall. Summer's dying. How quickly it goes, once it begins to die.

Door heard - George sits down - Fanny talks to George - He talks curtly to her -

FANNY

It seems queer how your mother can use such words.

GEORGE

What words?

FANNY

Words like "die" and "dying." I don't see how she can bear to use them so soon after your poor father . . .

GEORGE

Seems to me you're using them yourself.

FANNY

I? Never.

GEORGE

Yes, you did.

FANNY

When?

GEORGE

Just this minute.

FANNY

Oh! You mean when I repeated what she said?

GEORGE

Umhum.

FANNY

That's hardly the same thing, George.

GEORGE

I don't think you'll convince anybody that Mother's unfeeling.

FANNY

I'm not trying to convince anybody. I mean merely in my opinion—well, perhaps it's just as wise for me to keep my opinions to myself.

She rises slowly - Goes to right background - Talking - Exits -

FANNY

There is one thing I hope. I hope at least she won't leave off her full mourning the very anniversary of Wilbur's death.

EXT PORCH MCU - George leaning against railing - Staring off thoughtfully - Music heard -   **4 (7-10)**

EXT STEPS MLS - George sitting up on step at left foreground looking off thoughtfully - Music heard - Vision of Lucy comes on at right - Kneeling - Holds out her hands to him - She talks - Pleadingly - Music heard -   **5 (61-12)**

LUCY

George, you must forgive me! Papa was utterly wrong! I have told him so, and the truth is that I have come rather to dislike him as you do, and as you always have, in your heart of hearts.

GEORGE'S VOICE

Lucy, are you <u>sure</u> you understand me? You say you understand me, but are you sure?

LUCY

Oh, so sure! I shall never listen to Father's opinions again. I do not even care if I never see him again!

GEORGE'S VOICE

Then I pardon you.

Her vision exits - He leans back -

6 (16-8)   EXT PORCH MCU - George leaning back against post - Laughter heard - Vision of Lucy and boys comes on above at right behind him - They laugh - Talk - Sing indistinctly -

7 (24-4)   EXT PORCH MLS - George sitting up at left at top of steps staring off - Vision of Lucy and group of boys sitting on steps - They laugh and sing - Happily - George leaps up - Yells angrily - Vision exits -

GEORGE

Pardon nothing! Riffraff! Riffraff!

He goes up to background toward door - Yelling -

GEORGE

Riffraff!

He opens door - Exits through it - Slamming door -

FADE OUT

REEL 4 SECTION A

[DAY SEQUENCE

FADE IN EXT MANSION ELS - Mansion in background - Eugene and Isabel sitting on bench by tree at right near foreground - Music heard -

1 (34-4)

LAP DISSOLVE

EXT TREE MCU - Eugene at left takes hold of Isabel's hand - Music heard -

EUGENE

Isabel, dear.

ISABEL

Yes, Eugene?

EUGENE

Don't you think you should tell George?

ISABEL

About us?

EUGENE

Yes.

ISABEL

There's still time.

EUGENE

I think he should hear it from you.

EXT TREE CU - Isabel at right leaning against tree - Talks to Eugene at left - Music heard -

2 (28-0)

ISABEL

He will, dearest...soon...soon.

LAP DISSOLVE][48]

EXT MANSION LS - Camera shooting to mansion in background - Car coming on around drive left background - Goes to right background -

LAP DISSOLVE

---

[48] Material in brackets (beginning at reel 4A shot 1) moved to beginning of reel 3B.

INT DINING ROOM MLS - Ambersons, Minafers, and Eugene seated around table - Music heard[49] - Servant carrying tray crosses to door in background - Music stops -

MAJOR

I miss my best girl.

3 (6-11) INT DINING ROOM MS - Camera shooting over Major's left shoulder along table - Isabel at end of table facing Major - Fanny and George at left -

ISABEL

We all do. Lucy's on a visit, Father. She's spending a week with a school friend.

EUGENE'S VOICE

She'll . . .

4 (13-15) INT DINING ROOM MS - Camera shooting between Isabel at left and George at right both partly on - Major at opposite end of table - Jack and Eugene at left -

EUGENE

. . . be back Monday.

Fanny leans forward into shot -

FANNY

George, how does it happen you didn't tell us before? He never said a word to us about Lucy's going away.

MAJOR

Probably afraid to.

5 (5-2) INT DINING ROOM MCU - Camera shooting up at Major looking to right foreground -

MAJOR

Didn't know but what he might break down and cry if he tried to speak of it.

6 (16-5) INT DINING ROOM MS - Camera shooting over Major's shoulder -

MAJOR

Isn't that so, Georgie.

Major laughs -

FANNY

Or didn't Lucy tell you she was going?

---

[49] A repeat of the Herrmann's "Garden Scene" cue, which accompanied the sequence immediately preceding of Eugene and Isabel on the lawn of the Amberson mansion; eliminated in *RV*.

George looks around sullenly -

GEORGE

She told me.

MAJOR

At any rate, Georgie didn't approve. I suppose you two aren't speaking again?

Major laughs -

INT DINING ROOM MCS - Camera shooting across table - Jack at left - Eugene at center - Major at right -   **7** (39-3)

JACK

Gene, what's this I hear about someone else opening up a horseless carriage shop, somewhere out in the suburbs.

MAJOR

Ah, I suppose they'll drive you out of business, or else the two of you'll get together and drive all the rest of us off of the streets.

EUGENE

Well, we'll even things up by making the streets bigger. Automobiles will carry our streets clear out to the county line.

JACK

Well, I hope you're wrong, because if people go to moving that far, real estate values here in the old residence part of town will be stretched pretty thin.

INT DINING ROOM MCU - George looks to left foreground sternly -   **8** (6-8)

MAJOR'S VOICE

So your devilish machines are going to ruin all your old friends, eh Gene?

INT DINING ROOM MCS - Eugene partly on left foreground - Major in background at end of table -   **9** (13-14)

MAJOR

Do you really think they're going to change the face of the land?

EUGENE

They're already doing it, Major, and it can't be stopped. Automobiles are . . .

George heard interrupting -

"I don't think I
could survive that."

GEORGE'S VOICE

Automobiles[50] are a useless nuisance.

The two look to right foreground - Startled -

INT DINING ROOM MCU - Jack at left looking to right foreground - Frowning -   **10** (2-7)

INT DINING ROOM MCU - Isabel facing camera - Glances down - Embarrassed -   **11** (2-6)

INT DINING ROOM MS - Camera shooting between Isabel and George - Facing three men in background -   **12** (6-15)

MAJOR

What did you say, George?

GEORGE

I said automobiles are a useless nuisance.

INT DINING ROOM MS - Camera shooting over Major's shoulder -   **13** (4-15)

GEORGE

They'll never amount to anything but a nuisance and they had no business to be invented.

INT DINING ROOM MCU - Eugene at left looks down at table - Hurt - Fingers spoon -   **14** (8-2)

JACK'S VOICE

Of course you forget Mr. Morgan makes them—also did his share in inventing them.

INT DINING ROOM MCU - Jack at left of table -   **15** (4-10)

JACK

If you weren't so thoughtless he might think you rather offensive.

INT DINING ROOM MCU - George looking to foreground -   **16** (2-11)

Talks - Sarcastically -

GEORGE

I don't think I could survive that.

INT DINING ROOM MCU - Eugene looking to right foreground - Begins speaking - Fingers spoon - Glances down occasionally as he talks -   **17** (64-15)

---

[50] Previously George and Fanny have pronounced the word derisively, "ottomobiles." (The spelling is from Amalia Kent's cutting notes.)

EUGENE

I'm not sure George is wrong about automobiles...With all their speed forward they may be a step backward in civilization...It may be that they won't add to the beauty of the world or the life of men's souls—I'm not sure...But automobiles have come...and almost all outward things are going to be different because of what they bring...They're going to alter war, and they're going to alter peace...And I think men's minds are going to be changed in subtle ways because of automobiles...And it may be that George is right.

18 (2-6)   INT DINING ROOM CU - George glances down embarrassed -

19 (25-8)   INT DINING ROOM CU - Eugene looking down to right foreground -

EUGENE

It may be that in—ten or twenty years from now, if we can see the . . .

Looks up to right -

EUGENE

. . . inward change in men by that time . . .

Looks to right foreground -

EUGENE

. . . I shouldn't be able to defend the gasoline engine, but would have to agree with George...that automobiles had no business to be invented.

20 (3-1)   INT DINING ROOM CU - George looking to left frowning -

21 (6-14)   INT DINING ROOM CU - Eugene looking to right foreground - Glances down - Noise of his spoon firmly placed on table - He looks to right -

EUGENE

Well, Major . . .

He starts to rise -

22 (7-3)   INT DINING ROOM MCU - George rising -

EUGENE'S VOICE

. . . if you'll excuse me.

George glances to left as he hears -

EUGENE'S VOICE

Fanny?

FANNY'S VOICE

Oh, Eugene.

EUGENE'S VOICE

Isabel.

INT DINING ROOM MLS - Eugene and George standing behind table - Facing each other - Fanny and Isabel seated - Jack at right going to door in background - Major at left moves to escort Eugene to door -

23 (32-1)

EUGENE

I've got to run down to the shop and speak to the foreman.

MAJOR

I'll see you to the door.

EUGENE

Don't bother, sir. I know the way.

Fanny rises -

FANNY

I'll come too.

She walks past men through door - Major follows - Eugene stops - Looks back at George and Isabel - Goes out - Jack starts out - Looks back - Goes out - Closes door behind him - George resumes seat at table -

INT DINING ROOM MS - Camera shooting from Major's end of table - Isabel seated at other end of table - George at left -

24 (32-2)

ISABEL

Georgie, dear, what did you mean?

GEORGE

Just what I said.

ISABEL

He was hurt!

GEORGE

Don't see why he should be. Didn't say anything about him. Didn't seem to me to be hurt, he seemed perfectly cheerful. What made you think he was hurt?

ISABEL

I know him.

25 (49-13)   INT DINING ROOM MCS - George and Isabel at table in foreground - Jack opens door in background - Enters - Closes door behind him - Crosses left to fireplace - Camera pans to follow - Takes cigar from inner pocket - Stops before mantel in background - Turns and addresses George -

JACK

By Jove, Georgie, you are a puzzle!

GEORGE

In what way may I ask?

JACK

Well, it's a new style of courting a pretty girl, I must say, for a young fellow to go deliberately out of his way to try and make an enemy of her father, by attacking his business! By Jove!...That's a new way of winning a woman!

Jack turns to background and lights cigar - George throws napkin on table - Disgusted - Rises - Camera pans right - George hurrying to door in background - Isabel rises to follow - George opens door -

26 (264-10)   INT HALL MS - George rushing out doorway at right - Crosses hall - Camera pans left to follow - Fanny comes on from extreme left foreground - Whispers -

FANNY

George! You struck just the right treatment to adopt.

George turns to go to steps in background - Camera moves to follow -

FANNY

You're doing just the right thing!

GEORGE

Oh, what do you want?

Fanny follows him -

FANNY

Your father would thank you if he could see what you're doing.

GEORGE

Quit the mysterious detective business. You make me dizzy.

You don't care to hear that I approve of what you're doing?

GEORGE

For the gosh sakes, what in the world is wrong with you?

She starts up steps talking bitterly -

FANNY

Oh, you're always picking on me, always.

He follows her up steps - They argue - Camera following them up -

FANNY

Ever since you were a little boy!

GEORGE

Oh, my gosh!

FANNY

You wouldn't treat anybody in the world like this except old Fanny! "Old Fanny" you say. "It's nobody but old Fanny, so I'll kick her. Nobody'll resent it, I'll kick her all I want to!" And you're right. I haven't got anything in the world since my brother died—nobody—nothing!

GEORGE

Oh, my gosh!

FANNY

I never, never in the world would have told you about it, or even made the faintest reference to it . . .

He stops on steps - Camera pauses - She exits right -

FANNY'S VOICE

. . . if I hadn't seen that somebody else had told you, or you'd found out for yourself in some way.

GEORGE

Somebody else had told me what?

FANNY'S VOICE

How people are talking about your mother.

Music starts to play[51] - He pauses - Dumbfounded - Slowly goes up steps - Camera follows him up onto balcony - He stops facing Fanny -

GEORGE

What did you say?

FANNY

Of course, I understood what you were doing when you started being rude to Eugene.

They go to right - Start up another flight of steps - Camera moves to follow -

FANNY

I knew you'd give Lucy up in a minute if it came to a question of your mother's reputation . . .

GEORGE

Look here!

She stops - Turns - Looks down at him as they talk -

FANNY

. . . because you said that . . .

GEORGE

Look here! Just what do you mean?

FANNY

I only wanted to say that I'm sorry for you, George, that's all. But it's only old Fanny . . .

She turns - Goes up to right - He follows - Camera resumes moving -

FANNY

. . . so whatever she says, pick on her for it! Hammer her! Hammer her!

GEORGE

Uncle Jack said . . .

They confront one another on the landing -

FANNY

It's only poor old lonely Fanny!

---

[51] Herrmann's "Fantasia," contrapuntally scored and building to a stormy climax, originally accompanied the sequence of Fanny and George on the stairs.

Music heard -

GEORGE

. . . Uncle Jack said that if there was any gossip it was about you! He said people might be laughing about the way you ran after Morgan, but that was all.

FANNY

Oh, yes, it's always Fanny! Ridiculous old Fanny—always—always!

GEORGE

Listen! You said Mother let him come here just on your account, and now you say . . .

FANNY

I think he did. Anyhow, he liked to dance with me. He danced with me as much as he did with her.

GEORGE

You told me Mother never saw him except when she was chaperoning you.

FANNY

Well, you don't suppose that stops people from talking, do you?...They just thought I didn't count!..."It's only Fanny Minafer," I suppose they'd say! Besides, everybody knew he'd been engaged to her.

GEORGE

What's that?

FANNY

Everybody knows it. Everybody in this town knows that Isabel never really cared for any other man in her life!

GEORGE

I believe I'm going crazy. You mean you lied when you told me there wasn't any talk?

FANNY

It never would have amounted to anything if Wilbur had lived.

GEORGE

You mean Morgan might have married you?

No...because I don't know that I'd have accepted him.

GEORGE

Are you trying to tell me that—because he comes here and they see her with him—driving and all that—they think that they were right in saying that she was—she was in love with him before—before my father died?

FANNY

Why, George, don't <u>you</u> know that's what they say? You must know that everybody in town . . .

GEORGE

Who told you?

FANNY

What?

GEORGE

Who told you there was talk? Where is this talk? Where does it come from? Who does it?

FANNY

Why, I suppose pretty much everybody, I know it's pretty general.

He grabs her by shoulders shaking her - Shouting angrily -

GEORGE

Who said so?

FANNY

Why!

GEORGE

How did you get hold of it?

FANNY

Why!

GEORGE

You answer me!

FANNY

Why I hardly think it would be fair to give names!

GEORGE

Look here. One of your best friends is that mother of Charlie Johnson's across the way. Has she ever mentioned this to you?

FANNY

Why she may have intimated . . .

GEORGE

You and she have been talking about it! Do you deny it?

FANNY

Why, George!

GEORGE

Do you deny it!

FANNY

Why she's a very kind, discreet woman, George . . .

He turns - Rushes left down stairs - Exits as she talks -

FANNY

. . . but she may have intimated . . .

She leans over railing - Calling after him - Footsteps and music heard -

FANNY

George!...What are you going to do, George?[52]

She leans over to right foreground - Calling -

FANNY

George.

Music stops -

EXT DOOR CU - Door opening - Mrs. Johnson looks out to foreground - Surprised -   **27** (114-12)

MRS. JOHNSON

Mr. Amberson—heh, heh—I mean Mr. Minafer.

---

[52] In *RV* a door is heard slamming loudly at this point.

She opens door wider - Camera pans to follow - She exits left - Camera moves forward into Mrs. Johnson's living room -

                    MRS. JOHNSON'S VOICE

Eh, won't you come in please?

                    GEORGE'S VOICE

Thank you.

George comes on extreme left foreground - Goes into room - Camera following -

                    MRS. JOHNSON'S VOICE

Well, how nice to see you Mr. Minafer.

He stops - Back to camera -

                          GEORGE

Mrs. Johnson . . .

He turns to face left foreground -

                          GEORGE

. . . Mrs. Johnson, I've come to ask you a few questions.

Mrs. Johnson comes on left foreground - Stops -

                       MRS. JOHNSON

Certainly, Mr. Minafer. Anything I can do for you.

He turns away - They walk to background - Camera follows -

                          GEORGE

I don't mean to waste any time, Mrs. Johnson.

He turns to confront her -

                          GEORGE

You—you were talking about a—a scandal that involved my mother's name.

                       MRS. JOHNSON

Mr. Minafer!

She walks to left background past him -

GEORGE

My aunt told me you repeated this scandal to her.

She turns to face him -

MRS. JOHNSON

I don't think your aunt can have said that!

She comes to left foreground -

MRS. JOHNSON

We may have discussed some few matters that've been a topic of comment about town.

He crosses behind her to left - Looks over her shoulder -

GEORGE

Yes! I think you may have!

MRS. JOHNSON

Other people may be less considerate.

GEORGE

Other people! That's what I want to know about—these other people! How many? How many!

MRS. JOHNSON

What?

GEORGE

How many other people talk about it?

She crosses to left foreground - Camera pans to follow -

MRS. JOHNSON

Heh, really, this isn't a courtroom and I'm not a defendant in a libel suit.

GEORGE'S VOICE

You may be!

George comes on at right behind her - Talking angrily over her shoulder -

GEORGE

I want to know just who's dared to say these things, if I have to force my way into every house in town.

She whirls to face him -

GEORGE

I mean to know just who told you . . .

MRS. JOHNSON

You mean to know! Well you'll know something pretty quick! You'll know that you're out in the street. Please to leave my house!

He turns - Exits left - She glares after him -

28 (3-10)   INT BATHROOM ECU - Camera shooting down on water pouring out of spigot in bathtub - Pipes groan - Music heard[53] -

29 (6-1)   INT BATHROOM ECU - Jack bathing looking to left disgusted - Water heard - Music heard[54] -

JACK

Ohhhhh, now you have done it!

30 (34-0)   INT BATHROOM CU - George in foreground - Reflection of Jack bathing seen in mirror in background -

GEORGE

What have I done that wasn't honorable and right?

JACK

Awww.

GEORGE

Do you think these riffraff can go around town bandying my mother's good name?

JACK

They can now. Georgie...gossip's never fatal till it's denied.

GEORGE

If you think I'm going to let my mother's good name be . . .

JACK

Good name. Look, nobody has a good name in a bad mouth! Nobody has a good name in a—silly mouth, either.

[53] There is no record of any music recorded for the bathroom scene.
[54] Perhaps the transcriber means the loud groan from the water spigot, which underscores Jack's reaction.

George exits right foreground - His reflection seen in mirror going to Jack in tub in left background -

GEORGE

Didn't you understand me when I told you people are saying my mother means to marry this man?

JACK

Yes, yes, I understood you.

INT BATHROOM CU - George looking down to right foreground - Talking disgusted -

31 (3-4)

GEORGE

If such a—such an unspeakable marriage did . . .

INT BATHROOM CU - Jack bathing looks up to left foreground - Talks impatiently -

32 (19-9)

JACK

Unspeakable marriage!

GEORGE'S VOICE

. . . did take place do you think that would make people believe they'd been wrong in saying . . .

Jack shouts - Washing himself -

JACK

No. No, I don't believe it would. There would be more badness in the bad mouths and more silliness in the silly mouths. But that wouldn't hurt Isabel and Eugene. Why if they decided to marry . . .

INT BATHROOM CU - George looking down to right foreground - Incredulous - Pipes heard groaning -

33 (7-14)

GEORGE

Great gosh! You speak of it so calmly!

JACK'S VOICE

Why shouldn't they marry if they want to?

GEORGE

Why <u>shouldn't</u> they?

  JACK

             It's their own affair!

                                              GEORGE

             Why shouldn't they!

34 (2-9)   INT BATHROOM CU - Jack bathing - Looking up to left foreground - Shouting -

                                                JACK

             Yes, why shouldn't they!

35 (2-7)   INT BATHROOM CU - George looking down to foreground - Grimly - Music heard[55] -

                                          JACK'S VOICE

             I don't see anything . . .

36 (9-0)   INT BATHROOM CU - Jack bathing - Shouting impatiently -

                                                JACK

             . . . precisely monstrous about two people getting married when they are both free
             and care about each other. What's the matter with their marrying?

37 (15-14) INT BATHROOM CU - George looking down to right foreground - Shouts angrily -

                                              GEORGE

             Then it would be monstrous—monstrous if even this horrible thing hadn't hap-
             pened. Now in the face of all this—

             oh, that you can sit there and speak of it! Your own sister!

38 (3-10)   INT BATHROOM CU - Jack bathing looking up - Talks impatiently -

                                                JACK

             Ohhh, for heaven's sake, don't be so theatrical.

39 (1-5)   INT BATHROOM CU - George in foreground - Turns to background -

40 (1-2)   INT BATHROOM CU - Jack looking to left foreground - Calls sharply -

                                                JACK

             Come back here!

41 (5-5)   INT BATHROOM MCU - Camera shooting upward - George in background - Comes back up to
             camera -

---

[55] Perhaps the pipes groaned again.

INT BATHROOM CU - Jack looking to left foreground -   **42** (7-1)

> JACK
>
> You mustn't speak to your mother about this, Georgie! I don't think she's very
> well.

INT BATHROOM CU - George looking down to right foreground - Talks impatiently -   **43** (3-8)

> GEORGE
>
> Mother? I never saw a healthier person in my life.

INT BATHROOM CU - Jack looking up to left foreground - Talks sharply -   **44** (6-8)

> JACK
>
> She don't let anybody know. She goes to the doctor regularly.

INT BATHROOM CU - George looking to right foreground -   **45** (2-7)

> GEORGE
>
> Women are always going to doctors regularly.

INT BATHROOM CU - Jack in tub looking up to left - Talks warningly -   **46** (3-2)

> JACK
>
> I'd leave her alone, George.

INT BATHROOM CU - George in foreground - Turns quickly to background - Camera tilts   **47** (7-0)
down - He goes to door in background - Opens it - Goes out slamming door[56] -

> FADE OUT

---

[56] In *RV* Uncle Jack is heard yelling after George, "Come back here!"

REEL 4 SECTION B

DAY SEQUENCE

FADE IN INT ROOM MLS - Reflection of George in mirror - George in background unwrapping box - Comes to mantel - Music heard[57] - He puts picture up on mantel - His hands come on right foreground as he puts picture of Wilbur on mantel at right foreground - Hands exit as he looks around - Hands come on picking up picture - His reflection shown turning to background - **1** (52-0)

INT ROOM MS - George in background coming to foreground with picture - Music heard - Camera tilts upward following him to left foreground - He stops - Looks at picture - Puts it on table before camera - He turns - Camera pans - He goes to left - Sits down - Nearly exits - Back to camera - Car heard - **2** (29-0)

EXT STREET MLS - Camera shooting across to Mrs. Johnson's house from Amberson courtyard - Statue partly on at right - Music heard - Eugene comes on from right driving car - Stops in right foreground - Gets out - Walks to right foreground - Nearly exits - **3** (7-14)

EXT WINDOW MS - Camera shooting up to window - Music heard - Curtains part - George looks out - **4** (3-3)

INT WINDOW MCU - George looking out window - Eugene in extreme background coming up walk toward house - Music heard - **5** (5-8)

EXT WINDOW MCS - Camera shooting up to window - George looking down to left foreground - He closes curtains - Music heard - **6** (2-11)

INT VESTIBULE MCU - Detail of doors - Music heard - Bell heard - Maid comes on left on other side of glass doors - Crosses to right - Starts to open door - George comes on right - Crosses behind her - **7** (44-13)

GEORGE

You needn't mind, Mary. I'll see who it is and what they want. Probably it's only a peddler.

MARY

Thank you, Mister George.

Maid exits - Bell heard - Music heard - George opens door - Steps into vestibule in left foreground - Camera pans to follow him through vestibule to left - George with back to camera - He opens door showing Eugene standing on other side -

EUGENE

Good afternoon, George...Your mother expects to go driving with me, I believe.

Music stops -

---

[57] Herrmann's "Scène Pathétique" originally opened on the slamming of the bathroom door and played through shot 7; in *RV* it is the cue heard beginning with Eugene's arrival.

8 (6-7) | EXT DOORWAY MCU - Camera shooting over Eugene's left shoulder - Eugene at right foreground - Back to camera - George standing in doorway facing him -

EUGENE

If you'll be so kind as to send her word I'm here.

George talks sharply -

GEORGE

No.

9 (13-3) | INT DOORWAY MCU - Camera shooting over George's right shoulder - George at left foreground - Back to camera - Eugene facing him - Stares at him surprised - Smiles slightly -

EUGENE

I beg your pardon, I said . . .

George interrupts -

GEORGE

I heard you. You said you had an engagement with my mother, and I said <u>no</u>.

EUGENE

What's the matter?

10 (6-14) | EXT DOOR MCU - Camera shooting over Eugene's shoulder - George glaring -

GEORGE

My mother will have no interest in knowing that you came here today—or any other day.

11 (1-13) | EXT DOOR CU - Eugene looking to foreground -

EUGENE

I'm afraid I don't understand you.

12 (8-9) | INT DOORWAY CU - George looking to foreground -

GEORGE

I doubt if I can make it much plainer. But I'll try. You're not wanted in this house, Mr. Morgan.

13 (4-2) | EXT DOOR CU - Eugene looking to foreground grimly -

Now or at any other time. Perhaps . . .

INT DOORWAY CU - George looking to foreground -   **14** (1-12)

GEORGE

. . . you'll understand this!

INT VESTIBULE MCU - George standing left foreground - Back to camera - Slams outer door in   **15** (35-8)
Eugene's face - Eugene's profile visible through frosted glass door panel - Music heard[58] - After
long pause Eugene exits left - George turns slowly to right - Walks to vestibule door - Camera
pans to follow - He exits through doorway right - Slams door behind him -

INT HALL LS - George coming from hall in background - Comes into room in foreground -   **16** (30-10)
Music heard - He crosses to left foreground - Camera follows him to window at left - He looks
out through curtains - Turns - Comes to foreground - Sits down at left foreground back to
camera -

INT ROOM MLS - George sitting at right near foreground - Isabel coming on through doorway   **17** (181-12)
at left - Music heard - She looks around - Sees George - Talks to him -

ISABEL

Why Georgie! Dear, I waited lunch almost an hour for you, but you didn't come!

Bell heard ringing[59] -

ISABEL

Did you lunch out somewhere?

GEORGE

Yes.

Maid coming on right background - Passes before Isabel - Exits through doorway into hall at left -

ISABEL

Did you have plenty to eat?

GEORGE

Yes.

ISABEL

Are you sure?

Isabel turns - Calls into hall -

---

[58] Herrmann recorded two musical cues for the interval between George's turning Eugene away and Jack's return to tell
Isabel about it. "Waiting 1," scored for low winds, brass, and timpani, and very austere in character, began at the point
indicated in shot 15 and concluded with the ringing of the doorbell early in shot 17. "Waiting 2," similarly austere in
character, began just before the first lap dissolve in shot 17 and concluded in shot 18, again at the ringing of the doorbell,
with a chilling motif played on the vibraphone. In *RV* "Waiting 1" begins at the point originally indicated but continues in
place of "Waiting 2" after the deleted material. (That is, "Waiting 2" was eliminated entirely.)

[59] "Waiting 1" originally concluded at this point.

ISABEL

I think it's Mr. Morgan, Mary, tell him I'll be there at once.

MARY'S VOICE

Yes, ma'am.

Isabel comes toward table as she talks to George -

ISABEL

Wouldn't you like to have Aggie[60] fix something now for you in the dining room?
Or they could bring it to you here, if you think it would be cozier?

She sits down by table - Talking -

GEORGE

No.

George rises as she talks - He comes to left foreground - Standing partly on left foreground -

ISABEL

I'm going out driving, dear.

Maid comes in doorway left background - Talks to Isabel -

MARY

'Twas a peddler, ma'am.

ISABEL

Another one? I thought you said it was a peddler when the bell rang a while ago.

MARY

Mister George said so, ma'am; he went to the door.

ISABEL

There seem to be a great many of them.

Maid exits into hall - Isabel talking to George -

ISABEL

What did yours want to sell, Georgie?

GEORGE

He didn't say.

---

[60] The name by which everyone called Agnes Moorehead, changed from Maggie in Tarkington's novel. Welles loved covert allusions of this sort.

ISABEL

You must have cut him off rather short.

She looks at picture on table - Picks it up - Talking -

ISABEL

Gracious, you have been investing! Is it Lucy?

She looks at picture - Talks - George turns to her -

ISABEL

Oh! That was nice of you, Georgie. I ought to have had it framed myself, when I gave it to you.

She puts picture on table - He goes to her - Looks at her - Hurries to left - Goes through doorway - Exits in hall - She sits waiting - Music heard[61] -

LAP DISSOLVE

INT VESTIBULE CU - Glass door before camera - Music heard - George comes on on other side - Looks through to foreground - Music heard - He looks down - Turns slowly - Exits -

LAP DISSOLVE

INT ROOM MCS - Camera shooting through curtains - Isabel sitting by table looking to foreground - Photograph of Wilbur prominent at right - Music heard[62] -

INT ROOM CU - Isabel sitting at right foreground before camera - Bell heard ringing[63] - She looks to right - Rises - Moves to background to door - Camera pans to follow -   **18** (10-6)

INT HALL LS - Camera shooting down from balcony through hall - Jack comes on below at right - Removes hat - Isabel comes on from his right - They are barely heard -   **19** (76-1)

JACK

Isabel.

ISABEL

Yes?

JACK

I've just come from Eugene's.

He walks toward library in extreme background - Isabel follows -

ISABEL

Yes?

[61] "Waiting 2" originally began playing at this point.

[62] In *RV* "Waiting 1" resumes at this point.

[63] "Waiting 2" originally concluded at this point. In *RV* "Waiting 1" ends here. Also in *RV* the sound is of a door closing—logically, since Uncle Jack wouldn't have to ring to be let in.

He stops - Turns to her - Takes her arm - Leads her -

> JACK

I want to talk to you.

They go inside library - Jack closes double doors after them - Music starts to play - Camera tilts upward to George looking down over balcony - He looks up above as he hears Fanny in loud whisper -

> FANNY'S VOICE

Welll!

Camera tilt continues - Reveals Fanny above on second balcony -

> FANNY

I can just guess what that was about!

She hurries to left above - Exits - Camera tilts down to George - He comes down steps at left - Camera pans to follow - Music playing - He comes down to foreground - Crosses before camera - Nearly exits - Stops on lower landing - Looks up to Fanny on balcony in background - She talks in loud whispers -

> FANNY

He's telling her what you did to Eugene.

> GEORGE

You go back to your room!

> FANNY

You're not going in there!

> GEORGE

You go back to your room.

> FANNY

George!

She moves to left -

INT BALCONY MS - Camera shoots down staircase - Fanny hurrying down to George - Music heard -

> FANNY

George!

Camera pans across stair railings following her -

                              FANNY

    No you don't Georgie Minafer! You keep away from there!

She catches George - Takes hold of him -

                              GEORGE

        You let go of me!

She struggles as he tries to get away -

                              FANNY

        I won't! You come back here! And let them alone!

                              GEORGE

        Of all the ridiculous . . .

She puts hand over his mouth -

                              FANNY

        Hush up! Hush up! Go on to the top of the stairs—go on!

He goes up steps to right - She follows him - Camera panning - Music heard - They come up steps to right foreground -

                              FANNY

        It's indecent...It's like squabbling outside the door of an operating room!...The idea of you going in there now! Jack's telling Isabel the whole thing—and you stay here and let him tell her! He's got some consideration for her!

They stop before camera -

                              GEORGE

        I suppose you think I haven't?

                              FANNY

        You! Considerate of anybody!

                              GEORGE

        I'm considerate of her good name!

                              FANNY

        Oh!

GEORGE

Look here! It seems to me you're taking a pretty different tack.

FANNY

I thought you already knew everything I did! I was just—suffering, so I wanted to let out a little...Oh, I was a fool! Eugene never would have looked at me even if he'd never seen Isabel...and they haven't done any harm. She made—Wilbur happy, and she was a true wife to him—as long as he lived...And here I go, not doing myself a bit of good by it—and just ruining them.

GEORGE

You told me how all the riffraff in town were busy with her name, and the minute I lift my hand to protect her, you attack me and . . .

FANNY

Shh!

She looks over railing to left -

FANNY

Your Uncle's leaving.

JACK'S VOICE

I'll be back, Isabel.

George starts down steps to background - Stops at Fanny's entreaty -

FANNY

George, let her alone. She's down there by herself, don't go down.

He starts back up - Sound of door closing - He passes her - Comes to extreme foreground - Glances down to her at left -

FANNY

Let her alone.

George looks at her - Turns away - Exits right -

FADE OUT

DAY SEQUENCE

[1 (231-12)] FADE IN INT ROOM MCS - Camera panning to right showing Isabel standing by window reading letter - She comes slowly to foreground reading - Camera moving back - Eugene's voice heard - Music heard -

EUGENE'S VOICE

Dearest one. Yesterday I thought the time had come when I could ask you to marry me, and you were dear enough to tell me some time it might come to that. But now we're faced not with slander and not with our own fear of it, because we haven't any, but someone else's fear of it—your son's. And, oh, dearest woman in the world, I know what your son is to you and it frightens me.

She stops before camera - Turns - Goes back to background to windows - Reading - Camera following her -

EUGENE'S VOICE

Let me explain a little. I don't think he'll change. At twenty-one or twenty-two so many things appear solid and permanent and terrible which forty sees are nothing but disappearing miasma. Forty can't tell twenty about this; twenty can find out only by getting to be forty.

She turns around toward foreground - Reading -

EUGENE'S VOICE

And so we come to this, dear: Will you live your life your way or George's way?

She lowers letter - Looks off - Backs to right - Camera panning - She sits down - Reads -][64]

EUGENE'S VOICE

Dear, it breaks my heart for you, but what you have to oppose now is the history of your own selfless and perfect motherhood. Are you strong enough, Isabel? Can you make the fight?

Isabel looks up and faces foreground - Rises - Walks across dark room - Camera moving backward with her - She stops in partial light - Continues reading - Eugene's voice continues to be heard - Music continues -

EUGENE'S VOICE

I promise you that if you will take heart for it you will find so quickly that it's all amounted to nothing...You shall have happiness, and only happiness...I'm saying too much for wisdom, I fear...But oh, my dear, won't you be strong—such a little, short strength it would need.

---

[64] In *RV* the shot begins with Eugene in his study finishing the letter and beginning to read it to himself (in voiceover). At the end of the first segment ("it frightens me") there is a lap dissolve to a shot from the second-floor balcony of the Amberson mansion looking down to the first-floor reception hall; Eugene's voice continues reading. At the end of the third segment ("George's way") another lap dissolve returns to the action as in the *CC*, with Isabel seated reading the letter as Eugene's voiceover continues. Roy Webb replaced Herrmann's "First Letter Scene," a long, ethereal lyric melody for strings accompanied by harps and organ, which accompanied shots 1 through 3, with his own lugubrious "Eugene's Letter," heard in *RV*.

She pauses - Moves closer to camera[65] -

EUGENE'S VOICE

Don't strike my life down twice, dear. This time I've not deserved it.

She looks off tears in eyes - Lowers letter -[66]

INT ROOM CU - Camera shooting up at George - He lowers letter looking to foreground grimly - Music heard[67] - He turns - Goes to background - Camera pans down - He stops by fire in fireplace - Starts to put letter in fire - Hesitates - Looks around - Comes to left foreground - Camera moving back - He goes to left to door - Opens it - **2** (66-1)

INT HALL SECOND FLOOR MLS - Camera shooting down through columns in hall - George comes out door in background - Music heard - He crosses to right - Camera pans to follow - He exits right - Knock on door is heard - **3** (22-14)

ISABEL'S VOICE

Come in.

[INT BEDROOM LS - Isabel going to door right background - Opens it - George comes in - **4** (5-12)

INT ROOM MCS - Isabel standing by door at left - George coming in grimly - Comes to foreground - Exits left foreground as she closes door - She talks anxiously - **5** (8-9)

ISABEL

Did you read it, dear?

INT ROOM MS - George turning by fireplace in background - **6** (3-13)

GEORGE

Yes, I did.

INT ROOM MCS - Isabel moving to right to bench before dresser - Talking - **7** (6-3)

ISABEL

All of it?

She sits down facing foreground -

INT ROOM MS - George standing by fireplace in background holding letter - **8** (12-14)

GEORGE

Certainly.

He goes to right on other side of bed - Stops by divan - Talking -

---

[65] *RV* preserves one of film's most exquisite moments, when the light is reflected in Isabel's eyes. According to assistant cameraman Howard Schwartz, the intensity of the glow in her eyes was achieved by means of a light yellow filter intended for outdoor shooting and rarely used inside.

[66] *RV* lap dissolves to shot 3.

[67] A variation of Herrmann's "First Letter Scene," scored for low winds, brass, and low strings, with contorted theme fragments.

GEORGE

It's simply the most offensive piece of writing that I've ever held in my hands.

He sits down looking to foreground -

9 (6-10)   INT ROOM CU - George looking to foreground - Talking -

GEORGE

Don't you think that this is a pretty insulting letter for that man to be asking you to hand your son?

10 (3-2)   INT ROOM MCU - Isabel looking to foreground - Talks - Pleadingly -

ISABEL

You can see how fair he means to be.

11 (6-2)   INT ROOM CU - George looking to right foreground - Talking -

GEORGE

Do you suppose it ever occurs to him that I'm doing my simple duty?

12 (5-0)   INT ROOM MCU - Isabel seated looking to left foreground - Listening -

GEORGE'S VOICE

That I'm doing what my father would do if he were here?

13 (9-15) INT ROOM MS - George sitting on other side of bed right background - Rises - Goes to fireplace - Camera panning -

GEORGE

He said he and you don't care what people say but I know better.

He throws letter into fire -

14 (7-4)   INT ROOM CU - George by fireplace turning to foreground -

GEORGE

He may not care but you do.

15 (3-12) INT ROOM MCU - Isabel sitting facing foreground - Tears in eyes -

GEORGE'S VOICE

You're my mother, and you're an . . .

INT ROOM CU - George looking to right foreground -

16 (10-9)

GEORGE

. . . Amberson and you're too proud to care for a man who could write such a letter.

He moves to foreground -

INT ROOM MS - George in background before fireplace comes to right foreground - Camera pans to right - He passes Isabel seated at right foreground staring down - He goes to door - Opens it - Turns -

17 (23-3)

GEORGE

Well? What are you going to do about it, Mother?

INT ROOM CU - George standing in doorway looking to foreground -

18 (6-9)

GEORGE

What kind of an answer are you going to make to such a letter as that?

INT ROOM MCU - Isabel seated looking to foreground - Tears in eyes - Talks brokenly -

19 (11-5)

ISABEL

Why—I don't quite know, dear.

INT ROOM CU - George standing in doorway - Frowning - Talking bitterly -

20 (12-7)

GEORGE

It seems to me that if he ever set foot in this house again . . . I . . . I can't speak of it.

He turns - Exits in background -

INT ROOM MCU - Isabel seated looking to foreground - Tears in her eyes -][68]

21 (163-15)

FADE DISSOLVE[69]

NIGHT SEQUENCE

INT FLOOR CU - Letter is slipped under door on floor to foreground - Shadow moving - Music heard[70] -

LAP DISSOLVE

INT ROOM CU - Letter under door - Shadow moving across - George leans over - Picks it up - Camera pans up following him - He goes to bed in background opening letter - Lies down - Reads letter -

---

[68] The Bedroom Sequence (from shot 4 to here) was reshot by Robert Wise; the alternate version is printed just after the following deleted sequence.

[69] In his re-editing instructions Welles refers several times to a "half fade out half dissolve," which is apparently the meaning of this notation. See pp. 288–291.

[70] Herrmann's somber "Second Letter Scene," scored in three parts (two clarinets/eight violins and two violas/repeat clarinets), originally accompanied this sequence.

ISABEL'S VOICE

George, my own dearest boy, I think it is a little better for me to write to you like this, because I'm foolish and might cry again, and I took a vow once, long ago, that you should never see me cry. I've written Eugene just about what I think you would like me to.

He turns over on his stomach - Back to camera - Reads - Camera moving slowly closer to him -

ISABEL'S VOICE

He'll understand about not seeing him. He'll understand that though I didn't say it in so many words. He'll understand.

He opens page - Reads -

ISABEL'S VOICE

My darling, my beloved. I think I shouldn't mind anything very much as long as I have you all to myself—as people say—to make up for the long years away from me at college. We'll talk of what's best to do, shan't we? And for all this pain you'll forgive your loving and devoted . . .

INT ROOM CU - Camera shooting up at George's face - Letter before it - He whispers - Music heard -

22 (294-13)

GEORGE

Mother.

Gazes to foreground - Frowning -

FADE DISSOLVE

A different version of the sequence of George in Isabel's bedroom (shots 4 through the beginning of shot 21 in the CC) was directed by Robert Wise. The music cue for the Wise version, "Isabel's Bedroom Sequence," was composed by Webb.[71]

INT BEDROOM MS - Isabel seated at right - Door opens - George enters gravely - Closes it after him -

1 (50-1)

ISABEL

Did you read it, dear?

GEORGE

...Yes, I did.

ISABEL

...All of it?

[71] A black vertical bar designates reshot scenes; shot numbers and footage counts are from the *RV*.

...Yes.

He moves left - Puts letter on her bedside table - Stands at side of her bed -

ISABEL

...Well, what do you think, Georgie?

INT BEDROOM CU - George looking off left -   **2** (3-12)

GEORGE

What do you mean?

INT BEDROOM CU - Isabel looking to left -   **3** (2-9)

ISABEL

You can see how fair he . . .

INT BEDROOM CU - George looking to her in astonished reaction -   **4** (10-15)

ISABEL

. . . means to be.

GEORGE

Fair!...Fair, when he says that he and you don't care what people say?

INT BEDROOM CU - Isabel looking to left -   **5** (6-15)

ISABEL

What people say?...That Eugene loves me?

INT BEDROOM CU - George looking off right -   **6** (2-11)

GEORGE

He's always loved you.

INT BEDROOM CU - Isabel rises -   **7** (3-12)

INT BEDROOM MS - Isabel at right rising - Facing George across room - Music heard -   **8** (9-12)

ISABEL

That's true, Georgie.

INT BEDROOM CU - George becoming more agitated -   **9** (11-14)

GEORGE

But you're my mother! You're an Amberson! You just . . .

10 (3-9) INT BEDROOM CU - Isabel looking off left -

ISABEL

Yes, dear?

11 (25-7) INT BEDROOM CU - George dumbfounded - Glances downward - Sits on bed - Stares to foreground -

GEORGE

I don't know, Mother.

12 (4-4) INT BEDROOM CU - Isabel looking down to left foreground -

13 (329-10) INT BEDROOM MS - Isabel crosses to George seated on bed - Camera moves quickly toward them - She places hands on his head to console him - Strokes his hair - Stares off into distance -

ISABEL

I'll write Eugene...He'll understand...He'll wait...It'll be better this way...We'll go away for a while, you and I.

FADE DISSOLVE

DAY SEQUENCE

EXT STREET MCS - Lucy coming to foreground - George going past her toward background - Automobile engine heard - She stops - Turns to him and speaks -

LUCY

Hello.

She comes to left foreground looking back at him - He takes off his hat - Approaches her - She stops -

GEORGE

Lucy, you—haven't you . . .

LUCY

Haven't I what?

GEORGE

Nothing.[72] May I walk with you a little ways?

---

[72] "Haven't you heard what I did to your father?" is the sentence George fails to complete. She hasn't.

LUCY

Yes, indeed.

They move to foreground - George puts on hat - Traffic heard - They stroll down street past shops - Camera moves with them - People passing on walk - Reflections of moving traffic seen in shop windows -

GEORGE

I want to talk to you—Lucy.

LUCY

I hope it's about something nice. Papa's been so glum today he's scarcely spoken to me.

GEORGE

Well . . .

LUCY

Is it a funny story?

GEORGE

It may seem like one to you. Just to begin with—when you went away you didn't let me know! Not a word—not even a line.

LUCY

Why no. I just trotted off for some visits.

GEORGE

At least you might have done something.

LUCY

Why no, George. Don't you remember, we'd had a quarrel and we didn't speak to each other all the way home from a long, long drive! And since we couldn't play together like good children, of course it was plain that we oughtn't to play at all.

GEORGE

Play!

LUCY

What I mean is, we'd come to the point where it was time to quit playing—well, what we were playing.

GEORGE

At being lovers, you mean, don't you?

LUCY

Something like that. It was absurd.

GEORGE

It didn't have to be absurd.

LUCY

No, it couldn't help but be! The way I am and the way you are, it wouldn't ever be anything else.

GEORGE

This time I'm going away. That's what I wanted to tell you, Lucy. I'm going away tomorrow night. Indefinitely.

LUCY

I hope you have ever so nice a time, George.

They pass in front of "Bijou" movie theatre - Posters advertise Melies picture "Ghost at Circle X Camp"[73] and Jack Holt adventure[74] - Camera continues to move with them -

GEORGE

I don't expect to have a particularly nice time.

LUCY

Well, then, if I were you I don't think I'd go.

GEORGE

This is our last walk together, Lucy.

LUCY

Evidently! If you're going away tomorrow night.

GEORGE

This is the last time I'll see you—ever—ever in my life. Mother and I are starting on a trip around the world tomorrow and . . .

They stop before camera on corner - Face each other - People passing - Pharmacy in background -

GEORGE

. . . we've made no plans at all for coming back.

[73] Between 1910 and 1912 Gaston Méliès made over a hundred one-reel Westerns in Texas and California, including "Ghosts at Circle X Camp." See Paul Hammond, *Marvelous Méliès* (New York: St. Martin's, 1975), pp. 149–151.

[74] Westerns superstar Jack Holt (1888–1951) was Tim Holt's father.

LUCY

My, that does sound like a long trip. Do you plan to be traveling all the time or will you stay in one place for the greater part of it? I think it would be lovely . . .

GEORGE

Lucy!

LUCY

. . . to . . .

GEORGE

I can't stand this!

She laughs lightly -

GEORGE

I'm just about ready to go in that drugstore there and ask the clerk to give me something to keep me from dying in my tracks!

She laughs harder -

GEORGE

It's quite a shock, Lucy!

LUCY

What is?

GEORGE

To find out—just how deeply you've cared! To see how much difference this makes to you.

LUCY

George!

GEORGE

I can't stand this any longer!...I can't, Lucy.

He takes off hat - Speaks to her hopefully - She smiles lightly -

GEORGE

Good-bye, Lucy...It's good-bye.

He turns and walks away from her toward camera - Camera moves back - Her smile fades - He starts across street - Stops - She recomposes her smile - George looks back at her -

GEORGE

I think it's good-bye for good, Lucy.

He turns away again -

LUCY

Good-bye, George. I do hope you have the most splendid trip.

He puts on his hat - Hurries away - Exits left foreground - She waves after him - Smiling - Calling -

LUCY

Give my love to your mother!

Horns heard - People passing -

She turns toward drugstore - Hesitates - Walks toward entrance -[75]

---

[75] *RV* inserts a closeup of Lucy looking ruefully after George.

REEL 5 SECTION B

DAY SEQUENCE

INT DRUG STORE MCS - Whistling heard - Lucy approaching from left - Enters - Clerk passes in front of camera left to right - Exits - She stops at counter - Clerk comes on again from right -

1 (28-8)

LUCY

May I please have a few drops of aromatic spirits of ammonia in a glass of water?

He nods - Goes to right crossing store - Whistling - Camera pans to follow - Takes bottle from shelf - Turns around - Looks off to left - Stares - Surprised -[76]

NIGHT SEQUENCE

INT POOL HALL CU - Camera shooting up to clerk turning to foreground - Bragging -

2 (22-14)

CLERK

And if I hadn't been a bright, quick, ready-for-anything young fella . . .

Camera moves back - He turns with cue - Pushing markers above -

CLERK

. . . she'd a flummixed plum'![77]

He turns to background - Talking - Turns back to foreground -

CLERK

One of the prettiest girls that ever walked in our place and took one good look at me. I guess it must be true what some a' you town wags say about my face, huh?

FADE OUT

NIGHT SEQUENCE

FADE IN EXT PORCH MCS - Fanny sitting at right foreground - Major sitting on other side of her - Autos seen passing on street in far background - The two talk - Music heard[78] -

3 (281-12)

MAJOR

Funny thing. Those new houses were built only a year ago. They look old already. Cost enough money, though I guess I should have built those apartments after all.

FANNY

Housekeeping in a house is harder than in an apartment.

---

[76] *RV* uses an alternate take of the shot which makes clearer that Lucy has fainted: Clerk returns with bottle, looks downward over counter startled, exclaims "F'gosh sake, Miss!"

[77] That is, "plumb flummoxed," completely collapsed—or, as he goes on to imply, been literally knocked off her feet at the sight of him. The Clerk is former vaudeville comic and Mercury regular Gus Schilling, who usually has a cameo part in Welles's American films.

[78] Herrmann's "Second Nocturne," a cello solo accompanied by four alto flutes, eight violins, and two harps, played throughout this sequence.

"She'd a
flummixed plum'!"

MAJOR

Yes. Where the smoke and dirt are as thick as they are in the Amberson Addition, I guess the women can't stand it. Well, I've got one painful satisfaction—I got my taxes lowered.

FANNY

How did you manage such an economy?

MAJOR

I said it was a painful satisfaction. The property has gone down in value and they assessed it lower than they did fifteen years ago.

FANNY

But farther out . . .

MAJOR

Oh, yes, "farther out"! Prices are magnificent farther out and farther in, too! We just happen to be in the wrong spot, that's all.

FANNY

There seems to be so many ways of making money nowadays. Jack had some scheme he was working on before he went abroad.

MAJOR

Yes—that invention. Millions in it! Some new electric headlight.[79] He's putting half he's put by into it. Had a letter from him the other day asking me to go into it, too.

FANNY

He seemed certain it would pay twenty-five percent the first year, and enormously more after that! And I'm only getting four on my principal.

MAJOR

Isabel wants to come home. Her letters are full of it. Jack writes me she talks of nothing else. She's wanted to come for a long while. She ought to come while she can stand the journey.

FANNY

People are making such enormous fortunes out of everything to do with motor cars, it does seem as if . . . I wrote Jack I'd think it over seriously.

MAJOR

Well, Fanny, maybe we'll be partners. How about it? And millionaires, too!

He laughs -

FADE OUT

[79] *RV* deletes all but two passing references (in reel 7A shot 1) to the failed headlight scheme, thereby leaving it unclear why Fanny and Jack, who had their own means, end up penniless along with George.

220 THE MAGNIFICENT AMBERSONS

DAY SEQUENCE

FADE IN EXT BLDG MCS - Jack helping Lucy out of touring car - Jack talks as they go down walk to right background to entrance of mansion - Chauffeur closes door and exits left - Music heard -

4 (33-11)

JACK

[I wonder, Lucy, if history's going on forever repeating itself. I wonder if this town's going on building up things and rolling over them, as poor father once said it was rolling over his poor old heart. It looks like it.

They go up steps to entrance at right background - Jack talking - Camera panning slightly -

JACK

Well, here's the Amberson Mansion again, only it's Georgian instead of nondescript Romanesque; but it's just the same Amberson Mansion my father built long before you were born.][80]

EXT DOORS MCU - Lucy coming on at left foreground - Turns at right - Jack coming on at left - Talking - Music heard[81] - The two looking around to foreground -

5 (243-12)

JACK

You're pretty refreshingly out of the smoke up here.

Door behind them opens - Butler in doorway - Lucy talking -

LUCY

Yes, until the smoke comes and we have to move out farther.

JACK

No, no. You'll stay here. It'll be somebody else who'll move out farther.

He chuckles slightly - She takes his arm - They go into hall in background -

LAP DISSOLVE

INT ROOM MCS - Lucy sitting on divan at right foreground - Jack sitting by her at center - Eugene sitting in chair in left background - Fire in enormous fireplace in extreme background - Jack drinks from cup and places it on table -

JACK

I...found Isabel as well as usual.

Jack picks up cigar and fingers it -

---

[80] *RV* substitutes the following dialogue in shot 4:

"JACK

It's mighty nice of you, Lucy, you and Eugene, to have me over to your new house my first day back.

LUCY

You'll probably find the old town rather dull after Paris."

The change is not noticeable because both characters are facing away from the camera as they speak.

[81] Herrmann's "Romanza" cue, scored for five pairs of muted violins, introduced earlier in the sequence.

JACK

Only I'm afraid as usual isn't...particularly well...It struck me Isabel ought to be in a wheel-chair.

EUGENE

What do you mean by that?

JACK

Oh—she's cheerful enough. At least...she manages to seem so...She's pretty short of breath...Father's been that way for years, of course, but...never nearly so much as Isabel is now...I told her I thought she ought to make Georgie let her come home.

EUGENE

"Let her"?...Does she want to?

JACK

She doesn't urge it...George seems to like the life there in his grand, gloomy, and peculiar way...She'll never change about being proud of him and all that...He's quite a swell...But she does want to come...She'd like to be with Father, of course, and I think she's...well, she intimated one day that she was afraid it might even happen—that she wouldn't get to see him again...I think she was really thinking of her own state of health.

EUGENE

I see...and you say he won't let her come home?

JACK

Oh...I don't think he uses force...He's very gentle with her...I doubt if the subject is mentioned between them and yet . . .

Jack looks at Eugene as he talks -

JACK

. . . yet knowing my interesting nephew as you do...wouldn't you think that was about the way to put it?

Eugene nods -

EUGENE

Knowing him as I do—yes.

Yes, I should think that's about the way to put it.

Jack looks at Eugene - Smiling slightly embarrassed - Glances at Lucy in foreground -

FADE OUT

DAY SEQUENCE

FADE IN EXT STATION MS - Train noises heard - Camera shooting up toward entrance at left - George coming out carrying Isabel - Jack crosses in front of them - Rushes to open carriage door - Fanny following - Jack climbs in carriage - George starts to lift Isabel into carriage -

6 (9-7)

INT CARRIAGE MCS - Jack helping Isabel in - Seats her at right - George and Fanny get into carriage - It drives away to right background -

7 (254-1)

Autos come on - Honking at carriage - Some go to background - Others pass camera -

LAP DISSOLVE

INT CARRIAGE CU - Jack partly on in dark profile left foreground - Isabel and George sitting at right - Her head resting on his shoulder - She speaks weakly - Music heard[82] -

> ISABEL
>
> Changed...so changed.

> JACK
>
> You mean—you mean the town? You mean the old place is changed, don't you, dear?

> ISABEL
>
> Yes.

> JACK
>
> It'll change to a happier place, old dear, now that you're back in it—and going to get well again.

LAP DISSOLVE

INT HALL LS - George sitting at left foreground dejectedly - Jack standing on other side of him - Major standing in center looking to background - Nurse comes out of doorway in background - Comes to foreground passing Major - He turns - Talks as she comes to foreground -

> MAJOR
>
> Nurse, when are they going to let me see my daughter? I think she wants . . .

Nurse exits right foreground - Major comes to foreground - Stops before George and Jack - Major talking bewildered -

> MAJOR
>
> . . . I think she wants to see me.

[82] Herrmann's "Isabel's Return," with strings playing *tremolo* to suggest desperation, originally accompanied this shot but was removed in *RV*.

He stops - Talking bewildered - Door in background opening - Doctor standing in doorway -

MAJOR

A . . . a . . . a . . . I'm sure she wants to see me. I've got something to say to her too . . .

Jack goes to him - Major mumbling -

MAJOR

. . . if she don't want . . .

JACK

Father!

MAJOR

. . . to let me in to see . . .

Major turns to Jack - Jack looks at doctor in background - Major turns -Sees him - Major goes to background - Jack glances at George - Exits right foreground as Major goes into room in background - Fanny coming on up steps at right - Calls in whisper to George -

FANNY

George . . . George . . . George . . .

Isabel heard talking -

ISABEL'S VOICE

Father . . . Father . . .

FANNY

. . . George!

They glance to background - Major and doctor exit in room in background - Fanny comes to foreground - Whispering to George -

FANNY

Eugene is here, George!

GEORGE

Hm?

FANNY

He's downstairs.

GEORGE

What?

FANNY

Eugene is here.

George rises - Goes to her as she talks cautiously -

FANNY

He's downstairs. He wants to know if he can't see her. I didn't know what to say—
I said I'd see. I didn't know—the doctor said . . .

He talks grimly -

GEORGE

The doctor said we must keep her peaceful. Do you think that man's coming was
very soothing? Why it would be like taking a stranger into her room. Doesn't he
know how sick she is?

He goes to right behind her - Fanny staring to foreground as he talks impatiently -

GEORGE

You tell him the doctor said she had to be quiet and peaceful. That's what he did
say, isn't it?

She turns slowly - Goes down steps to right - Exits - He looks after her -

[NIGHT SEQUENCE[83]

INT HALL MLS - Eugene sitting at right foreground before camera - Fanny enters at left background - Crosses to right - He rises - Exits left as camera moves up closer to her - She stops -

1 (73-0)

FANNY

The doctor said she must be kept quiet.

She comes to left foreground -

EUGENE'S VOICE

If I could only look into the room and see her . . .

Eugene comes on at left by Fanny - Talks to her -

EUGENE

. . . just for a second.

She talks tensely -

FANNY

The doctor said she mustn't see anyone.

EUGENE

All right, Fanny.

He turns - Exits left - She looks after him - Turns - Goes to left background - Watching Eugene going down hall to door in background - Camera panning - He opens door in background - Goes out - Exits -

EXT ENTRANCE MLS - Left angle shot - Eugene's shadow on door at left background - Music heard[84] - He comes out entrance - Comes to right foreground down steps - Exits right of camera -]

2 (26-6)

The foregoing sequence as it appears in RV:

FADE DISSOLVE[85]

INT HALL MS - Eugene standing with topcoat on and hat in hand - Sam comes on right - Approaches Eugene -

SAM

Mr. George'll be right down, Mr. Morgan.

---

[83] The following sequence in which Eugene is prevented from seeing Isabel was reshot by the film's assistant director, Freddie Fleck. The Fleck version is printed immediately after the *CC* version.

[84] Herrmann's "The Departure," an austere orchestral chorale, originally began at this point; it continued through shots 3 to 6, which survive with this musical cue in *RV*.

[85] See footnote 69.

EUGENE

Thank you.

Sam crosses in front of Eugene - Exits left foreground - Camera moves slowly in toward Eugene - Eugene looks off left - Walks left toward stairs - Camera moves to follow - George comes on right at foot of stairs - He and Eugene face one another -

EUGENE

I've come to see your mother, George.

GEORGE

I'm sorry, Mr. Morgan.

Eugene stares piercingly - Shakes his head -

EUGENE

Not this time, George.

Eugene forces his way past George - Starts up stairs -

EUGENE

I'm going up to see her.

GEORGE

The doctor said that . . .

Eugene whirls - Glares at George in extreme left foreground - George continues angrily -

GEORGE

. . . she had to be kept quiet.

EUGENE

I'll be quiet.

Fanny comes on from left down stairs crying - Faces Eugene -

FANNY

I don't think you should right now...The doctor said . . .

Fanny sobs uncontrollably -

JACK'S VOICE

Fanny's right, Gene.

Camera pans right and tilts up to Jack on stair landing -

JACK

Why don't you come back later?

Camera tilts down and pans back to group on stairs - Fanny continues sobbing - George crosses between Fanny and Eugene and goes up stairs - Somber music heard - Eugene turns and goes back down stairs -

EUGENE

All right.

He goes to left foreground in direction of door - Camera pans to follow -

LAP DISSOLVE

EXT WINDOW MCS - Camera shooting up to window - George approaches - Opens and looks through curtains - Music continues -   **3** (3-8)

INT WINDOW LS - George's reflection on window at left close to camera - He looks grimly out at Eugene in extreme background going through entrance gates - Eugene gets into automobile -   **4** (7-5)

NURSE'S VOICE

She wants to see you.

INT ROOM CU - George turning head to face right background - Walks to background as camera pans to follow - Nurse seen by door in extreme background - George slowly approaches door -   **5** (26-6)

INT ROOM MCS - Door in center opening - George enters - Nurse follows him into room and closes door - George pauses - Approaches bed and kneels down - Camera pans and tilts to follow - George brings face close to Isabel's face on bed - Light through curtain throws lace pattern on their faces - She speaks weakly - Music heard -   **6** (170-12)

ISABEL

Darling, did you get something to eat?

GEORGE

Yes, Mother.

ISABEL

All you needed?

GEORGE

Yes, Mother.

ISABEL

Are you sure you didn't—catch cold coming home?

GEORGE

I'm all right, Mother.

He picks up her hand in his - Kisses it -

ISABEL

That's sweet...sweet.

GEORGE

What is, Mother darling?

ISABEL

My hand against your cheek. I <u>can</u> feel it...I wonder...if Eugene and Lucy know that we've come home.

GEORGE

I'm sure they do.

She glances up directly at him -

ISABEL

Has he asked about me?

He lowers her hand - Answers with difficulty -

GEORGE

Yes...he was here.

ISABEL

Has he gone?

GEORGE

Yes, Mother.

ISABEL

Oh...I'd like to have seen him...just once.

She stares off wistfully into distance -

NURSE'S VOICE

She must rest now.

Shadow crosses slowly over Isabel as curtains offscreen are drawn - George turns ruefully away - Exits - She looks after him -

LAP DISSOLVE

7 (118-10) INT ROOM LS - Jack sitting at left foreground - Fanny at right - Door in background opens - The two rise - Major rising on bed in background - George comes in - Comes to foreground - Fanny exits hurriedly - George stops before Jack - Talks sharply - Jack going to background to Major -

GEORGE

The doctor in New York said she might get better! Don't you know he did? Don't you know he said she might?

Major lies down - Jack stops by him - George moving to right - Jack goes to doorway in background - Stands in it -

INT BEDROOM CU - Major propped up on bed - Sleeping fitfully - Music heard - He awakens - Rises and walks toward camera - Camera moves back - Jack comes on left - Crosses in foreground - Exits right - Major stumbles after him - Camera pans to follow -

FANNY'S VOICE

George!

Fanny facing camera in extreme foreground with arms around George - Major exits in background behind them -

FANNY

She loved you! She loved you!

Oh, how she did love you!

FADE OUT

NIGHT SEQUENCE

8 (343-5) FADE IN INT ROOM CU - Major staring into camera - Firelight flickering on his face - Music heard -

NARRATOR'S VOICE

And now Major Amberson was engaged in the profoundest thinking of his life.

He was occupied with the first really important matter that had taken his attention since he came home after the Gettysburg campaign, and went into business.

And he realized that everything which had worried him or delighted him during this lifetime

between then and today

—all his buying and building and trading and banking—that it was all trifling and waste beside what concerned him now. For the Major knew now that he had to plan how to enter an unknown country, where he was not even sure of being recognized as an Amberson.

Not sure of anything, except that Isabel would help him if she could.

> JACK'S VOICE

That's true, Fanny. You know it's a funny thing about the deed of the house. Father . . .

> FANNY'S VOICE

But it must go right, we saw with our own eyes how perfectly it worked in the shop.

> JACK'S VOICE

I'm only glad you didn't go into the confounded thing, to the extent I did.

> FANNY'S VOICE

But the light was so bright no one could face it, and so there can't be any reason for it not to work. It simply must.

> JACK'S VOICE

It certainly was a perfect thing in the shop. Well our headlight[86] just won't work, Fanny.

> JACK'S VOICE

Father...Father . . .

Major glances to right -

> MAJOR

Huh?

> JACK'S VOICE

The house was in Isabel's name, wasn't it?

He nods slightly -

---

[86] See footnote 79.

MAJOR

Yes.

JACK'S VOICE

Can you remember—when you gave her the deed, Father?

He shakes his head slightly - Looks into camera -

MAJOR

No—no, I can't just remember.

GEORGE'S VOICE

It doesn't matter.

JACK'S VOICE

The whole estate is about as mixed up as an estate can get.

I haven't helped out any by this infernal headlight scheme.[87]

You ought to have that deed, George.

GEORGE'S VOICE

No, don't bother.

Major continues to stare into camera - Music continues -

MAJOR

Huh—it must be, in the sun...There wasn't anything here, but the sun in the first place...the sun. The earth came out of the sun...and we came out of the earth...so—but whatever we are we must have been in the earth.

We go back to the earth we came out of—so the earth goes back to the sun it came out of—and in a little while we'll all be back in the sun together, and time means nothing. Just nothing at all. I wish . . .

He glances to right foreground - As he hears -

GEORGE'S VOICE

Did you want anything, Grandfather?

MAJOR

Huh?

---

[87] See footnote 79.

GEORGE'S VOICE

Would you like a glass of water?

Major talks slowly -

MAJOR

No—no, I—I don't want anything at all. I wish somebody could tell me . . .

LAP DISSOLVE

DAY SEQUENCE

EXT CEMETERY MS - Camera shooting up to two tombstones - For Major and Isabel - Music heard[88] -

FADE OUT

---

[88] Herrmann's "Short Chorale" for low brass and winds originally accompanied this shot.

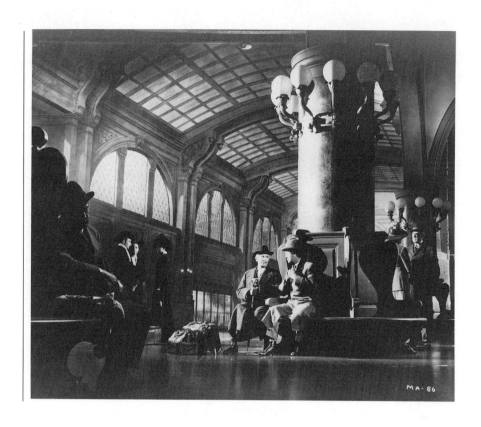

REEL 6 SECTION B

DAY SEQUENCE

FADE IN INT R.R. STATION LS - People around in foreground - Others coming on in foreground going to background - General station noises heard - Jack and George sitting on bench at right near foreground - Bells heard - Jack talks to George - George taking out wallet -

JACK

Just a hundred, Georgie, I know you can't spare it, but I really must have something to tide me over in Washington 'til things are settled.

Man heard calling trains indistinctly - Man at left foreground - Rises - Goes to left - Exits - Camera moves up close to the two - George glances around -

JACK

Nobody's looking.

George hands money to Jack - People moving in background -

JACK

We'll survive, Georgie—you will especially. For my part, I'll be content with just surviving. An ex-Congressman can always be pretty sure of getting a consulship somewhere. Oh, I'll live pleasantly enough with a pitcher of ice under a palm tree, and native folk to wait on me—that part of it will be like home.

GEORGE

I wish you'd take more.

George putting wallet in pocket -

JACK

There's one thing I'll say for you, young George. You haven't got a stingy bone in your body. That's the Amberson stock in you.

They rise as Jack talks - Camera following them - Station noises heard - Train whistle heard -

JACK

Well, I may not see you again, Georgie. From this time on it's quite probable we'll only know each other by letter until you're notified as my next of kin that there's an old valise to be forwarded to you and maybe some dusty curios from the consulate mantelpiece.

Jack at left foreground facing George at right foreground - General station noises heard -

1 (317-4)

JACK

Well...odd way for us to be saying good-bye...one wouldn't have thought it, even a few years ago, but here we are...two gentlemen of elegant appearance in a—state of bustitude. Enh, you can't ever tell what'll happen at all, can you...Once I stood where we're standing now, to say good-bye to a pretty girl—only it was in the old station before this was built—we called it the "depot."...We knew we wouldn't see each other again for almost a year. I thought I couldn't live through it. She stood there, crying...Don't even know where she lives now, or if she is living...If she ever thinks of me she probably imagines I'm still dancing in the ballroom of the Amberson Mansion...She probably thinks of the Mansion as still beautiful—still the finest house in town...Ah, life and money both behave like—loose quicksilver in a nest of cracks...When they're gone you can't tell where, or what the devil you did with 'em! But I—believe I'll say now while there isn't much time left for—either of us to get any more embarrassed, I...believe I'll say I've always been fond of you, Georgie, I can't say I've always liked you...but we all spoiled you terribly when you were a boy, but you've had a pretty heavy jolt, and you've taken it pretty quietly and . . .

Jack glances around at sound of train pulling in -

JACK

. . . well with the train coming into the shed, you'll forgive me for saying there have been times when I thought you ought to be hanged, and just for a last word there may be somebody else in this town who's always felt about you like that—fond of you, I mean, no matter how much it seems you ought to be hanged. You might try . . .

Jack glances toward sound of conductor -

CONDUCTOR'S VOICE

[Calling names of towns]

Jack begins backing to left -

JACK

I must run. I'll send back the money as fast as they pay me, so good-bye and God bless you, Georgie.

Jack runs with suitcases to left background toward station platform - Others pass back and forth - George in extreme left foreground with back to camera watches him go -

George turns to right foreground - Exits -

FADE OUT

In RV a substantial portion of the remaining film was taken out of order and inserted without apparent logic at this point:

LAP DISSOLVE to Eugene and Lucy walking in their garden as she tells the tale of the overbearing Indian "Loma-Nashah" (reel 7A shot 2).

LAP DISSOLVE to Fanny and George in kitchen realizing they face financial disaster; Fanny slumps against an unheated boiler (new version of reel 7A shots 1 through 4, original version resumes with shot 5) FADE OUT.

FADE IN to George in Bronson's office seeking a high-risk job with a premium income (reel 7A after LAP DISSOLVE in shot 5) FADE OUT.

TRANSITION #1...[89]

2 (138-4) FADE IN EXT STREET LS - Camera shooting upward toward building in background - Camera moves slowly to left down street throughout montage of dissolves - Music heard -

NARRATOR'S VOICE

George Amberson Minafer walked homeward slowly through what seemed to be the strange streets of a strange city...for the town was growing . . .

LAP DISSOLVE

EXT GRAIN ELEVATORS ELS - Camera shooting up -

NARRATOR'S VOICE

. . . and changing.

LAP DISSOLVE

EXT ELECTRICAL GENERATOR ELS - Camera shooting up -

NARRATOR'S VOICE

It was heaving up in the middle incredibly...It was spreading incredibly.

LAP DISSOLVE

EXT FACTORY ELS - Camera shooting up to traffic sign - "Automobiles SLOW" - Factory in background -

NARRATOR'S VOICE

And as it heaved and spread . . .

LAP DISSOLVE

EXT STRUCTURES LS AND MS - Superimposed shots of steel scaffolding and factory exterior -

---

[89] Unfamiliar notation.

NARRATOR'S VOICE

. . . it befouled itself and darkened its sky.

LAP DISSOLVE

EXT ALLEY MLS - Camera shooting up - Clothes hanging on lines behind apartment building in background - Camera moving to left -

NARRATOR'S VOICE

In this alley he'd fought with two boys at the same time, and whipped them.

LAP DISSOLVE

EXT STREET MLS - Camera shooting to shabby house and yard in background - Music heard - Camera moving slowly to left -

NARRATOR'S VOICE

On that sagging porch a laughing woman had fed him and other boys with dough-nuts and gingerbread.

LAP DISSOLVE

EXT STREET MLS - Camera shooting over to fence across street to building in background - Music heard - Camera moving to left -

NARRATOR'S VOICE

Yonder the relics of the iron picket fence he'd made his white pony jump, on a dare.

LAP DISSOLVE

EXT HOUSE MLS - Camera moving past house in background to left - Music heard -

NARRATOR'S VOICE

And in the shabby stone-faced house behind he'd gone to children's parties, and when he was a little older he'd danced there often and fallen in love with Mary Sharon and kissed her, apparently by force, under the stairs in the hall.

LAP DISSOLVE

EXT HOUSE MS - Camera moves left in front of row of tenement houses - Music heard -

NARRATOR'S VOICE

This was the last "walk home" . . .

LAP DISSOLVE

The fall of the house of Amberson: preliminary treatment for a matte painting, by later-to-be-renowned space artist Chesley Bonestell.

EXT BUILDINGS MS - Camera shooting up to exterior of larger apartment houses -

NARRATOR'S VOICE

. . . he was ever to take up National Avenue to Amberson Addition . . .

LAP DISSOLVE

EXT BLDG MS - Camera shooting up to sign - "New Hope APARTMENTS Single Rooms" -[90]

LAP DISSOLVE

EXT STREET MLS - Camera moving slowly down street to left background - Two houses at right background - Music heard -

NARRATOR'S VOICE

. . . and the big old house at the foot of Amberson Boulevard . . .

LAP DISSOLVE

EXT AMBERSON MANSION MLS - Camera shooting through gates to house in background - Music and Narrator heard - Camera moving closer to gate -

NARRATOR'S VOICE

Tonight would be the last night that he and Fanny were to spend in the house which the Major had forgotten to deed to Isabel.

Tomorrow they were to move out...Tomorrow everything would be gone.

FADE OUT

NIGHT SEQUENCE[91]

[FADE IN INT BEDROOM CU - George in foreground - Camera moving back - Music and Narrator heard - George kneeling by dismantled bed -

3 (152-8)

NARRATOR'S VOICE

The very space in which tonight was still Isabel's room would be cut into new shapes by new walls and floors and ceilings. And if space itself can be haunted as memory is haunted, then it may be that some impressionable overworked woman in a "kitchenette," after turning out the light, will seem to see a young man kneeling in the darkness, with arms outstretched through the wall . . .

LAP DISSOLVE

INT ROOM MLS - George kneeling by bed at right background - Music and Narrator heard -

---

[90] At this point in *RV* the screen fades to black and remains black as the narrator continues.

[91] The following sequence was to have opened with a shot representing the point of view of George as he moves around inside the deserted mansion. Stanley Cortez and a crew spent four days working out the elaborate mechanics of the shot. (Going up the stairs proved especially difficult.) It has always been assumed that the footage was a casualty of Wise's re-editing. The footage does not, however, appear in the *CC*. It may be that Welles was unhappy with what Cortez shot. Another possibility is that Welles never intended to use it in the first place. Antagonism between Welles and Cortez had steadily increased during production because of Cortez's painstakingly slow working pace. While Cortez and a crew were off working on the deserted mansion footage, principal photography continued under RKO studio cinematographer Harry Wild. The assignment, then, may have been a diversion constituting Cortez's unofficial demotion. After all, it is hard to imagine Welles leaving such tantalizingly challenging material entirely in someone else's hands if he was really serious about it. See footnote 112.

NARRATOR'S VOICE

. . . clutching at the covers of a shadowy bed. It may seem to her that she hears the faint cry, over and over . . .

GEORGE

Mother, forgive me...God forgive me.

Music heard - Lights dim - Narrator heard - George kneeling by bed -][92]

---

[92] *RV* eliminates the second part of shot 3 (after the lap dissolve), moves George's line asking forgiveness to the beginning, and continues with the following substitute narration:

"NARRATOR'S VOICE

Something had happened...a thing which—years ago—had been the eagerest hope of many, many good citizens of the town...and now it came at last: George Amberson Minafer had got his comeuppance...He got it three times filled...and running over...But those who had so longed for it were not there to see it, and they never knew it...Those who were still living had forgotten all about it and all about him." FADE OUT

The changes are not noticeable because George's back is always to the camera.

REEL 7 SECTION A

DAY SEQUENCE

[INT KITCHEN MCU - Fanny sinking down on floor by boiler - George partly on standing at right of camera - She stares up at him mouth open - Talks hysterically to him -

1 (496-13)[93]

FANNY

You want to leave me in the lurch!

GEORGE'S VOICE

Get up, Aunt Fanny.

FANNY

I can't. I—I'm too weak. You're going to leave me in the lurch!

GEORGE'S VOICE

Aunt Fanny! I'm only going to make eight dollars a week at the law office. You'd have to be paying more of the expenses than I would.

FANNY

I'd be paying—I'd be paying?

GEORGE'S VOICE

Certainly you would. You'd be using more of your money than mine.

FANNY

My money!

She laughs hysterically -

FANNY

I have twenty-eight dollars. That's all.

GEORGE

You mean until the interest is due again.

FANNY

I mean that's all. I mean that's all there is. There won't be any more interest be-cause there isn't any principal. I know, I told Jack I didn't put everything in the headlight, but I did—every cent except my last interest payment and—and it's gone.

---

[93] Originally a single uninterrupted take lasting more than five minutes. Mercury Theatre business manager Jack Moss shot an alternate, shorter version of the first four minutes for *RV*. The Moss version is given in the text just after the footage it replaced.

GEORGE'S VOICE

Why did you wait till now to tell me?

FANNY

I couldn't tell till I had to. It wouldn't do any good—nothing does any good, I guess in this old world! I knew your mother'd want me to watch over you and try to have something like a home for you. And I tried—I tried to make things as nice for you as I could. I walked my heels down trying to find a place for us to live. I walked and walked over this town. I didn't ride one block on a streetcar. I wouldn't use five cents no matter how tired I . . .

She laughs wildly - Hysterically -

FANNY

. . . oh—and now you don't want—you want—you want to leave me in the lurch!

She laughs wildly - George talking - Impatiently -

GEORGE'S VOICE

Aunt Fanny! Aunt Fanny—get up! Don't sit there with your back against the boiler. Get up, Aunt Fanny!]

LAP DISSOLVE[94]

INT KITCHEN MCU - Fanny with back to camera at left foreground - George comes on right and faces her -

GEORGE

Please try and understand. It's not doing either of us any good going on arguing this way. That place you picked out . . .

FANNY

But this boarding house is practical...and we could be together.

GEORGE

How? On eight dollars a week? I'm only going to be getting eight dollars a week at the law office. Why, you'd be paying more of the expenses than I would.

FANNY

I'd be paying?...I'd be paying!

GEORGE

Certainly you would. We'd be using more of your money than mine.

---

[94] The preceding material within brackets was reshot for *RV* by Jack Moss. Moss's version follows. Shot numbers and footage counts are from *RV*.

FANNY

My money?...My money!

She laughs - Then sobs -

FANNY

I've—I've got twenty-eight dollars. That's all.

GEORGE

Twenty-eight dollars!

FANNY

That's all...I know I told Jack I didn't put everything in the headlight[95] company but—I did...every cent...and it's gone.

GEORGE

Why did you wait till now to tell me?

FANNY

I couldn't tell till I had to...It wouldn't do any good.

GEORGE

Oh my gosh.

George turns away from her to right foreground - Disdainful - Fanny pulls him by sleeve to face her again - Whines -

FANNY

Ohhh, I know what you're gonna do...You're—you're gonna leave me in the lurch!

GEORGE

I'm only asking you to be reasonable. To try and understand that it's impossible for either of us to go on this way.

Fanny sinks down on floor with back to boiler -

GEORGE'S VOICE

Will you get up?!

Fanny sobs in reply -

FANNY

I can't...I'm too weak.

---

[95] The first of only two allusions remaining in *RV* to the ill-fated headlight scheme in which Fanny and Uncle Jack lost all their money. See footnote 79.

2 (6-9) INT KITCHEN MCU - Camera shooting up - George looking off lower left foreground -

GEORGE

Oh—none of this makes any sense. Will you get up?

3 (63-15) INT KITCHEN MCU - Camera shooting down to Fanny seated against boiler - Looking off right -

FANNY

I knew your mother'd—want me to watch over ya—and try and make something like a home for ya. And I tried...I tried to make things as nice for ya as I could.

GEORGE'S VOICE

I know that.

FANNY

I walked my heels down—looking for a place for us to live...I—I walked and walked over this town...I—I didn't ride one block on a streetcar...I wouldn't—use—five cents no matter how tired I was.

She cries -

4 (5-15) INT KITCHEN MCU - George looking off lower left foreground -

GEORGE

For the gosh sakes will you get up! Don't sit there with your back against the boiler.

Camera shooting down to Fanny - George partly on at right - [96]

GEORGE

Get up, Aunt Fanny!

FANNY

It's not hot! It's cold! The plumbers disconnected it...I wouldn't mind if they hadn't...I wouldn't mind if it burned—I wouldn't mind if it burned me, George!

George leans down - Pulls her to her feet - Shakes her - She laughs wildly and uncontrollably - Camera pulls back - They come to foreground -

GEORGE

Oh Aunt Fanny for gosh sakes, get up!

Camera moves back through doorway as they come through -

---

[96] Beginning of original Cortez footage in *RV*, where it is "Shot 5 (132-6) INT KITCHEN MCS." The difference is evident in Cortez's more expressionistic lighting and softer focus.

GEORGE

Now stop it! Stop it! Listen to me, do you hear me? Stop it, now, stop it. Listen to me now!

They pass through several rooms of deserted mansion - Fanny calming down - Camera continues moving back -

GEORGE

There, that's better. Now let's see where we stand...Let's see if we can afford this place you've picked out.

FANNY

I—I'm sure the boarding house is practical, George. I'm sure it's practical.

GEORGE

I know it must be practical, Aunt Fanny.

FANNY

And...and it is a comfort to be among nice people.

GEORGE

It's all right, I was thinking of the money, Aunt Fanny. You see . . .

Camera continues moving back - George leads her left into drawing room - Camera pans to follow - Fanny agitated - Twisting handkerchief -

FANNY

There's—there's one great economy. They—they don't allow tipping. They—they have signs that prohibit it.

GEORGE

That's good. But the rent's thirty-six dollars a month. And dinner's twenty-two and a half for each of us. I've got about a hundred dollars. A hundred dollars, that's all. We won't need any new clothes for a year. Perhaps . . .

They stop in shadows before slatted window - Furniture covered with sheeting in background - Shafts of light fall across room -

FANNY

Oh, longer! So—so you see . . .

GEORGE

Yes, I see. I see that thirty-six and forty-five make eighty-one...At the lowest we'll need a hundred dollars a month.

He moves from her - Looks out window - Says bitterly -

GEORGE

And I'm going to be making thirty-two.

LAP DISSOLVE[97]

[DAY SEQUENCE

INT OFFICE MCU - Camera shooting upward - George crossing left to right in extreme foreground - Passes secretary who holds door into Bronson's office open - Camera pans to follow - Reveals Bronson standing in background looking to right foreground -

BRONSON

The real flair!

Bronson comes to right foreground - Camera pans to follow showing George standing at extreme right foreground - Bronson pats him on shoulder -

BRONSON

Real flair for the law.

They go around desk to right background - Camera pans to follow -

BRONSON

That's right. Couldn't wait 'til tomorrow to begin! The law is a jealous mistress and a stern mistress.

Bronson sits at his desk -

GEORGE

I can't do it. I can't take up the law.

BRONSON

What?

GEORGE

I've come to tell you that I've got to find something quicker—something that pays from the start.

BRONSON

I can't think of anything just this minute that pays from the start.

---

[97] In *RV* the entire "unheated boiler" sequence, as revised—the Moss footage plus the remainder of the original footage—was placed earlier (see *CC* reel 6B), between the train sequence (shot 1) and the last walk home sequence (shot 2).

GEORGE

Well, sir, I've heard that they pay very high wages to people in dangerous trades—people that handle touchy chemicals or high explosives—men in the dynamite factories. I thought I'd see if I couldn't get a job like that. I wanted to get started tomorrow if I could.

BRONSON

Georgie, your grandfather and I were boys together. Don't you think I ought to know what's the trouble?

GEORGE

Well, sir, it—it's Aunt Fanny.

George moves to window in background - Traffic noises heard outside -

GEORGE

She's set her mind on this particular boarding house—seems she put everything in the headlight company...and, well, she's got some old cronies and I guess she's been looking forward to the—games of bridge and the—harmless kind of gossip that goes on in such places...Really, it's a life she'd like better than anything else...and it struck me that she's just about got to have it.

Bronson rises - Goes to window at left - Camera pans to follow - George turns to look at him as he talks -

BRONSON

I got her into that headlight business with Jack,[98] I feel a certain responsibility myself.

GEORGE

I'm taking the responsibility. She's not your aunt, you know, sir.

Bronson comes around desk to left foreground - George follows - Camera moves backward - Bronson turns back to camera - Moves to background as he talks -

BRONSON

Well, I'm unable to see, even if she's yours, that a young man is morally called upon to give up a career at the law to provide his aunt with a favorable opportunity to play bridge whist.

George crosses to left in front of Bronson - Stops - They turn to face one another -

BRONSON

All right, all right. If you'll promise not to get blown up I'll see if we can find you the job.

---

[98] This conversation contains the second of the two remaining allusions in *RV* to the headlight scheme.

Bronson comes to extreme left foreground - Turns and faces George -

BRONSON

You certainly are the most practical young man I ever met!

FADE OUT][99]

[DAY SEQUENCE

2 (317-1) FADE IN EXT GARDEN MS - Lucy and Eugene in background walking to foreground - Camera shooting up - Moving backward as they advance - He knocks pipe on hand - Music heard -

LUCY

Did you ever hear the Indian name for that little grove of beech trees?

EUGENE

No...and you never did either.

She laughs - They stop - He turns to face her -

EUGENE

Well?

LUCY

The name was "Loma-Nashah" and it means "They-Couldn't-Help-It."

EUGENE

Doesn't sound like it.

LUCY

Indian names don't.

They continue advancing to foreground - Camera continues moving back -

LUCY

There was a bad Indian Chief lived there, the worst Indian that ever lived. And his name was—it was . . .

They stop again - Eugene turns to face her -

LUCY

. . . "Vendonah." Means "Rides-Down-Everything."

---

[99] In *RV* the entire sequence in Bronson's office was placed earlier (see *CC* reel 6B), between the train sequence (shot 1) and the last walk home sequence (shot 2).

EUGENE

What?

She turns to face him -

LUCY

His name was Vendonah, same thing as Rides-Down-Everything.

EUGENE

I see . . .

Lucy laughs nervously -

EUGENE

. . . go on.

LUCY

Vendonah was unspeakable. He was so proud that he wore iron shoes and walked over people's faces with them. So at last the tribe decided that it wasn't a good enough excuse for him that he was young and inexperienced—he'd have to go. So they took him down to the river and put him in a canoe, and pushed him out from shore; and the current carried him on down to the ocean—and he never got back...They didn't want him back, of course. They hated Vendonah...but they weren't able to discover—any other warrior they wanted to make chief in his place...They couldn't help feeling that way.

EUGENE

I see. So that's why they named the place, "They-Couldn't-Help-It."

LUCY

Must have been.

They resume walking to foreground - Camera moving back - They stop and face one another again -

EUGENE

So—you're going to stay in your garden...You think it's better just to—keep walking about among your flower beds till you get old...like a pensive garden-lady in a Victorian engraving. Hm?

LUCY

I suppose I'm like that tribe that lived here, Papa. I had too much unpleasant excitement. I don't want any more...in fact—I don't want anything but you.

> EUGENE

You don't?

He glances sharply off to right -

> EUGENE

What was the name of that grove?

He quickly faces her again -

> LUCY

"They-Couldn't" . . .

> EUGENE

The Indian name, I mean.

> LUCY

Oh—"Mola-Haha."

They laugh together -

> EUGENE

"Mola-Haha"...that wasn't the name you said.

> LUCY

Oh, I've forgotten.

> EUGENE

I see you have...Perhaps you remember the chief's name better.

Lucy glances off to right -

> LUCY

I don't.

He puts his arm around her - Draws her near -

> EUGENE

I hope some day you can forget it.

They walk partly off arm in arm in extreme right foreground -

> LAP DISSOLVE][100]

---

[100] In *RV* the entire sequence of Eugene and Lucy walking in their garden was placed earlier (see *CC* reel 6B), between the train sequence (shot 1) and the last walk home sequence (shot 2).

EXT STREET MS - Camera shooting up to crowd - Two interns carrying George on stretcher to ambulance at right foreground - Policeman off heard shouting to crowd in Irish accent - Young man in driving coat also shouting - Another policeman standing by him - Car partly on left foreground - Others heard talking indistinctly -

POLICEMAN'S VOICE

All right, stay back there, now!

DRIVER

He run into me much as I run into him, and if he gets well—he ain't going to get not one single cent out of me!

Policeman comes on in foreground and approaches driver - Camera moves closer to them - Second policeman joins them - Camera shooting up at them -

DRIVER

I'm perfectly willing to say I'm sorry for him, an' so is the lady with me.

Irish policeman in center talks to other policeman at right -

POLICEMAN

Wunnderful the damage one of these little machines can do, you'd never believe it.

Policeman turns to driver - Commands him -

POLICEMAN

All right, Sonny, back in your car, back in your car.

Policeman takes driver by shoulder and pushes him toward car - Driver heard faintly -

DRIVER'S VOICE

We're both willin' to say—understand?

Two policemen turn to background - Begin dispersing crowd - Camera following them -

POLICEMAN

All right, stay back there, now!

POLICEMAN

I guess he ain't got much case to give that fellow . . .

They talk indistinctly - Crowd noise heard -

POLICEMAN

. . . and that's all he did . . .

"Riffraff!"

They talk indistinctly - Going to background - Truck passing -

POLICEMAN

... broke both his legs for him and gosh knows what all.

They stop - Face each other - Policeman at right talks -

SECOND POLICEMAN

I wasn't here then—what was it?

POLICEMAN

Riffraff!

FADE OUT

FADE IN INSERT #1 - Front page of Indianapolis *Daily Inquirer* - Headlines -   **3 (7-4)**

INQUIRER
AUTOMOBILE BUTCHERY!

Governor Flays
Auto Deaths
PROMISES SWIFT ACTION

(Picture of car)[101]

INSERT #2 - Detail - Camera zooming in on article in paper -   **4 (11-1)**

TODAY'S TOLL
Serious Accident

G. A. Minafer, Akers Chem-
ical Co., both legs broken.

G. A. Minafer, an employee of
the Akers Chemical Company

---

[101] *RV* substitutes headline **AUTO CASUALTIES MOUNT**, probably to lessen potentiality of offense to interests concerned. In center of page is cartoon of skeleton driving automobile over row of bodies. At left of page is column, "Stage Views—Jed Leland" with inset photograph of Joseph Cotten, an allusion (like the name *Inquirer*) to *Citizen Kane*.

[NIGHT SEQUENCE[102]

INT FACTORY MCU - Eugene sitting in shadows at right - He rises - Goes to window at right - Looks out - Music heard -

1 (13-13)

INT ROOM CU - Eugene looking grimly to foreground - Glances to right -

2 (25-3)

LAP DISSOLVE

EXT FACTORY MS - Car parked inside gate on drive - Eugene coming out office building left foreground - Comes to car -

LAP DISSOLVE

EXT CAR MCU - Driver behind wheel - Eugene coming on outside window at left -

EUGENE

I won't go home now, Harry. Drive to the City Hospital.

HARRY

Yes, sir. Miss Lucy's there. She said she'd expected you'd come there before you go home.

EUGENE

She did?

HARRY

Yes, sir.

Eugene gets into car - Driver starts it -

EXT FACTORY MS - Car inside gates on drive - Comes out to foreground - Exits left foreground -

3 (76-11)

LAP DISSOLVE

EXT HOSPITAL MLS - Camera shooting across street to hospital - Car drives on at right - Stops before entrance - Eugene gets out - Goes up steps - Exits -

WIPE DOWN LAP DISSOLVE[103]

EXT HOSPITAL MLS - Camera shooting across street to hospital - Car parked before it - Eugene comes out in background - Comes down steps to car - Gets in - Car drives to left - Exits -

LAP DISSOLVE

---

[102] The entire closing sequence in which Eugene visits Fanny at the boarding house where she resides was scrapped, and a much shorter version shot by Freddie Fleck was substituted. Fleck's version is given below just after the original sequence it replaced.

[103] Apparently designates a transition which begins as a WIPE and continues as a LAP DISSOLVE.

EXT STREET LS - Camera shooting from street to tall buildings in background - Lights in some windows - Car comes on right foreground - Stops before building at right - Eugene gets out - Traffic noise heard -

4 (10-9) EXT HOUSE MLS - Eugene in foreground - Going through gates to house in background -

5 (103-14) EXT DOOR MCU - Scene in darkness - Music stops - Doorbell heard - Door opens showing man in hall looking to foreground - Eating - Talking record heard indistinctly[104] - Camera moving up close to him - He turns - Goes to background - Camera pans to left - Showing landlady rising from table in room left background - She comes through to foreground - Man stops by doorway in background - She comes through to right - Exits - Camera swings to left to mirror - Showing women in room in background - Reflection of Eugene and landlady in foreground -

LANDLADY

What may I do for you, sir?

---

[104] The record playing in the background during this sequence is an adaptation of a verbal routine "No News; or, What Killed the Dog" performed by Joseph Cotten and Norman Foster in the style of the popular vaudeville and radio team "The Two Black Crows" (George Moran and Charles Mack). In a grimly ironic sense it recapitulates the fate of the Ambersons.

"One time a wealthy man was ordered by his physicians to go away to the mountains for a rest. He went home and told the members of his family what the doctor had said. He said, 'Now, while I'm away I don't wish to be annoyed by letters or telegrams. In fact, I do not wish to receive *any* news of *any* kind.' So he went away and was gone about six weeks. He returned to the city very much improved in health and very anxious to hear some news from home. He got off the train and was met by his colored servant and the following conversation ensued:

Man: Well, Henry, how is everything? Have you any news for me?

Henry: No suh, no suh, they ain't no news, suh. Everything is jus' 'bout the same as when yo'all went away.

Man: Well, well—nothing happened?

Henry: No, suh, no suh, nothing happened. They ain't no news for you.

Man: Well, you know I'm just dying for some word from home, Henry, any little thing no matter how trifling.

Henry: No, suh, no suh, they ain't no news for you, suh, there ain't nothing to tell you, suh, exceptin' just one thing. Since you been away your dog died.

Man: Oh, my dog died, eh? Well that's too bad. What killed the dog?

Henry: Well, suh, it seems that the dog et some burned hoss flesh and dat's what killed the dog.

Man: Well, where did the dog get the burned horse flesh to eat?

Henry: Well, suh, you know your barn burned down and after the fire had cooled off the dog went in and et some of the burned hoss flesh and dat's what killed the dog.

Man: Oh, my barn burned down, eh?

Henry: Oh, yes suh, yes suh, that old barn burned down.

Man: Well, how did the barn catch fire?

Henry: Well, suh, you see the sparks from the house floated over and ketched on the barn and burned the barn and burned all the cows and horses and after the fire cooled off the dog went in and et some of the burned hoss flesh and dat's what killed the dog.

Man: Oh, my house burned down too?

Henry: Yes suh, yes suh, yo' house burned down. That's completely destroyed.

Man: Well, how in the world did the house catch fire?

Henry: Well suh, they had some candles in the house and one of the candles fell over, ketched on the curtain, and the sparks from the curtain ketched the roof and burned the house down, and burned the barn down, and after the fire cooled off the dog went in and et some of the burned hoss flesh and dat's what killed the dog.

Man: We had candles in the house, when I have gas and electricity? Why, I never knew there was a candle in the house.

Henry: Yes suh, they had candles burning all around the coffin.

Man: The coffin—why, who's dead?

Henry: Oh, yes, suh, yes suh, that's another little thing I forgot to tell you about. Since you been away your mother-in-law died.

Man: Oh, my mother-in-law died, eh?

Henry: Oh, yes suh, yes suh. She'd dead. You needn't worry about her no more.

Man: Well, what on earth killed my mother-in-law?

Henry: Well suh, I don't know exactly what killed her but around the neighborhood they all say it was from the shock of your wife runnin' away with the chauffeur—but outside of dat dey ain't no news."

EUGENE

I'd like to see Miss Fanny Minafer, please.

                                      LANDLADY

Just a moment.

Landlady's reflection goes to room in background - She talks - Eugene walking slowly to background -

                                      LANDLADY

Miss Minafer, there's a gentleman to see you.

Fanny rises from table in background - Women watching curiously - She comes to Eugene - He talks to her -

                                      EUGENE

Hello, Fanny.

                                      FANNY

Hello, Eugene.

They come to foreground as he talks -

                                      EUGENE

I missed you at the hospital. I'm sorry.

Their reflections cross to right - As she talks -

                                      FANNY

There's nothing to worry about.

Camera pans to right - The two come on right foreground - Going into room at left background as she talks - Women in mirror watching curiously -

                                      FANNY

The doctor told me he's going to get him all well.

                                      EUGENE

Yes.

                                      FANNY

I saw Lucy there.

                                      EUGENE

Yes.

INT ROOM MCS - Fanny coming on at right - Talking - Eugene following her - Man eating at table in background - Talking record heard indistinctly -

6 (4-0)

FANNY

Lucy looks very well.

EUGENE

Yes.

She sits down at left - They look at man in background - Fanny talks to him - Chair squeaking - Man exits right background -

FANNY

Will you excuse us, Mr. Fleck?[105] You feeling any better?

Eugene talks to Fanny - She rocks -

EUGENE

Yes, she got there before I did. How are you, Fanny?

FANNY

Oh, I'm fine . . .

INT ROOM MS - Camera shooting over victrola in foreground - Record going around - Man sitting on lounge in background reading - Indistinct talking from record heard -

7 (19-8)

FANNY'S VOICE

. . . fine.

Man rises - Throws book down - Crosses to right - Glances at Fanny and Eugene in background - Eugene standing - Camera pans to follow man crossing to right - Others exit - He goes out into hall closing doors -

INT ROOM MCS - Two looking to foreground - Eugene turns - Looks at Fanny rocking at left background - Chair squeaking - Record heard -

8 (31-2)

EUGENE

You look fine.

He sits down -

EUGENE

About your nephew . . .

FANNY

George?

---

[105] Another covert use of names of those involved in the production.

I thought at first I wouldn't go to the hospital.

FANNY

No?

INT ROOM MCU - Eugene sitting glancing to left foreground - Talking - Chair and record heard -   **9** (15-8)

EUGENE

I thought it would be hard not to be bitter, but of course I went.

INT ROOM MCU - Camera shooting up at Fanny seated rocking - Chair squeaking - She looks to foreground unemotionally -   **10** (7-15)

INT ROOM MLS - Camera shooting over victrola in foreground - Fanny sitting rocking in background - Needle on record in foreground scratching -   **11** (3-9)

INT ROOM MCS - Camera shooting past Eugene sitting at right of camera - Glances at Fanny sitting in background soberly rocking - Victrola needle heard scratching on record - He jumps up - Camera pans as he goes to left background to victrola -   **12** (7-14)

INT ROOM MCU - Camera shooting up to Fanny sitting rocking glancing to left - Talks - Scratching of record heard -   **13** (5-2)

FANNY

Think they'll get married—after all?

INT ROOM MLS - Camera shooting over victrola in foreground - Past Eugene standing partly on by it - Fanny sitting in background rocking - Eugene's hand lifting needle off record - Stops victrola as he talks -   **14** (5-8)

EUGENE'S VOICE

Think so, Fanny.

INT ROOM MLS - Eugene turning from victrola in background - Looks to right foreground - Talks - Chair heard squeaking -   **15** (11-15)

EUGENE

Lucy says so.

He comes toward foreground -

INT ROOM MCS - Fanny sitting rocking - Eugene's shadow passing over her - He comes on at left before camera - Sits down at right foreground -   **16** (80-1)

EUGENE

Funny how much like her, he looks.

She talks coldly -

FANNY

Who?

EUGENE

George.

FANNY

Oh.

EUGENE

Like Isabel.

FANNY

Oh.

She smiles slightly - Talks to him -

FANNY

Well, it's nice to see you, looking well.

EUGENE

Thanks, Fanny.

He looks off to left - Talking - Glancing at her as he hesitates - She listens stony-faced -

EUGENE

I just wanted to come here—and—you were always so close to Isabel—she was so fond of you. You know what he said to me when I went into that room?

INT ROOM CU - Fanny's face before camera - She looks to foreground - Talks sharply -   **17** (2-14)

FANNY

George?

EUGENE'S VOICE

He said . . .

INT ROOM CU - Eugene's face before camera - He talks slowly - Sadly -   **18** (16-8)

<small>REEL 7B   269</small>

EUGENE

. . . "You must have known my mother wanted you to come here today so that I could ask you to forgive me."

19 (4-1) | INT ROOM CU - Fanny's face before camera - She glances down - Chair squeaking -

20 (7-4) | INT ROOM CU - Eugene's face before camera - He glances to left - Smiles slightly -

EUGENE

We shook hands.

21 (4-15) | INT ROOM CU - Fanny looking off to left foreground - Makes noise - Rocking squeaking heard -

FANNY

Hm.

22 (16-8) | INT ROOM MCS - Camera shooting past Eugene sitting at right of camera talking wistfully - Fanny rocking in background -

EUGENE

I wish you could have seen Lucy.

He looks down - Rises - Exits left -

23 (38-11) | INT ROOM CU - Fanny rocking glances slightly to left - Eugene's shadow passes over her face - She looks up to left as shadow exits - She rocks - Chair squeaking -

EUGENE'S VOICE

Fanny, you're the only person I'd tell this to, but it seemed to me as if someone else was in that room down there at the hospital . . .

She stops rocking - Squeaking stops - She stares off tensely - Eugene's shadow passing over her face -

24 (26-1) | INT ROOM MCU - Camera shooting up at Eugene standing at right in shadow - He crosses to left foreground - Coming closer to camera - Camera panning to left - He stops - Looks down to left -

EUGENE

. . . and that through me she had brought her boy under shelter again—that I'd been true at last to my true love.

25 (12-3) | INT ROOM CU - Fanny staring off to left - Starts rocking - Squeaking heard - She looks down -

FANNY

Yes.

INT ROOM MCU - Camera shooting upward - Eugene standing at right before camera in shadow - Turns to right - | **26** (3-0)

INT ROOM CU - Fanny seated staring down - Rocking - Squeaking heard - Eugene's shadow passes over her face - Exits - | **27** (5-7)

INT ROOM MCU - Fanny sitting partly on at right rocking - Eugene standing before her at left - In shadow - Talks to her - | **28** (25-9)

EUGENE

Well, I'll say good-night, Fanny.

Fanny rises slowly - Draws up - Exits left - He turns - Exits after her -

INT HALL MCS - Mirror before camera - Reflections showing women sitting in room in background around table - Door at right of mirror opens - Eugene and Fanny come out - Camera pans to right as they come to right foreground - Door heard closing as they stop in foreground - Man passes behind them - Exits left - Fanny looks down - Door heard closing - She glances at Eugene smiling grimly - Talks - Man coming out in hall in background watching - | **29** (65-7)

FANNY

Well, good-night, Eugene.

Man exits in background - Eugene smiles slightly - Talks to Fanny -

EUGENE

Good-night, Fanny.

He comes to left foreground - Camera pans - She exits - He crosses - Exits - Showing reflections in mirror of Fanny standing looking after him - Women in room in background watching her curiously - Fanny turns - Goes to women around table in background - Exits -

EXT STREET LS - Car parked at right before boarding house - Tall buildings at end of street in background - Light in windows - Music heard[106] - Car starts - Drives to background - Traffic passing on across street in background - Car turns corner in background - Exits - | **30** (40-6)

FADE OUT][107]

The version of the preceding sequence used in the RV:

INT LIBRARY MS - Eugene at desk reading newspaper - Lucy at right looking over his shoulder - Music heard[108] - Eugene puts down newspaper and looks pensively to foreground - | **1** (74-5)

LUCY

What are you going to do, Papa?

Eugene clasps hands - Continues stare without reply - Lucy begins to move around desk away from him -

---

[106] Herrmann's "End Title" originally began at this point and played through to the end of the credit sequence. It was a reuse of the "First Letter Scene" cue (reel 5A shots 1 to 3).

[107] The original ending of the film.

[108] The music heard in *RV*, "Eugene and Lucy at Desk," was composed by Webb in a conventional, densely orchestrated melodramatic idiom.

LUCY

I'm going to him.

She hesitates - Hand on edge of desk - Looks back at Eugene -

LUCY

You coming, Papa?

Eugene continues stare - Lucy pauses - Walks resolutely to foreground - Exits extreme right foreground - Camera pans and tilts to follow -

2 (177-2) INT LIBRARY MCS - Eugene still lost in thought - Music continues - Eugene glances up at sound of door closing - Rises - Walks to foreground - Smiling - Exits extreme right foreground - Camera pans to follow -

LAP DISSOLVE

INT HOSPITAL CORRIDOR MS - Music heard[109] - Door opens in background - Eugene comes out - Closes it after him - Fanny comes on right - Approaches him -

FANNY

How is he?...How is Georgie?

Eugene nods reassuringly -

EUGENE

He's going to be all right.

Eugene takes Fanny's arm - They walk down corridor toward camera -

EUGENE

Fanny, I wish you could have seen Georgie's face when he saw Lucy...You know what he said to me when we went into that room?...He said . . .

They continue down corridor - Camera moves back -

EUGENE

. . . "You must have known my mother wanted you to come here today...so that I could ask you to forgive me."...We shook hands.

They look at one another as they walk - Smiling - Face forward again - Sign seen on left wall in background - "Miss Haran, Head Nurse"[110] -

EUGENE

I never noticed before how much like Isabel Georgie looks.

---

[109] The music heard in *RV*, "Fanny Returns," was composed by Webb in the same clichéd Hollywood idiom.
[110] Shifra Haran was Welles's private secretary.

Fanny nods approvingly - They stop - Camera stops - Both stare pensively offscreen -

                              EUGENE

You know something, Fanny?

Eugene turns to look at her -

                              EUGENE

I wouldn't tell this to anybody but you . . .

Eugene looks offscreen again - They begin walking toward camera again - Camera resumes moving back - Continues moving throughout shot - Pans right to CU of Fanny looking offscreen right foreground - Tears on face -

                         EUGENE'S VOICE

. . . but it seemed to me as if someone else was in that room . . .

Fanny casts gaze upward - Camera holds on her face as Eugene continues -

                         EUGENE'S VOICE

. . . and that through me she—brought her boy under shelter again . . .

Camera pans left to CU of Eugene looking offscreen left foreground - He continues walking slowly to foreground -

                              EUGENE

. . . and that I'd been true at last...to my true love.

Eugene looks questioningly at Fanny - Camera pulls back to MS of them both - She smiles radiantly - Looks upward - Music rises to crescendo - Camera stops - They exit in extreme foreground on either side of camera - Corridor empty - Door to George's room seen in extreme background -

                                                    FADE OUT

BLACK SCREEN - Music Heard[111] -   **31 (55-2)**

                         NARRATOR'S VOICE

Ladies and gentlemen,

that's the end of the story.

The Magnificent Ambersons . . .

---

[111] Webb replaced Herrmann's "End Title," which was considered too downbeat, with his own composition, "Cast," an upbeat, densely orchestrated arrangement of *Toujours ou jamais*.

FADE IN - CU OF COVER OF BOOK

A PULITZER PRIZE NOVEL

THE MAGNIFICENT
AMBERSONS

BOOTH TARKINGTON

NARRATOR'S VOICE

. . . was based on Booth Tarkington's novel. Stanley Cortez . . .

LAP DISSOLVE

INT SET CU - Camera shooting up at 35mm Mitchell camera -

NARRATOR'S VOICE

. . . was the photographer.[112]

LAP DISSOLVE

CU of hand drawn musical score -

NARRATOR'S VOICE

Bernard Herrmann wrote and conducted the music.[113]

LAP DISSOLVE

NARRATOR'S VOICE

Mark Lee Kirk . . .

CU blueprint of exterior of Amberson mansion -

NARRATOR'S VOICE

. . . designed the sets. Al Fields . . .

LAP DISSOLVE

---

[112] Welles's first choice was Gregg Toland, who had worked on *Citizen Kane*. With Toland unavailable, Welles instructed Richard Wilson, his chief production assistant, to find someone with a strong individual style who was also very fast (like Toland). In the course of screening samples of the work of more than thirty cinematographers, Wilson came across *Badlands of Dakota*, a 1941 B western directed by Alfred E. Green and shot by Cortez with considerable visual flair. On the basis of seeing just the first two reels of this film, Welles decided on Cortez.

Cortez shot *The Magnificent Ambersons* with a standard Mitchell camera, a 30mm lens usually set at f-stop 4.2 (sometimes 4.0 or 4.5), and plus-X film stock. He achieved depth by means of split focus (setting the focus plane between the foreground subject and the background) and, in the dark scenes, by means of lighting contrast, often using cross lighting for greater effect. (Interview with assistant cameraman Howard Schwartz, October 26, 1987; Cortez's own accounts are inconsistent and unreliable.) The result was a much softer look than in *Citizen Kane*, where Toland had used a self-blimping Mitchell BNC, a 24mm lens with the aperture narrowed ("stopped down") to f-stop 8 and sometimes all the way to f-stop 11 or even 16, Super-XX film stock, and strong frontal lighting.

Acutely conscious of the tremendous career opportunity *The Magnificent Ambersons* represented, Cortez worked very meticulously, which went against Welles's need for great speed. Antagonisms festered, and toward the end Welles had Cortez unofficially replaced. See footnote 91.

[113] The rescoring and rerecording were carried out without Herrmann's knowledge. When he heard the results, he threatened legal action if his name was not removed from the film. Only 30 minutes of Herrmann's original score of 56 minutes remain intact in *RV*, and 6 minutes, 45 seconds composed by Webb are added. I am grateful to Christopher Husted of the Bernard Herrmann Archive at the University of California, Santa Barbara, for detailed information on the original score and the rescoring and rerecording. For a thematic analysis of Herrmann's score, see Kathryn Kalinak, "The Text of Music: A Study of *The Magnificent Ambersons*," *Cinema Journal* 27, no. 4 (Summer 1988), 45–63.

MCU of chair and set dressing -

NARRATOR'S VOICE

. . . dressed them. Robert Wise . . .

LAP DISSOLVE

CU of film going around rewind -

LAP DISSOLVE

NARRATOR'S VOICE

. . . was the film editor. Freddie Fleck . . .

CU pages of *Magnificent Ambersons* shooting script turning -

NARRATOR'S VOICE

. . . was the assistant director. Edward Stevenson . . .

LAP DISSOLVE

CU of dress material -

NARRATOR'S VOICE

. . . designed the ladies' wardrobe. The special effects were . . .

LAP DISSOLVE

CU of optical printer -

NARRATOR'S VOICE

. . . by Vernon L. Walker. The sound recording was . . .

LAP DISSOLVE

CU of hands working recording machine dials -

NARRATOR'S VOICE

. . . by Bailey Fesler and James G. Stewart. Here's the cast:

FADE OUT

FADE IN CU of Eugene - Music heard -   **32** (81-6)

NARRATOR'S VOICE

Eugene . . . Joseph Cotten.

LAP DISSOLVE

CU of Isabel -

NARRATOR'S VOICE

Isabel . . . Dolores Costello.

LAP DISSOLVE

CU of Lucy -

NARRATOR'S VOICE

Lucy . . . Anne Baxter.

LAP DISSOLVE

CU of George -

NARRATOR'S VOICE

George . . . Tim Holt.

LAP DISSOLVE

CU of Fanny -

NARRATOR'S VOICE

Fanny . . . Agnes Moorehead.

LAP DISSOLVE

CU of Jack -

NARRATOR'S VOICE

Jack . . . Ray Collins.

LAP DISSOLVE

CU of Bronson -

NARRATOR'S VOICE

Roger Bronson . . . Erskine Sanford.

LAP DISSOLVE

CU of Major -

NARRATOR'S VOICE

Major Amberson . . . Richard Bennett.

LAP DISSOLVE

INT SET ECU - Microphone before camera - Light shining in background from skylight -

NARRATOR'S VOICE

I wrote the script and directed it...My name is Orson Welles...This is a Mercury Production.

Microphone swings up to background toward skylight - Music rises to crescendo -

LAP DISSOLVE

TITLE #1 -

IATSE

APPROVED
MPPDA
CERTIFICATE
NO. 7800

RKO
RADIO
PICTURES
REG. U.S. PAT. OFF.

RCA
SOUND SYSTEM

COPYRIGHT MCMXLII RKO RADIO PICTURES, INC.
ALL RIGHTS RESERVED

The characters and events depicted in this photoplay are fictional. Any similarity to actual persons, living or dead, is purely coincidental.

FADE OUT

5

EDITING *AMBERSONS*:
A DOCUMENTARY HISTORY

The long ordeal of editing and reediting *The Magnificent Ambersons* can be said to have begun on January 22, 1942, the day principal photography on the picture officially closed, and it ended on June 8, the day on which RKO President George Schaefer approved a final cut and declared the picture ready for release. It was a bewilderingly complicated process involving several key players thousands of miles away from one another attempting to communicate intricate and sometimes sensitive details via such unreliable media as shortwave radio and international telephone hookup, in circumstances made even more difficult by a world war. That a significant number of their communications have survived—enough at least to provide a reasonably clear view of the course of events as they unfolded—is truly remarkable. These documents can be found in two principal collections: the RKO Radio Pictures archive (henceforth RKO) now housed in the Theater Arts Library at UCLA, and the Orson Welles manuscript collection at Lilly Library, Bloomington, Indiana (hereafter Lilly). The most important of these documents are reprinted here, with a running contextual commentary and, in matters bearing directly on the nature of the film's editing, numerical indicators (in brackets) of the location of the pertinent contents in the cutting continuity.

Midway through shooting on *The Magnificent Ambersons,* Welles entered into an agreement to undertake a major filming project in South America early the following year. By the time shooting on *The Magnificent Ambersons* closed, Welles was almost entirely occupied with preparations for South America and with fulfilling other commitments in advance of his departure. Over the following two weeks, Robert Wise, the film's editor, assembled a rough cut of *Ambersons* (without music, special effects, and certain scenes), which he took to Miami to screen for Welles as he was passing through on his way to South America. They spent February 5, 1942, together at the Fleischer Studios in Miami, recording Welles's voiceover narration and working out his plan for the final cut. At this point there was at least a month's postproduction work yet to be done. Welles left it in Wise's hands and issued a directive clarifying Wise's role:

Because of the enormous amount of work Bob Wise has to do on *Ambersons*, because of the necessity of speed and of some central authority, I would like you to make clear to all department heads that his is the final word. He is to have a free hand in ordering prints, dissolves, further work from [special effects head] Verne Walker, and anything else of a similar nature. It boils down to this: I want to know that he won't be slowed up at any point because his authority is questioned. I dictate this at the airport just before departing. Orson

(Telegram, Welles to Moss, February 6, 1942, RKO)

The instructions were to be relayed by Jack Moss, business manager for the Mercury Theatre, who had been left behind at the studio as coordinator of Mercury operations and general overseer of Welles's interests. Moss, who lacked experience in film production or supervision, had inherited the role more or less by default because all the Mercury production talent was either in South America or had dispersed on pursuits of their own. Moss was never comfortable in this role nor was he taken seriously by the studio. On *The Magnificent Ambersons* Moss and Wise were to work together as a team, with Wise as supervisor of postproduction and Moss as surrogate producer. So there would be no confusion, Welles stated exactly what he expected of Moss:

Please start running *Ambersons* nightly and taking active production charge. Get in Norman [Foster], Jo [Cotten], Dolores [Costello] for jury as many times as possible. Every opinion must be covered by an alternate. Stop. You have been away from *Ambersons* long enough to be fresh and you know I trust you completely.

(Telegram, Welles to Moss, February 28, 1942, Lilly)

Moss and Wise were in steady communication with Welles almost from the time he arrived in Rio. Wise was sending new or redone footage of individual scenes as soon as they were ready, and Welles's elaborately detailed comments soon began flowing back by cable. Moss spoke with him by telephone or shortwave radio or exchanged cables almost daily concerning *The Magnificent Ambersons, Journey Into Fear* (on which he was keeping watch), and matters involving the South American project.

Welles's intention was for Wise to bring the completed film to him in Rio for a final check. He instructed Wise to prepare and bring along alternate shots, dissolves, and sounds wherever possible, plus a spare music track, to give him the widest possible latitude in making changes. Schaefer himself approved Wise's travel, but Wise's application to leave the country was denied at the last minute because of wartime restrictions. Welles partisans have always maintained that the studio defaulted on its promise. It is difficult to see how the government could have denied the request if it had been argued forcefully, especially since Welles had agreed to undertake the South American project at the request of the State Department in the first place. On the other hand, RKO did have a reason for being lukewarm in the matter. Schaefer was desperate to have *The Magnificent Ambersons* ready for a wide release during Easter week (one of the best times of the year for the box office) in order to maximize recoupment on the studio's $1,000,000 investment, and there was undoubtedly concern that sending Wise in those uncertain times and with Welles's uncertain ways could result in a delay that would jeopardize the plan. In any case, whether Wise's actual presence at a fine-tuning of the picture would have made a crucial difference to the final outcome is another question.

The print and additional footage were shipped on March 11 and arrived in Rio on March 15. Meanwhile, the studio went ahead with preview arrangements, a customary practice. The first preview was held at the Fox Theatre in Pomona on Tuesday, March 17. The regular feature that evening was *The Fleet's In*, a rousing wartime musical starring Dorothy Lamour and William Holden. Next day, Welles prodded Schaefer for news:

> . . . Eager hear reactions *Ambersons* preview.
>
> (Telegram, Welles to Schaefer, March 18, 1942, RKO)

The first response came not from Schaefer but from Moss:

> [Pomona preview] unsatisfactory general comment too long but despite impatience they were over and over again held by drama previewing again tonight Pasadena different type audience we will phone you tomorrow full report both previews.
>
> (Telegram, Moss to Welles, March 19, 1942, Lilly)

Moss was characteristically upbeat. The Pomona preview had been a disaster. Schaefer was so unsettled by it that he immediately began to think the unthinkable. He asked his legal experts if it would be possible to take the picture out of Welles's hands. Ross Hastings, RKO Legal Counsel, responded:

> You asked me concerning our rights in connection with the cutting of The Magnificent Ambersons.
>
> Orson Welles has the right to make the first rough cut of the picture or to cut the picture in the form of the first sneak preview if it is to be previewed. Thereafter he agrees to cut the picture as directed by us.
>
> I am not really informed as to the facts, but I know that the picture has been previewed, and assume that this preview was in the form in which he cut the picture, or at least in the form as to which he controlled the cutting. In view of the fact that from this point on he is obligated to cut as directed by us, and in view of the further fact that he is now not available for cutting, it is my opinion that we have the right to cut the picture.
>
> (Hastings to Schaefer, March 19, 1942, RKO)

Under his original RKO contract, Welles had the unprecedented right of final cut—that is, a provision that his films could only be released in a form determined by him. However, *The Magnificent Ambersons* was covered by a later, compromise contract lacking this guarantee and circumscribing his rights in the manner indicated. The legend persists that RKO took advantage of Welles by breaking his contract when he was out of the country and not in a position to defend himself. However much one may deplore the action, when RKO recut *The Magnificent Ambersons* it was acting within its contractual rights. The second preview was held at the United Artists Theatre in Pasadena on Thursday, March 19. The evening's regular feature was *Captains of the Clouds*, a wartime adventure starring James Cagney. The next day, Schaefer finally wrote a typewritten letter sent via air mail special delivery and marked "Personal-Confidential." Richard Wilson, who was with Welles when it arrived, always remembered his utter devastation and the deep gloom into which he sank:

Dear Orson:

I did not want to cable you with respect to The Magnificent Ambersons as indicated in your cable of the 18th, only because I wanted to write you under confidential cover.

Of course, when you ask me for my reaction, I know you want it straight, and though it is difficult to write you this way, you should hear from me.

Never in all my experience in the industry have I taken so much punishment or suffered as I did at the Pomona preview. In my 28 years in the business, I have never been present in a theatre where the audience acted in such a manner. They laughed at the wrong places, talked at the picture, kidded it, and did everything that you can possibly imagine.

I don't have to tell you how I suffered, especially in the realization that we have over $1,000,000 tied up. It was just like getting one sock in the jaw after another for over two hours.

The picture was too slow, heavy, and topped off with somber music, never did register. It all started off well, but just went to pieces.

I am sending you copies of all the preview cards received to date. They speak for themselves and do not tell the whole story because only a small percentage of people make out cards. I queried many of those present and they all seemed to feel that the party who made the picture was trying to be "arty," was out for camera angles, lights and shadows, and as a matter of fact, one remarked that "The man who made that picture was camera crazy." Mind you, these are not my opinions—I am giving them to you just as I received them.

The punishment was not sufficient, and as I believed in the picture more than the people did, I hiked myself to Pasadena again last night, feeling sure that we would get a better reaction. We did, but not, of course, in its entirety. There were many spots where we got the same reaction as we did in Pomona. I think cutting will help considerably, but there is no doubt in my mind but what the people at Pasadena also thought it was slow and heavy. The somber musical score does not help.

While, of course, the reaction at Pasadena was better than Pomona, we still have a problem. In Pomona we played to the younger element. It is the younger element who contribute the biggest part of the revenue. If you cannot satisfy that group, you just cannot bail yourself out with a $1,000,000 investment—all of which, Orson, is very disturbing to say the least.

In all our initial discussions, you stressed low costs, making pictures at $300,000 to $500,000, and on our first two pictures, we have an investment of $2,000,000. We will not make a dollar on Citizen Kane and present indications are that we will not break even. The final results on Ambersons is still to be told, but it looks "red."

All of which again reminds me of only one thing—that we must have a "heart to heart" talk. Orson Welles has got to do something commercial. We have got to get away from "arty" pictures and get back to earth. Educating the public is expensive, and your next picture must be made for the box-office.

God knows you have all the talent and ability for writing, producing, directing—everything in Citizen Kane and Ambersons confirms that. We should apply all that talent and effort in the right direction and make a picture on which "we can get well."

That's the story, Orson, and I feel very miserable to have to write you this.

My very best as always.

(Schaefer to Welles, March 21 [sic], 1942, RKO)

On Monday Moss sent a voluminous wire containing a precise outline of the film's contents at each of the previews, a warning about what was brewing behind the scenes, and a compromise proposal for reediting the film worked out in committee. Moss's wire is so intimidatingly detailed it will be presented in separate components. (Telegram, Moss to Welles, March 23, 1942, Lilly)

Pomona Preview

Dear Orson as cabled Pomona preview generally unsatisfactory Stop Pasadena preview better reception Stop Following is way picture was previewed Pomona Stop Continuity as picture was shot to end of carriage scene Jack and Major Stop Fade out here drop porch scene fade in on Eugene Isabel at tree Stop Continuity follows as shot up to new scene George finds Isabel unconscious Stop Made your big cut and come to group in hall exterior Isabel's room Stop Continuity again as shot up to Indian legend dropped this and accident Stop Fade in on accident insert continue to end as shot

In the absence of evidence to the contrary, it has been assumed that the film was previewed in Pomona in the form corresponding to the cutting continuity of March 12.

Studio documents seem to corroborate this. For instance, the footage count entered on the preview comments report is exactly the same as on the cutting continuity: 11,858. But this may mean no more than that the transcriber picked up the footage tally from another document. The reported footage calculates as a running time of over 131 minutes, which correlates with Schaefer's reference to taking punishment for over two hours. But Schaefer may have calculated a running time in his head from the footage count on his preview notice rather than doing an actual timing. For someone like Schaefer who attended hundreds of previews, thinking in that way would have become second nature. Besides, the extreme hostility of the preview reaction would have made the experience seem longer than it was. On the other hand, some of the major departures indicated in Moss's wire do have solid foundation in studio records.

Out, according to Moss, was the so-called "first porch scene" with Isabel, Fanny, and George (cutting continuity, reel 3B, after lap dissolve in shot 3 through shot 7, approximately 5 minutes 30 seconds). The "new scene" Moss refers to in which "George finds Isabel unconscious" is in neither the cutting continuity nor the release version. Identification of it is found in a daily production report of March 10 indicating that Wise shot an "added scene" of George and Isabel in her bedroom. This could only have been done at Welles's instruction, probably by telephone since no written record has been found, and is confirmation that he was making major changes before he received Wise's new version. This new scene served as the bridge over the "big cut" Welles ordered—the elimination of all footage between Isabel's receiving Eugene's letter and the family gathered in the hallway outside her room just before her death. This includes: the scenes of George and Isabel discussing Eugene's letter, Isabel's letter telling George she will renounce Eugene slipped under George's door, George's walk with Lucy on the street, the drugstore and poolroom, the "second porch scene" with Fanny and the Major, Jack's visit to the Morgans, and Isabel's return (reel 5A shot 4 through reel 5B to second lap dissolve in shot 7, approximately 13 minutes 40 seconds). With the new scene and big cut, the sequence of events is as follows: Isabel receives Eugene's letter, falls unconscious, and dies shortly after. (For confirmation of this interpretation of the big cut, see Welles's cable of March 27 below.) Since the new scene was shot too late to be included in the shipment of March 11, Welles could not have seen the film in this version before the preview. Also out were Eugene and Lucy's walk in their garden discussing an "Indian Legend" and the automobile accident (reel 7A shot 2, approximately 3 minutes 30 seconds). Both of these, as well as the "first porch scene," were in the March 11 print and apparently ordered cut by Welles after he had screened it in Rio.

Altogether, the changes amount to a loss of approximately 22 minutes, making the running time at Pomona around 110 minutes. The "big cut" is nothing less than startling. Another surprise is the elimination of the "Indian Legend," a scene of exquisite beauty. It is open to question whether the shortened version screened at Pomona was superior to the original.

Pasadena Preview

and following is way picture was previewed at Pasadena Stop First cut factory scene second cut first porch scene third cut bathroom Jack and George scene Stop Continuity again as shot put back all film your big cut except Major Fanny in second porch scene Stop Continuity as shot to end railroad Jack goodbye scene followed by Fanny's boiler scene Bronson's office George's walk home Indian legend accident lap out accident omitting quote riffraff unquote Stop Lap from newspapers to Eugene exiting hospital to process shot Eugene says quote take me to Miss Minafers unquote to boarding house Stop Boarding house cut down Stop Put line quote that's end of story unquote under fade out matte shot street Stop

Moss and Wise quickly recut the film for Pasadena. They restored Welles's "big cut," the "Indian Legend," and the automobile accident, and put into effect an alternate plan they had devised in early March with the intention of having Wise present it to Welles in Rio.

This involved: (1) Eliminating four scenes outright: the visit to the Morgan automobile factory (reel 3A shots 19 and 20, approximately 2 minutes); the first porch scene with Isabel, Fanny, and George (reel 3B, after lap dissolve in shot 3 through shot 7, approximately 5 minutes 30 seconds); the bathroom scene with Jack and George (reel 4A shots 28 through 47, about a minute and a half); and the second porch scene with Fanny and the Major (reel 5B shot 3, slightly over three minutes). (Omission of the factory scene is difficult to fathom, since it is as brilliantly choreographed as anything in the film. Despite Ray Collins's superb performance, the bathroom scene was probably a negative overall because of the magnitude of George's overreaction; in the release version the scene is in, but much of George's dialogue has been cut. Both porch scenes involved long, single-take conversations that apparently pleased no one. Neither scene was ever shown to a theater audience.)

It also involved: (2) Moving George's last walk home and kneeling at his mother's bed (reel 6B, shots 2 and 3) from after the parting with Jack at the train station to later, resulting in this order of events: the parting at the train station, Fanny at the unheated boiler, George in Bronson's office, the last walk home, the Indian legend, the automobile accident. (In this position the scene of George's "comeuppance" became the culmination of the decline in the Ambersons' fortunes rather than just an episode along the way.)

They now made other minor changes. When George was lying in the street with both legs broken, one policeman heard him utter his familiar epithet "riffraff" (reel 7A, just above shot 3); this was removed, since it suggested that George hadn't repented at all. Eugene learned of George's accident in his office and was shown being driven to the hospital (reel 7B shots 1 to 3); since no hospital scene ensued, this was deemed superfluous and a single shot was substituted of Eugene asking to be taken to Fanny's boardinghouse. The boardinghouse sequence with which the film ended (reel 7B shots 5 to 29), an extended conversation almost 6 minutes long, was trimmed; eventually it would be replaced altogether by the brief scene of Eugene and Fanny in the hospital corridor.

The Moss-Wise changes amounted to a reduction of approximately 15 minutes, making the running time at Pasadena around 117 minutes, 7 minutes longer than at Pomona. Their single most important change was to restore all of Welles's audacious "big cut." While audience composition partly explains the difference in preview results between Pomona and Pasadena, story content cannot be entirely discounted: the two audiences saw very different versions of the film.

Compromise Plan

> Schaefer and his associates advocate many drastic cuts mainly for purposes of shortening length Stop Bob Wise Joe Cotten and myself have conferred analyzing audience reactions exercising our best judgment and we believe the following suggested continuity would remove slow spots and bring out heart qualities of picture Stop The suggestions follow

In all but a few essential respects, the film as it was eventually released corresponds to the following plan. (Material within brackets indicates whether or how the recommendation was eventually acted on.)

> switch continuity opening reel from quote less time we have to spare unquote cut to quote during earlier years this period unquote play down to quote without sense of sin unquote cut back to quote in those days had time for everything unquote play through Gene falling on bass viol lap to quote magnificence of Ambersons conspicuous as brassband unquote cut from quote stationary washstands unquote speech to Gene at door Stop Reason for foregoing to keep fall through bass viol and Eugene turned away closer together Stop [changes adopted; see notes to reel 1A, shots 4 through 13] Cut last two speeches sewing circle Stop [reel 1A shot 36, change not adopted] Continuity through to George on horsecart after quote George returned same stuffing unquote lap to nite snow shot quote when he returned for holidays unquote losing FOTA club Stop [changes adopted; see reel 1A shot 65 to reel 1B shot 7] Continuity through to end quote family likes to have someone in Congress unquote [reel 1B shots 7 to 16] then lap to all boys saying quote hello unquote to Lucy play through to point George on stairs with Lucy says quote having fine time will you excuse us unquote lap to group walking in to punch bowl Major says quote eggnog anybody unquote play through to end of quote thanks for letting my name be Lucy unquote cut from this to Gene saying quote goodbye Ive got this dance with her unquote Stop [cuts in ballroom sequence adopted; see notes to reel 1B shot 16 through reel 2A shot 1] Continuity continues fade out hall scene fade in snow sequence drop stable Stop [change adopted; stable scene, reel 2B shot 12 after lap dissolve to shot 13, dropped] Snow sequence plays through to closeup Lucy singing after George says quote how about that kiss unquote from her closeup cut to longshot iris out Stop [partly adopted; reel 2B shots 72 to 82 dropped] After tombstone [departure from recommendation; shot of tombstone, reel 3A shot 3 replaced with action shot] go to factory drop diploma [change adopted; diploma, reel 3A shot 4, dropped] and kitchen scene [major departure from recommendation; kitchen scene to Fanny's tearful exit retained, reel 3A shot 4 after lap dissolve; only end of kitchen scene and excavations outside dropped, reel 3A near end of shot 4 through shot 18] Stop From

interior factory lap to Gene and Isabel at tree [change adopted; reel 4A shot 1 and shot 2 to first lap dissolve moved to beginning of reel 3B] from this lap to George Lucy on cart [reel 3B shots 1 and 2] Stop Fade out on this drop Major Jack in carriage [departure from recommendation; carriage, reel 3B shot 3, retained; however, first porch scene, continuation of reel 3B shot 3, not specifically mentioned here, dropped] fade in dining room Stop Continuity again as shot [reel 4A shot 2 after lap dissolve through shot 27] drop bathroom [major departure from recommendation; bathroom scene retained, though much of George's dialogue omitted, reel 4A shots 28 through 47] cut from George coming in with packages to Gene arriving [change adopted; George's business with father's picture, reel 4B shots 1 and 2, dropped] play through to fade out Fanny on stairs [reel 4B shots 3 through 20] Stop Play first part Eugene's letter over extreme high up long shot interior Amberson mansion Stop Slight reverberation on his voice no music lap to Isabel seated music starts play through to quote this time I've not deserved it unquote [change adopted with one alteration; new shot of Eugene seated at desk begins letter scene, then cut to high angle shot inside mansion, reel 5A shot 1] cut to George in hall on door slam Stop Shoot new scene with George and Isabel her bedroom [change adopted; reshot by Wise, see reel 5A shots 4 through 21] lap to letter under door much shorter make new track Isabel's letter to play over George [major departure from recommendation; second letter scene, reel 5A shots 21 and 22, dropped] Stop Later two as outlined in Wise's letter [reference unknown] Stop Play through street scene and drugstore [reel 5A shot 22 after lap dissolve through reel 5B shot 1] drop poolroom [change adopted; poolroom, reel 5B shot 2, dropped] drop Major and Fanny on porch [change adopted; second porch scene, reel 5B shot 3, dropped] fade in exterior Morgan mansion and play through Stop Fade out sooner interior of mansion play through exterior railroad station lap sooner to carriage [reel 5B shot 4 to shot 7 second lap dissolve] drop hallway shot exterior Isabel's room [change adopted; hallway scene, reel 5B shot 7 after second lap dissolve, dropped] Stop Shoot new scene in which Eugene first time asserts self when George attempts stop him going upstairs to see Isabel then Fanny pleads with Eugene not to go up to come back later [change adopted; new scene shot by Fleck, see reel 6A shots 1 and 2] and in meantime Isabel dies Stop Lap from Isabel's deathbed scene to Major on bed play through [reel 6A shots 3 to 7] Stop Cut headlight talk Major's fireside scene [change adopted; see reel 6A shot 8] fade in railroad station on line quote well this is an odd way for us to be saying goodbye unquote [change adopted; first part of railroad station scene cut, see reel 6B shot 1] follow with Fanny's boiler scene [change adopted; major restructuring in latter third of film, see reel 6B end of shot 1] Stop Shoot new scene Bronson's office stressing George's distress and need of more than eight dollars week [departure from recommendation; Bronson scene, reel 7A shot 1 after lap dissolve, not reshot] Stop In walk home cut from quote darkened its sky unquote to quote this was the last walk home unquote [change adopted; cut made in reel 6B shot 2] after quote big old house at end of Amberson Boulevard unquote cut to quote tomorrow everything would be gone unquote [change adopted; cut made in reel 6B shot 2] this over shot of mansion [departure from recommendation; shot of mansion, reel 6B shot 2, dropped] Stop Then lap dissolve to longshot George at bed long pause then quote Mother forgive me God forgive me unquote [changes adopted; shot shortened, George's lines moved to head of scene, new narration inserted, see reel 6B shot 3] Stop Play on through to end as in Pasadena preview [major departures from recommendation: Indian legend, reel 7A shot 2, moved to before boiler scene, see reel 6B shots 1 to 2; more radical changes in ending in release version than in Pasadena version—Eugene and Lucy receiving news of George's accident together replaces Eugene alone, reel 7B shots 1 to 3; scene in hospital corridor replaces boardinghouse sequence, reel 7B shots 4 to 30] Stop Please cable or phone your decisions and instructions love from all.

To reiterate, there were only five major departures from this set of recommendations in the release version of the film: the kitchen and bathroom scenes stayed in; the scene of Isabel's letter to George was taken out; the Indian legend remained in but was moved from near the end and placed between Jack's departure and Fanny at the boiler; and the ending was completely reshot. Although it may be true, as Wise has always asserted, that he recut the picture strictly on his own, clearly his model was this early compromise plan put forward jointly by Wise, Cotten, and Moss.

Welles immediately rejected the compromise plan out of hand and once again asked for Wise:

> My advice absolutely useless without Bob [Wise] here. Sure I must be at least partly wrong, but cannot see remotest sense in any single suggested cut of yours, Bob's, Jo's Stop. Realize I haven't seen completed film in audience reaction but cannot even begin discussing on proposals as received without doing actual work on actual film with Bob here.

> (Telegram, Welles to Moss, March 25, 1942, Lilly)

If the studio had originally been lukewarm about sending Wise, one can imagine how a revival of the plan would have been met in these circumstances. Once again, however, Moss was unrealistically upbeat:

> Every effort being made secure immediate passage for Bob Stop We all agree your decisions Ambersons dependent upon actual work with actual film Stop.

> (Telegram, Moss to Welles, March 25, 1942, Lilly)

Either Welles was told directly that sending Wise was out of the question or he had learned by now to read between the lines of Moss's communications, since he now began to prepare his own detailed plan for recutting the film. The following communication represents Welles's most sustained effort to reassert control over the production. It picks up at the end of the ballroom sequence; instructions concerning the earlier material would come later. As will be noted, he has begun to come around on some of the Wise-Moss-Cotten recommendations. Wise has often spoken with exasperation of receiving thirty-page cables from Welles containing detailed cutting instructions. This is surely one of the ones he had in mind. Although it has been transcribed by the studio in a format resembling a shooting script, the original document would easily have extended to that length. Because of the density of detail, it will be treated part by part as with the Moss wire. (Telegram, Welles to Moss, March 27, 1942, RKO)

Reel 2

This is preliminary list Amberson cuts details follow tomorrow morning.

After -

FULL SHOT - Ballroom following "A Yachtsman" instead of dissolve to Joe and Dolores waltzing half fade out half dissolve to stable scene same timing going out of ballroom as before same timing coming into stable as before.

Also -

Try starting scene same line on Wilbur CLOSE SHOT Tim walking in.

Also -

On same line try FADING IN as door opens throwing light on Tim, Dolores - they looking camera left at end of WALKING SHOT in half.

I will say this again for clarity color -

Joe blows out light on black screen.

FADE IN second floor mansion on Tim's line "Look here, Father, about this man Morgan" and so on through remainder of scene fading out same timing as present dissolve as Tim walks up half laughing after Jack goes back in room.

In other words -

This eliminates full late night sequence on first floor also exterior mansion automobile TWO SHOT and Tim, Dolores walk along dark hall from stairway to Wilbur's room. This cuts nothing which promotes story or reveals character where not otherwise revealed.

FADE IN - REFLECTION SHOT same timing as before. Cut next two shots.

Go -

From REFLECTION to SCENE SIXTEEN camera under auto

Then -

Continue Snow Sequence as before, finishing as before except instead irising down and out half fade out half dissolve to next scene.

Welles proposes to go directly from the lap dissolve in reel 2A shot 1 to the scene of Eugene and Lucy putting the car away after they arrive home ("stable scene," reel 2B, after lap dissolve in shot 12). He would then go back and pick up the scene on the bedroom hallway of the Amberson mansion at reel 2B shot 2 and play it through to the end (lap dissolve in shot 12). The material eliminated would run from the end of reel

2A shot 1 through reel 2B shot 1 (slightly over 4 minutes) and the resulting continuity would be: end of ball—Lucy in stable asking her father about George—George at home asking the others about Eugene. There is a logical symmetry to this scheme, but it is astonishing that Welles would propose deleting Isabel and Eugene dancing alone after the ball is over, what many regard as the single most beautiful shot in the film. In the snow scene, he would cut two brief establishing shots at the beginning (reel 2B shots 14 and 15) and—another great surprise—the iris out at the end.

Reels 3 and 4

Next scene is SCENE ONE - Reel Three Auto coming towards us smoke music on to George, Lucy in buggy as before.

Play through -

George-Lucy scene to Major Jack trimming last few frames on crane shot so Major's buggy does not start out of frame before we cut in side.

Suggest trying very fast lap to -

Interior Major's Buggy. Play through Major Jack scene which is vital to picture. Fade out end of scene to -

FADE IN beginning Funeral Scene door of mansion with crepe. Or if music works well for it make transition half fade out half dissolve. Placing funeral here makes it less arbitrary gives it slight angle. Another advantage is beautiful time transition from horseless carriage in snow early automobile on street. From end of funeral FULL SHOT try going to -

"Wilbur Minafer—Quiet man—Town will hardly know he's gone."

Remake this TWO SHOT against back of flowers to match interior library. Phone me to get correct reading for line.

Following suggestion experimental:

Try going from TWO SHOT of citizens to choker of Fanny then half fade out half dissolve from Fanny's face to night MATTE SHOT mansion rain then -

DISSOLVE into kitchen - starting kitchen scene as before. Also try alternate start of kitchen scene on Fanny's line -

"So Eugene came to the station to meet you."

In any event diploma insert and music definite cut.

Also definite cut fadeout kitchen scene Jack's line -

"I really don't know of anything much Fanny has got except her feeling about Eugene."

FADEOUT just before Tim reacts to houses outside. Fadeout is half fade out half dissolve.

Goes -

From here to First Porch Sequence - SCENE THREE, Reel three. Cut establishing shot. Come in on porch scene to carry maximum possible pause before Fanny's line -

"Are you laughing about something."

Play Porch Scene through Fanny's exit -

"The very anniversary of Wilbur's death."

and -

CLOSEUP of Tim leaning against railing starting off. Before full SHOT including Lucy's vision

DISSOLVE TO

The changes in this section are more radical. Welles would completely rearrange the order of events, playing George and Lucy's buggy ride and the Major and Jack's carriage ride (reel 3B shots 1 to 3 to lap dissolve) before Wilbur's funeral (reel 3A shots 1 to 3). In addition to the advantages Welles indicates, this would get on more directly with the development of George and Lucy's relationship and permit an earlier introduction of the fact that the Ambersons' fortunes are declining with the changes in the town. The shots of a tombstone and George's diploma would be removed (reel 3A shot 3 after lap dissolve and shot 4); instead, a chorus of townspeople would pronounce Wilbur's epitaph, and Fanny's new line would signal the move forward in time. The kitchen scene (reel 3A shot 4) would continue as shot up to Jack's summary line about Fanny, but the balance of this shot and the following sequence involving George and Jack discovering the foundations for houses on the lawn of the Amberson mansion would be eliminated (reel 3A end of shot 4 through shot 18, around one minute). The factory sequence would also be eliminated (reel 3A shots 19 and 20, around two minutes), but the first porch scene (not included in either preview version) would be included except for the vision of Lucy (a genuine curiosity) and the ending (another "riffraff" from George), reel 3B after lap dissolve in shot 3 through shot 4.

Reel 4

Day Sequence SCENE ONE - Reel four, Exterior Mansion Eugene and Isabel - then play through to end of Jack George bathroom scene as in present version making only following short cut color scene thirty-seven, Reel four cut George's line beginning -

"Then it would be monstrous in the face of all this."

In other words cut from -

"What's the matter with their marrying"

to-

"Oh, that you can sit there and speak of it."

FADE OUT

slamming door timing as in present version.

FADE IN - SCENE THREE, Reel four - Exterior Eugene entering in car. This cuts George's entrance in parlor unwrapping picture sitting down before window.

Tone down big up in music over vestibule setup otherwise continuing unchanged through Fanny's line -

"Let her alone."

FADE OUT

end Reel four.

Reel 4A (Eugene and Isabel discussing whether they should tell George, dinner for Eugene and its aftermath, confrontation with Mrs. Johnson, bathroom scene with George and Jack) would play as shot except for the single line deletion in shot 37. The opening of reel 4B showing George unwrapping his father's picture at the fireplace mirror would be deleted (shots 1 and 2, just under a minute), but the rest of the reel— George turning Eugene away, Isabel waiting, Jack arriving with the bad news, Fanny and George on the stairs—would be played according to the plan.

Reel 5

Very slow FADE IN following new scene Interior Eugene's house desk near window late afternoon - backlight TIGHT SHOT Joe writing almost in silhouette sound of pen as he signs name then puts down pen - look back to top of page - as he reads to himself, his lips not moving - his voice reading letter heard on track with music as in present letter sequence. New text of letter as follows -

SOUND

"Yesterday I thought the time had come when I could ask you to marry me, and you were dear enough to tell me sometime it might come to that. But now we come to this dear—Will you live your own life your way or George's way?——Oh, Dearest woman in the world, I know what your son is to you and it frightens me. Dear, it breaks my heart for you but what you have to oppose now is the history of your own selfless and perfect motherhood. Are you strong enough, Isabel? Can you make the fight?"

Now CUT or QUICK DISSOLVE to Isabel seated as she looks up from letter then rises. Here is added line for Eugene's narration for this place -

"I know you aren't quite well dear — But...."

Then go on with letter -

"I promise you that if you will take heart for it ....."

and so on through -

DISSOLVE TO

George. Then play through George entering Isabel's room, including new scene where he finds her unconscious which should be terrific if camera in close enough and moving with him as he drops to feel—takes her in his arms for fade out. Again emphasize tremendous importance this shot be beautifully done—music very strong.

FADE OUT

FADE IN on Interior Hall - REEL FIVE - Family waiting outside Isabel's room. Play through until just before Fanny's entrance.

Reel 5 involves Welles's most drastic and controversial changes. The opening is to be reshot so that instead of the camera being on Isabel throughout the voiceover reading of Eugene's letter, he is to be seen first finishing it and looking it over as the reading begins; a new, shorter text is supplied (shot 1). Welles is still insisting that the rest be played as at the Pomona preview—George crosses to Isabel's room (shot 3), finds her unconscious (the "new scene"), and next the family is gathered in the hallway outside her room just before her death (reel 5B after second lap dissolve in shot 7). Once again, the "big cut" is being called for—the scenes of George and Isabel discussing Eugene's letter, Isabel's letter to George, George's walk with Lucy on the street, the drugstore and poolroom, the "second porch scene" with Fanny and the Major, Jack's visit to the Morgans, and Isabel's return (reel 5A shot 4 through reel 5B to second lap dissolve in shot 7, approximately 13 minutes 40 seconds). Additionally, the last few feet of reel 5B, in which George tells Fanny that Eugene cannot see Isabel, are to be eliminated by the following means:

Reel 6

Then -

CUT or QUICK DISSOLVE to SCENE ONE - REEL SIX - Silhouette of Eugene waiting downstairs. If possible repeat frames before Fanny's entrance to lengthen pause. This cuts scene between Fanny and George about whether Eugene should be allowed to see Isabel.

Play through from Fanny Eugene Scene to and including Major's death scene with these dialogue changes in offstage voices over Major's face: Jack's speech should read -

"I am only glad you didn't put as much money in it as I did."

Instead of -

"Go into the confounded thing to the extent I did."

Jack's next line should read -

"Our headlight just won't work, Fanny. We should have taken Gene's advice."

Instead of -

"It certainly was a perfect thing in the shop. Well, our headlight just won't work, Fanny."

George's off stage lines to grandfather -

"Did you want anything?"

And -

"Would you like a glass of water?"

Spoken too sharply and pronounced too carefully. Effect unpleasant. Remake.

Also -

Off stage voices this sequence all slightly too high.

I will repeat for clarity:

Entire Isabel death sequence stands as in present version. Dialogue between George and Fanny only cut between fade in Hall Scene and fade out Major's death.

All Cemetery Scenes cut so use footage allowed for in music to hold over on flickering low key image Major's face screen going black just as death music finishes.

Narration here also throughout entire picture slightly too low consonants and sibilants too sharp. This must be filtered out also music sometimes fights me.

Following Major's Death scene FADE IN Railway Scene as present version only conductor must be calling trains over dark screen continuing as we fade in and on through till first finish of effect as already laid in track. General station sounds should be slightly higher at very start of scene. Railway Scene uncut. FADE OUT at end.

Except for the line changes and other minor adjustments, reel 6A (Eugene turned away a second time, Isabel's death, the Major's death) are to be played according to plan. The beginning of reel 6B (Jack's farewell at the train station) is also to be played according to plan. Originally, George's walk home was to be next in order, but Welles has now come over to the major restructuring of events previously advocated:

Reel 6 Revised

FADE IN Lucy Eugene Garden Scene. Play through but sneak out music under Lucy's line -

"Rides down everything."

Build in blank spots. Bird calls and rustle of breeze in trees. FADE OUT at end of scene same timing as present dissolve.

then QUICK FADE IN Kitchen Scene as Fanny falls to floor.

"You want to leave me in the lurch."

Same timing as present version. Play through Fanny George Scene and George Bronson Scene as in present version only addition this line for secretary.

"Mister Minafer."

As door opens on dissolve into office line this fading up with fade in. FADE OUT at end Bronson office.

FADE IN Walking Home Sequence. Image stays too long in clear on words -

NARRATOR

"It befouled itself and darkened its sky."

Flat side of building dull and meaningless. Also iron picket fence looks new. Should be very broken down, even nonexistent. Last image in this sequence should be sign reading -

INSERT

NEW HOPE APARTMENTS

Hold on this longer.

FADE OUT

Definitely cut MATTE SHOT front of mansion if necessary cut lines -

NARRATOR

"Tonight would be the last night that he and Fanny were to spend in the house which the Major had forgotten to deed to Isabel."

Narration reading -

"And the big old house at the foot of Amberson Boulevard — Tomorrow they were to move out and so on....."

Rest of sequence plays through as in present version.

After Narrator's lines -

"Faint cry over and over...."

Take longer pause before George's line -

"Mother, forgive me. God, forgive me."

On Narrator's lines -

"Came at last."

Music should have sneaked down and almost out returning to level of present version under words -

"Those who had so longed for it."

The revised order was to be as it appears in the release version: after Jack's and George's farewell at the train station, Eugene and Lucy in their garden (from reel 7A shot 2), Fanny at the boiler (from reel 7A shot 1 to lap dissolve), George in Bronson's office (from reel 7A shot 1 after lap dissolve), then George's walk home and plea for forgiveness (reel 6B shots 2 and 3).

Reel 7

FADE OUT as in present version slight pause then continue with narration sent you last week. Without music and on black screen play narration through to finish after last words of this -

"By an automobile."

FADE IN Eugene's car coming to stop in front of boarding house. Then play boarding house scene through as in present version. Only change necessary here is comic record. Norman sounds too legitimate. Get Ray to play straight man who should sound like tight voiced vaudevillian.

As Wise says in letter, final FADEOUT should be slowed traffic effects. Better.

As to credits, these must be done in plaque style. One half plaque style or negative effect. Indeed, any effect but straight cuts as in present version. If no photographic tricks satisfactory, suggest pen and ink drawings in somewhat simplified Gibson Style white lines on black field or some such vague pleasant stylish effect. Very worried visual problem end titles but theory seems to work.

Opening Title Mercury Productions should be as set by me before leaving. Similar to Kane.

In the original plan the scene of Eugene and Lucy in their garden would have been followed by the automobile accident (reel 7A shot 2 after lap dissolve); Welles's narration to a black screen is now to replace the actual playing of the accident scene. Eugene's visit to the hospital is now eliminated (reel 7B shots 1 to third lap dissolve in shot 3, slightly over a minute) and Eugene goes directly to Fanny's boardinghouse. This long sequence is to be played as intended except that the comic record heard in the background of Joseph Cotten and Norman Foster imitating The Two Black Crows is to be rerecorded with Mercury veteran Ray Collins replacing Foster. The cast credit sequence is to be completely redesigned. For the opening title and its similarity to *Kane*, see footnote 3 to the cutting continuity.

Early the following week, Wise completed the full report on the preview reactions Welles had requested. Wise does not differentiate between the Pomona and Pasadena previews. It is worth noting, however, that he makes particularly favorable comments on every scene of Welles's "big cut," which he and Moss restored for Pasadena but Welles is still asking for in his March 27 wire:

Dear Orson,

You asked for a detailed report of preview audience reactions and I have never tackled a more difficult chore. What I mean is, it's so damn hard to put on paper in cold type the many times you die through the showing—the too few moments you are repaid for all the blood and suffering that goes into a show.

With God's help and a sigh, here's a rough breakdown of the previews:

To start with, the audience seemed very restless and impatient during the first three or four reels of the show. It's not that there were any bad reactions or laughs during this part of the picture, but I had figured on more chuckles and general enjoyment.

Things like Joe's fall on the fiddle, the derby hat, shoes, different clothes, etc., got only a part of the laughs I'd expected.

The F.O.T.A. Club got only one laugh. That was at the boys crossing their arms and saying, "Welcome, friend of the Ace." The balance of the scene got nothing.

Uncle John and the olive business, I had figured on both for quite a number of laughs, got very few. This was true of a lot of the lines, particularly those of Lucy kidding George, which I had always felt were more amusing.

The scene downstairs after the ballroom seemed to play very well, and the scene upstairs in the hallway between George, Aunt Fanny and Uncle Jack was a wow. They really loved it. The stable scene between Eugene and Lucy fell rather flat.

The snow sequence, especially the part of starting the car, the pushing, cuts of George pushing and coughing, all played very well and got good laughs. However, it did seem to drag along when we got into the later dialogue and the song. However, the lack of expected laughs that I have pointed out in this part of the picture is not the important thing to stress. The really important thing is the length of the film and the definite audience disinterest and inattention during all this.

During the scene of characters filing past Wilbur Minafer's casket the audience laughed at the shot of Mrs. Johnson. This badly affected the balance of the scene.

The kitchen scene between George, Aunt Fanny and Uncle Jack played to laughs all the way through with an especially big one on Fanny's hysteria and crying. The same was true of George and Uncle Jack in the rain.

The factory, George and Lucy on the cart, the Major and Jack in carriage, Eugene and Isabel under the tree all went well by comparison.

The dinner sequence played beautifully, especially Joe's long speech about the automobile. They got a big kick out of Uncle Jack's line to George: "That's a new way of winning a woman."

We again got laughs from Aunt Fanny in several spots on the stair scene where she tells George that people are talking about his mother, as well as a couple in Mrs. Johnson's scene especially on her line: "Please to leave my house."

The bathroom scene did not get any particular laughs but one got the impression in this scene, as well as the rain scene where George and Jack yelled at each other, that they resented the hysterical sort of boy that George seems to be in these scenes.

There was a feeling of restlessness when George unwrapped the picture and did the business with it in the drawing room. But they were held by the scene at the door where George turns Eugene away.

There was a little laugh at the discovery of Fanny up at the top of the stairs but the audience settled down and were interested for the balance of that scene.

There was also some bad laughter at the start of Eugene's letter to Isabel.

On the cut of George reading Eugene's letter we got, not a laugh, but a reaction that said: "Oh, God, here he is again." There was a great lack of sympathy for George through this particular part of the picture.

Scene in Isabel's bedroom and her letter to him seemed to play well enough and the scene on the street between George and Lucy went beautifully. They got right away that Lucy still liked him and was giving him the needle. That she fainted in the drugstore does not seem clear, but we have tried to remedy this by putting in one of the other takes where the clerk says, after he apparently sees her on floor: "For gosh sakes, Miss."

The scene of Uncle Jack and Lucy at the exterior of the Morgan mansion all through the scene with Eugene, Jack and Lucy, the railroad station where they bring Isabel home, and the scene in the carriage all played well. The scene in the hallway outside of Isabel's room got rude laughs on Major Amberson speaking to the nurse and on his walk back to Isabel's bedroom.

As I think you already know, Aunt Fanny repeatedly calling George got loud laughs and varied audible mimics from the audience.

The scene downstairs between Fanny and Eugene, Eugene's departure, George at the window, George's scene with Isabel in the bedroom, the scene in George's bedroom where they are all waiting, and finally the Major on the bed to the fade out played, once again, to impatience and restlessness.

I'm sorry to say that there was some laughter at the first preview on the Major's wonderful speech in the fireside scene. This, however, wasn't repeated at the second preview.

The railroad station went well. The walk home did just all right. Here again there was that same impatience. Fanny in the boiler scene again got laughter in a few spots.

Bronson's office, the garden scene, the accident, on down to the boarding house played all right. The boarding house got us several laughs, one on the man's face when the door opens and several through the scene on Fanny's strange behavior, and here again we could feel great restlessness.

At Pomona we got a big hand and what seemed to be a sigh of relief on your line: "That's the end of the story." At both previews there were too many people who walked out all during the show. This can be attributed, I think, to the great length and slow pace. The picture does not seem to bear down on people.

Please believe me that notwithstanding all in this report, we are all certain that the basic quality of the show was appreciated and it is merely a matter of gentle, tireless and careful study and work to resolve the "Magnificent Ambersons" into a real proud Mercury production.

Warmest regards.

/s/ Bob Wise

(Letter, Wise to Welles, March 31, 1942, Lilly)

In the meantime, Welles had made up his mind about the credit sequence: he would use it to help alleviate the problem of the film's profoundly downbeat effect:

To leave audience happy for Ambersons remake cast credits as follows and in this order: first, oval framed oldfashioned picture very authentic looking of Bennett in Civil War campaign hat. Second, live shot of Ray Collins, no insert, in elegant white ducks and hair whiter than normal seated on tropical veranda ocean and waving palm tree behind him—Negro servant serving him second long cool drink. Third, Aggie [Moorehead] blissfully and busily playing bridge with cronies in boarding house. Fourth, circular locket authentic oldfashioned picture of Costello in ringlets looking very young. Fifth, Jo Cotten at French window closing watch case obviously containing Costello's picture tying in previous shot; sound of car driving away Jo turns, looks out window and waves. Sixth, Tim Holt and Anne Baxter in open car—Tim shifting gears but looking over shoulder—as he does this, Anne looking same direction and waving, they turn to each other then forward both very happy and gay and attractive for fadeout. Then fade in mike shot for my closing lines as before.

(Telegram, Welles to Moss, April 2, 1942, RKO)

As solutions go, this one could only have raised doubts about how fully Welles comprehended the gravity of the situation. By this time, Schaefer had imposed a temporary moratorium on further activity on the film. Although he had ordered Joseph Cotten called back from New York for retakes the day before (April 1), his communications with Welles over the next two weeks suggest he was genuinely looking for a compromise solution. But during this same time, the situation on Welles's South American venture was getting worse, and this unquestionably had a major impact on Schaefer's final decision. It was communicated to Wise around the middle of April that he do whatever was necessary to get *The Magnificent Ambersons* in releasable form. At that point, full authority over the reediting was transferred to Wise. For a time, instructions continued to come in from Welles. Moss duly passed them on, but Wise was free to do with them as he wished.

The recut version was first tested in preview at Inglewood on May 4. No precise details are available, but there were still serious enough doubts that shipment of the print to New York for Schaefer's final review was postponed for two weeks. A new version was previewed at Long Beach on May 12 with encouraging results; although complaints persisted about the depressing nature of the story, the preview comments were two thirds favorable and filled with praise for the film's intelligence and unique directorial style. The Long Beach version ran eighty-seven minutes; it contained the scene of George unwrapping his father's picture (reel 4B shots 1 and 2) but was missing the scene of Eugene and Isabel at the tree (reel 4A shot 1 and shot 2 to lap dissolve) and the drugstore scene (reel 5B shot 1). When Schaefer saw it in this form, he ordered the picture scene eliminated and the two other scenes restored. A new version incorporating these changes was shipped to New York on June 5. Schaefer screened it on June 8 and cleared it for release.

The release version ran eighty-eight minutes ten seconds. It was test-marketed in July to spotty results and in effect abandoned by the studio. By this time Schaefer had been deposed as studio head and Welles's services had been terminated. Wise's career flourished under the new regime. Moss's summary judgment to Richard Wilson after he and Welles had returned from South America: "If only Orson could communicate his genius by telephone."

CAST

Eugene Morgan	Joseph Cotten
Isabel Amberson	Dolores Costello
Lucy Morgan	Anne Baxter
George Minafer	Tim Holt
Fanny Minafer	Agnes Moorehead
Jack Amberson	Ray Collins
Major Amberson	Richard Bennett
Roger Bronson	Erskine Sanford
Sam the Butler	J. Louis Johnson
Wilbur Minafer	Don Dillaway
Uncle John Minafer	Charles Phipps
Mrs. Johnson	Dorothy Vaughn
Mrs. Foster	Ann O'Neal
Townspeople Outside Amberson Mansion	Elmer Jerome, Maynard Holmes, Edwin August, Jack Baxley, Harry Humphrey
Barber	Jack Santoro
Men in Barber Shop	Lyle Clement, Joe Whitehead, Del Lawrence
Women in Sewing Room	Katherine Sheldon, Georgia Backus
George as a Boy	Bobby Cooper
"Terrorized" Laborer	Heenan Elliott
Elijah	Drew Roddy
Men Idling in Sunshine	Bert LeBaron, Jim Fawcet, Gil Perkins
Man in Apron	Henry Rocquemore
Guests at Ball	Nina Gilbert, John Elliott
Lucy's Stunt Person	Helen Thurston
George's Stunt Person	Dave Sharp
Servant in Dining Room Scene	Jess Graves
Mary the Maid	Olive Ball
Drugstore Clerk	Gus Schilling
Irish Policeman	James Westerfield
Young Driver at Accident	William Blees
Second Policeman	Philip Morris

Performers in Deleted Scenes

Members of George's Club
Fred Kinney	Mel Ford
Charlie Johnson	Bob Pittard
Unnamed	Ken Stewart
Eugene's Driver	Ed Howard
Landlady of Boarding House	Lil Nicholson
Man in Boarding House	B. Emery

BIBLIOGRAPHY

Special Collections

Orson Welles Collection.

    Manuscipts Department, Lilly Library, Indiana University, Bloomington, Indiana.

Orson Welles Collection.

    RKO Pictures Files, Theater Arts Library, UCLA.

Roger Hill Orson Welles Correspondence File.

    Private collection.

Charles Higham Research Collection.

    Archives of Performing Arts, University of Southern Calfornia.

George Schaefer Collection.

    Western Heritage Center, Laramie, Wyoming.

Unpublished Interviews

William Alland (October 28, 1987), Lois Bader-Stein (various), Grace Blum (October 26, 1987), Linwood Dunn (October 26, 1987), Amalia Kent (October 25, 1987), Howard Schwartz (October 26, 1987), Ruth Warrick (May 7, 1988), Orson Welles (various), Richard Wilson (various), Robert Wise (various).

Print and Broadcast Interviews

Cortez, Stanley.

"American Film Institute Seminar." *American Cinematographer.* November 1976: 1238–1239, 1242–1243, 1246–1247.

Charles Higham. *Hollywood Cameramen: Sources of Light.* Bloomington: Indiana University Press, 1970. Pp. 98–119.

Welles, Orson.

Koval, Francis. "Interview with Orson Welles." *Sight & Sound.* December 1950: 314–316. Reprinted in: *Filmmakers on Filmmaking.* Edited by Harry M. Geduld. Bloomington: Indiana University Press, 1967.

Powell, Dilys. "The Life and Opinions of Orson Welles." London *Sunday Times.* February 3, 1963: 21.

Tynan, Kenneth. "Playboy Interview: Orson Welles." *Playboy.* March 1967: 53–64.

The Orson Welles Story. Arena (BBC television series), broadcast May 18 and 21, 1982. Revised version broadcast in U.S. as *With Orson Welles: Stories From a Life in Film* (Turner Network Television), February 5, 1990.

Audience Participation Sessions

Welles Press Conference at the Boston Opening of *F for Fake,* January 7, 1977.

Stanley Cortez Question-Answer Session at the American Museum of the Moving Image, March 22, 1986.

Miscellaneous

The Magnificent Ambersons. Campbell Playhouse, radio broadcast, October 20, 1939. Available on *The Magnificent Ambersons* Criterion Videodisc.

The Magnificent Ambersons. Laser Videodisc Critical Edition. Produced by Robert Stein and Robert Carringer. The Criterion Collection. Los Angeles: Voyager, 1986.

The Magnificent Ambersons. The Australian Philharmonic Orchestra conducted by Tony Bremner. Preamble PRCD 1783. Liner notes by Christopher Husted. Issued 1990. A reconstruction of Bernard Herrman's score for the original version of the film.

The Magnificent Ambersons. Fiction version by Lee Pennington. *Photoplay* 20 (April 1942): 44–46, 96–100.

Unpublished Thesis

Reitz, Carolyn Lee. "The Narrative Capabilities of Prose and Film." Ph.D. thesis, University of Texas at Austin, 1978. See: *DAI* 39 (1978), 1887A.

Books

Bazin, André. *Orson Welles.* Translated by Jonathan Rosenbaum. New York: Harper and Row, 1978.

Brady, Frank. *Citizen Welles: A Biography of Orson Welles.* New York: Scribners, 1989.

Carringer, Robert. *The Making of* Citizen Kane. Berkeley, Los Angeles, London: University of California Press, 1985.

Cotten, Joseph. *Vanity Will Get You Somewhere.* San Francisco: Mercury House, 1987.

Fennimore, Keith J. *Booth Tarkington.* New York: Twayne Publishers, 1974.

France, Richard, ed. and introd. *Orson Welles on Shakespeare: The W.P.A. and Mercury Theatre Playscripts.* New York: Greenwood Press, 1990.

Higham, Charles. *The Films of Orson Welles.* Berkeley: University of California Press, 1970.

———. *Orson Welles: The Rise and Fall of an American Genius.* New York: St. Martin's Press, 1985.

Hill, Roger. *One Man's Time and Chance: A Memoir of Eighty Years 1895/1975.* Private Printing, 1977.

Houseman, John. *Run-Through: A Memoir.* New York: Simon and Schuster, 1972.

Leaming, Barbara. *Orson Welles: A Biography.* New York: Viking, 1985.

———. *If This Was Happiness: A Biography of Rita Hayworth.* New York: Viking, 1989.

Palmer, Christopher. *The Composer in Hollywood.* London: Marion Boyars, 1990.

Perry, David G., and Kay Busey. *Social Development.* Englewood Cliffs, N.J.: Prentice-Hall, 1984.

Runyan, William McKinley. *Life Histories and Psychobiography: Explorations in Theory and Method.* New York: Oxford University Press, 1982.

Sturges, Preston. *Preston Sturges.* Adapted and edited by Sandy Sturges. New York: Simon and Schuster, 1990.

Tarkington, Booth. *Penrod.* Garden City, N.Y.: Doubleday, Page, 1914.

———. *Seventeen.* New York: Harper and Brothers, 1916.

———. *The Magnificent Ambersons.* Garden City, N.Y.: Doubleday, Page, 1918.

———. *Alice Adams.* Garden City, N.Y.: Doubleday, Page, 1921.

Wood, Bret. *Orson Welles: A Bio-Bibliography.* New York: Greenwood Press, 1990.

Woodress, James. *Booth Tarkington: Gentleman from Indiana.* Philadelphia and New York: J. B. Lippincott, 1955.

Articles

Bates, Kirk. "Hollywood Jeers While Watching Orson Welles on Slippery Limb." February 6, 1940: 1–2; "When Welles Loses Sleep He Makes It Up, and How!" February 7, 1940: 1–2; "Kenosha Is Indignant Over Some Orson Welles Stories." February 8, 1940: 1–2. Milwaukee *Journal.*

Bates, Robin, with Scott Bates. "Fiery Speech in a World of Shadows: Rosebud's Impact on Early Audiences." *Cinema Journal* 26, no. 2 (Winter 1987): 3–26.

Beatty, Jerome. "Big Show-Off." *American,* February 1947: 38–39, 138–140.

Boyum, Joy Gould. "*The Magnificent Ambersons:* Reversing the Bias." In *Double Exposure: Fiction Into Film,* 230–242. New York: Universe Books, 1985.

Brady, Thomas. "Genius Under Stress." *New York Times,* November 16, 1941: X.5.

Carringer, Robert L. "The Scripts of *Citizen Kane.*" *Critical Inquiry* 5, no. 2 (Winter 1978): 369–400.

Drake, Herbert, with marginal notes by Orson Welles. "Orson Welles—Still a Four-Ply Genius." *Look,* August 19, 1947: 50–51, 53–55.

Farber, Stephen. "*The Magnificent Ambersons.*" *Film Comment,* Summer 1971: 49–50.

Johnston, Alva, and Fred Smith. "How to Raise a Child." *The Saturday Evening Post,* January 20, 1940: 9–11, 94–96; January 27, 1940: 24–25, 51–54; February 3, 1940: 27, 38, 40, 45.

Kael, Pauline. "Raising Kane." *The New Yorker*, February 20, 1971: 43–89, and February 27, 1971: 44–81. Reprinted in *The* Citizen Kane *Book*. Boston: Little, Brown, 1971.

Kalinak, Kathryn. "The Text of Music: A Study of *The Magnificent Ambersons*." *Cinema Journal* 27, no. 4 (Summer 1988): 45–63.

Maloney, Russell. "Profiles: 'This Ageless Soul.'" *The New Yorker* October 8, 1938: 22–27.

Pollock, Dale. "'Ambersons' Lost Footage Part of DGA Sesh on Orson." *Variety*, November 22, 1978: 7, 9.

Sklar, Robert. "Welles before *Kane:* The Discourse on a 'Boy Genius.'" *Persistence of Vision*, no. 7 (1989): 63–72.

Smith, Julian. "Orson Welles and the Great American Dummy—Or, The Rise and Fall and Regeneration of Benjamin Franklin's Model American." *Literature/ Film Quarterly* 2, no. 3 (Summer 1974): 196–206.

Tynan, Kenneth. "Orson Welles." *Show* (October 1961: 65–69; November 1961: 60–65). Reprinted in Kenneth Tynan. *Profiles*. New York: Harper Perennial, 1990.

Vandour, Cyril. "Holt & Sons." *Photoplay* 21, no. 6 (November 1942): 47, 89–90.

Vermilye, Jerry. "Spoken Credits." *Films in Review*, June/July 1959: 382.

Welles, Orson. "My Father Wore Black Spats" and "A Brief Career as a Musical Prodigy." *Vogue* (Paris), December 1982:184–187.

Wigod, Sheldon. "Three Faces of *The Magnificent Ambersons*." In *Transformations: From Literature to Film*. Edited by Douglas Radcliff-Umstead, 84–90. Kent, Ohio: Kent State University, 1987.

Designer: Robert Ross

Compositor: Modern Design

Text: 10/12 Garamond

Display: Garamond

Printer: Malloy Lithographing, Inc.

Binder: John H. Dekker & Sons

RE-20561-86 (Robert Carringer,
        Univ. of Illinois)